Limits to Culture

Limits to Culture

Urban Regeneration vs. Dissident Art

Malcolm Miles

PlutoPress
www.plutobooks.com

First published 2015 by Pluto Press
345 Archway Road, London N6 5AA

www.plutobooks.com

British Library Cataloguing in Publication Data
A catalogue record for this book is available from the British Library

ISBN   978 0 7453 3435 6   Hardback
ISBN   978 0 7453 3434 9   Paperback
ISBN   978 1 7837 1308 0   PDF eBook
ISBN   978 1 7837 1310 3   Kindle eBook
ISBN   978 1 7837 1309 7   EPUB eBook

This book is printed on paper suitable for recycling and made from fully managed
and sustained forest sources. Logging, pulping and manufacturing processes are
expected to conform to the environmental standards of the country of origin.

10   9   8   7   6   5   4   3   2   1

Typeset by Stanford DTP Services, Northampton, England
Text design by Melanie Patrick
Simultaneously printed by CPI Antony Rowe, Chippenham, UK
and Edwards Bros in the United States of America

Contents

List of Illustrations

All images are the author's unless otherwise stated

Introduction

This is a book about how culture has become a mask of social ordering under neoliberalism, and about some of the dissenting practices that have emerged in the past few years against that trend or as alternatives to it.

Despite claims to the contrary, culturally led urban redevelopment does not bring the social or economic regeneration of communities, and is not a means to social inclusion so much as a relatively low-cost way to address failures in other policy areas. New art museums are said to generate employment and attract cultural tourism or investment, and a few spectacular cases – Barcelona and Bilbao – are quoted; but conditions differ from one place to another, so that a model is unlikely to be replicated (while the benefits are disputed in supposedly successful cases). I have nothing against public investment in cultural resources, which is preferable to spending on military adventures, bailing out private-sector banks, or building new roads; but I ask more from spending on the arts than support for property redevelopment, and am not persuaded that the arts drive urban renewal (in the sense of regenerating local economies and communities). In some cases there might be benefits but these tend to be unevenly distributed and often the impact is gentrification. Anyway, the game is up.

After the 2007–08 crisis in global financial services, and austerity, money for the arts has decreased while governments have become out-sourced providers of governmental services to transnational corporations. If the project of capital is the total containment of all elements of life in profit mechanisms, culture is part of its soft policing. If that seems bleak or cynical, culture's co-option to the regime of globalisation follows its function in liberal improvement in the nineteenth century, when new art museums opened access to high culture to the lower classes as a means to greater productivity and social stability. In the past few decades, public art, cultural quarters and flagship cultural institutions have become further means of ordering, now in service of property development.

In brief, culture has been co-opted to redevelopment in service, not of local needs, but of the symbolic economies by which cities compete globally. Within the new, immaterial economy, art fits well enough with rebranding. In London in the 2000s, the Millennium Dome and Tate

Modern were flagships of the rebranding of Britain as Cool Britannia, although contrasting in their capacity to deliver the smoke-and-mirrors effect. Since the crash, what has emerged as a distinct redevelopment sector has allowed the cultural mask to slip; schemes are overtly seen as urban clearances designed to move the poor and unproductive to the geographical as well as the social and economic margins. In place of inner cities, now, urban villages cater for the dwelling and consumption needs of young professionals in the new economy, defined, in one rather dubious analysis, as a 'creative class'.

A number of tendencies and trajectories merge, collide or slip into entropy. The civic values which were a modern outcome of nineteenth-century liberal reformism gave way in the 1980s to managerialism, which transmuted into an imperative to consume, and a totalitarian denial of alternatives. Against this, dissident art has a role of resisting the erasure of the alternative imaginaries which might one day be realised as a better world. The work of art collectives is discussed in the book's later chapters, and gives me hope for change of some kind, although real political change (at least through representational systems) is unlikely at present.

Occupy showed, in the winter of 2011–12, that direct democracy is possible if ephemeral. If another kind of politics has emerged then there might at some point be another kind of cultural work as antidote to affirmative culture and the affluent society. Nonetheless, the book ends on an ambivalent note, reflecting on an incidental occurrence outside art, but no less cultural. Well, I do not work in the Answers Department at the university: my job is more reframing the questions.

Two sources

The title, *Limits to Culture*, echoes *Limits to Medicine* by Ivan Illich. With Herbert Marcuse and André Gorz, Illich was a contributor to the radical Left in the 1960s and 1970s, looking beyond the affluent society towards a liberation of consciousness. In *De-schooling Society*,[1] Illich argued that formal education restricts a potential for experiential learning while the institutionalisation of learning signifies a general institutionalisation of life. This could be compared to the radical, vernacular, living-based pedagogy proposed by Paolo Freire;[2] and prefigures an emphasis on direct democracy in radical movements. In *Limits to Medicine*, Illich argued that society had become medicalised to the detriment of health but in service of productivity: 'The medicalisation of industrial society brings its imperialistic character to ultimate fruition.'[3] Illich also observed that an excessive fear of mortality characteristic of society's medicalisation occurred when, 'megadeath came upon the scene' in the form of nuclear weapons.[4] Like Marcuse and Gorz, Illich aligned each issue to a world order – which Marcuse called the affluent society[5] – which restricts a human urge to liberation not merely by default but instrumentally. Culture might then be a means to freedom, able to evade the dominant state of self-coercion and political repression: 'Body-sense is experienced as an ever-renewed gift of culture.... Cultured health is bounded by each society's style in the art of living.'[6]

I want to juxtapose Illich's writing from the era of protest and intentional communities with Peter Sloterdijk's *In the World Interior of Capital*. If Marcuse and Illich pointed to a new totalitarianism of capital which was as oppressive as the totalitarianism of the Soviet Union, I think Sloterdijk deepens the argument historically by locating the beginning of globalisation literally in the invention of the globe and the voyages of colonisation of the late fifteenth and early sixteenth centuries. Hence a universal system enabled the total sight of the world, but the story does not end with an all-seeing gaze; it leads to a total economic system, or globalised capitalism, which assimilates every human and natural phenomenon. That is, what began as a quest for exploitation has become a total imperative to consume, and to do so in ways which entrench the underlying value-system. Sloterdijk writes,

> As for capitalism, we can only now say that it always meant more than the relations of production; its shaping power had always gone much further than can be encapsulated in the thought figure of the 'global market'. It implies the project of placing the entire working life, wish life, and expressive life of the people it affected within the immanence of spending power.[7]

The implication here is that cities are (re)produced by this mechanism. A specific outcome is, I argue, the co-option of culture and urban spaces to the trajectory of capital. The end of that trajectory is wealth accumulation by an elite whose power is political-economic, as the state declines as fabled protector of the common wealth (or well-being). Culture, in the form of culturally led urban redevelopment, lends an aura of universal benefit to the property market, and recodes space as elite zones producing new margins outside them.

In German Idealism, the end of history was the attainment of Reason. In the late twentieth century, it was announced that history was over: the market had triumphed and there was no alternative. Furthermore, the so-called free market was said to be self-correcting. After the 2007 crash and exposure of casino-capitalism this has become untenable: the market does not correct itself, and is evidently irrational. In parallel, the culture of urban redevelopment schemes (or the cultural sector generally) tends towards a version of high culture adapted to new elites in the immaterial economy; it differs from the anthropological sense of cultures as shared articulations and expressions of meanings and values in ordinary lives. This translates, in this book, into a contrast between the cultural apparatus of redevelopment and the efforts of artists and artist-collectives to develop a range of cultural practices both embedded in their social situations and, at the same time, at a critical distance from consumerist culture.

My conjecture is more modest than Sloterdijk's although, like him, I am a theorist not an empiricist; I am not a social scientist and do not do data; nor do I have any talent for fieldwork (I don't like meeting people I don't know); but if that puts me in a historicist milieu, I am also English, not given to Wagnerian flights of text, and probably out of my depth when dealing with world-historical meta-narratives. In that context, the trajectory which I propose in this book connects nineteenth-century urban improvements to today's culturally led urban redevelopment as a means of control, sets out a counter-culture, and does that mainly through the evidence and arguments of published research. If I make a contribution it is in making new connections between the ideas and findings published in different, disparate literatures.

The book

In Chapter 1 I set the scene, critically contextualising the cultural turn of the 1980s–1990s in a de-industrialised estate. I look at iconic cases of culturally led redevelopment, the recoding of sites as cultural zones, the demarcation of cultural quarters and insertion of new flagship cultural venues in the wastes left by de-industrialisation. Chapter 2 examines the notion of a cultural class, questioning the use of the category but accepting a link between culturally led redevelopment and gentrification as the lifestyle associated with the professionals in the new economy of immaterial production taken as driving the process. Then, Chapter 3 looks back to expressions of civic values and ideas of national identity at the Festival of Britain in 1951, and compares the festival to celebrations of its 60th anniversary in 2011, and to the failure of the Millennium Dome in 2000. This is not a plea for a return to a lost world, because clocks do not run backwards, but raises questions as to what place civic or shared values have now or might have in new ways one day.

Chapter 4 is shorter and constitutes an experiential, at times journalistic, interlude; I record impressions formed of some of the new art museums around England funded mainly by the National Lottery, which I visited in March 2014. But I offer some contextual material from critical museology, as well. Chapter 5 resumes the critical discourse, moving to a historical perspective: an expansion of public museums (such as the Tate Gallery, opened in 1897) in the nineteenth century is aligned with fear of social unrest, after what seemed to be an opening of cultural events to new publics in Georgian London but which, on investigation, reproduces social divisions in a time of rapidly expanding wealth. Chapter 6 maps the book's arguments onto public spaces, seen in the 1990s as enabling social mixing and social cohesion, and asks to what extent urban redevelopment actually conceals a democratic deficit, and whether new ideas and tactics for social change really occur in public spaces which were designed for the display of power, or elsewhere, otherwise.

This leads me to the work of artists and artist-collectives whose practices I read as dissident, or at least as outside the strictures of redevelopment; and to alternatives modes of producing urban space. This begins at the end of Chapter 6 and is the substance of Chapter 7. It is not for me to say what artists should do but I try to summarise what I think they have done. The cases cited in Chapters 6 and 7 follow contact with artists and artists' groups. Where possible I have sent them drafts for comment.

At the end, Chapter 8 is a short reflection on whether art has a role in social change after Occupy, which I read as an instance of the direct production of a new society. I ask how cultural work finds paths outside the institutional structures by which it has been drawn into market economics, and whether aesthetics retains a possibility for dissent. Is Beauty radically other? Can art break the institutional ties of Culture? I don't know.

1

Cultural Turns:
A De-industrialised Estate

The strangeness of cities becomes familiar. Perhaps it began in the 1900s, with the frenetic ambience of electric light and tramcars, and the crowds which thronged metropolitan cities. But this was an optimistic world, soon to be fractured by an industrialised war that would redraw the map of Europe. In the inter-war years, European cities became sites of democracy as well as technology, and of growing diversity through migration. The whole continent was devastated again, with the bombing of civilian targets to an unprecedented extent, before a sense of renewed civic values and humanism prevailed in the post-war era. There was austerity, and bomb sites remained; yet there was a renewed hope in the 1950s and economic expansion in the 1960s, culminating in the prospect of really changing the world in May 1968. That failed. Europe, and the rest of the world, has moved politically to the Right and economically to free market irrationality ever since. It sometimes seems as if the project of Enlightenment became tenuous in the 1930s and 1940s but has finally been encapsulated in an unrecoverable past in today's neoliberal realm of de-industrialisation: a new wasteland characterised by corporate greed, human rights abuses and environmental destruction. If there is a post-industrial state of mind, it is produced by an economic system but as much enhanced by design. The steel and glass corporate towers, non-places of travel, labyrinthine malls and new art museums in cool industrial sheds amid signs of gentrification, all contribute to a new, post-Enlightenment sense of the sublime. It is characterised by both scale and visual language: the 800,000 square metre Euralille and the 20-hectare CCTV building in Beijing, for instance, both designed by Rem Koolhaas, are daunting;[1] and the steel, glass and pale grey cladding of post-industrial urban sheds and towers creates an other-worldly coldness, a feeling of alienation which is as much a source of awe as the Alps were for eighteenth-century travellers on the grand tour.

The new centres in their shiny splendour produce new margins. What was ordinary becomes marginal and residual. Contrasts deepen, real or imagined barriers emerge. Cities split. Owen Hatherley describes the redevelopment of Salford in Greater Manchester as generating a new, 'dead centre' in this enclave of wholesale reconstruction, entered from one side by an elegant bridge designed by Santiago Calatrava but from the other by bleak dual carriageways, dreary retail parks and old office complexes in down-at-heel Trafford.[2] Salford houses two flagship museums, the Lowry and a branch of the Imperial War Museum, and Media City, where parts of the BBC have moved. Walking in Salford Quays, Hatherley co-opts the weather:

> Looking out through torrential rain … at this, the most famous part of the most successfully regenerated ex-industrial metropolis, we can't help but wonder; is this as good as it gets? Museums, cheap speculative housing, offices for financially dysfunctional banks? What of the idea that civic pride might mean a civic architecture … ?[3]

Yes, but civic pride is a nineteenth-century value, the last flowering of which occurred in the 1950s (as in the Festival of Britain). These towers contain rather than house their occupants, as cheap housing warehouses the poor; and Hatherley imagines, 'barricading oneself into a hermetically sealed, impeccably furnished prison against an outside world … assumed to be terrifying'.[4] As digital communications systems link the enclaves of the immaterial economy of financial services, media and public relations along never-closing electronic highways, the city becomes a sleepless world where humans operate in systems more extensive than their imaginations. Sleep is, in any case, according to art theorist Jonathan Crary, no use, 'given the immensity of what is at stake economically'.[5] Manchester is a city which never sleeps, or which cannot because the night-economy of alcohol and clubs is as important as its day-time commerce. Permanent consumption compensates the operatives of late capitalism for routine alienation; it is the only game in town, the sole (if soulless) remaining imperative, enforced by the soft policing of the news-entertainment-culture sector.

Time!

If Slavoj Žižek is accurate when he says that these are the end-times,[6] the question is what is ending. Perhaps it is modernity and the values it espoused of freedom and human happiness. In the nineteenth century, this was translated into efforts to ameliorate the material conditions of the poor; the improvements – sewers, clean water, housing – were genuine, and culture in the form of new public art museums was one of them, but the strategy was always repressive: the prevention of revolt. Since the 1980s, culture has been co-opted to urban redevelopment, first as public art – since institutionalised to the point of offering a choice between bland new public monuments, corporate logos or visual pollution – then as the participation of artists in the design of environments (from over-designed parks and piazzas to wobbly bridges) and of publics in projects aimed at dealing with the new category of social exclusion. Following the 2007 financial services crisis (the crash) the regeneration industry has emerged in a more brutal guise, looking less to culture for an aura of respectability as it gets on with postcode clearances.

Meanwhile Beauty is radically other to the world produced by capital.[7] Like art's uselessness, or the autonomy claimed for modernism, Beauty is not productive but convulsive. It is met in unexpected moments and encounters which fade before they can be grasped, yet lingers in the mind, and is not at all confined to art. Beauty fractures capital's routines, breaking the chains of consumer culture in the awareness, suddenly, of 'the incommensurability of the voice of poetry'.[8] And the moment, however ephemeral, is transformative.[9]

To speak of such moments is utopian, and always has been. But utopianism was the content of modernism, which became (at some point in the late twentieth century) encapsulated in a no longer accessible (hence mystified) past. Art historian Tim Clark argues that modernism and socialism ended at the same time: 'If they died together, does that mean that … they lived together, in century-long co-dependency?'[10] I must leave that for another book, saying here only that globalisation renders both modernism and socialism as obsolete as old wireless sets.

Globalisation concentrates capital in companies which appropriate powers previously vested in states, and produces super-elites. When national regulation is an obstacle, companies go to transnational bodies; the super-rich enjoy unlimited mobility and avoid the inconvenience of paying tax. For sociologist Martin Albrow, no single sovereign power can claim 'legitimate authority' over transnational institutions, so that the 'decentred and delinked' structures of the new world order become a 'vacant discursive space' where, 'people refer to the globe as once they referred to the nation, hence globalism'.[11] Zygmunt Bauman writes that, as states are 'no longer capable of balancing the books', they become instead 'executors and plenipotentiaries of forces which they have no hope of controlling politically'.[12] Peter Sloterdijk reads capital as aiming to put 'working life, wish life and expressive life ... [all] within the immanence of spending power'.[13] In this context, some of the systems employed by global capital reproduce the practices of the eighteenth century: journalist James Ridgeway reports that: 'Children are traded in large numbers ... [as] a source of low-cost labour' in the sex industry.[14] The global oil industry looks to Arctic exploration now that burning fossil fuels has melted much of the ice, just as colonialists previously pillaged rainforests. After 9/11, an older pattern of private security has been revived, and Naomi Klein writes of 'the Bush team' devising a role for government, in which the job of the state is, 'not to provide security but to purchase it at market prices',[15] Again, design plays its part in the production of a fear which serves the security sector, which has little connection with genuine safety. And design is central to the gleaming images which compensate for money's trashing of the city, reproduced in glossy tourist brochures and the promotional material for waterside redevelopment schemes, employing star architects in de-industrialised sites 'to sprinkle starchitect fairy dust'.[16] The signs of change are highly visual, sometimes but not always economically successful, and often socially divisive.

Conspicuous division

The chasm between wealth and deprivation is especially visible in redevelopment zones next to neighbourhoods of residual poverty. David Widgery, a doctor in Limehouse, watched the building of Canary Wharf in London's old Docklands, observing that, '[It] remains curiously alien, an attempt to parachute into the heart of the once industrial East End an identikit North American financial district ... a gigantic Unidentified Fiscal Object.'[17] A UFO, a strange object from another world, the design style which characterises enclaves of the global city of financial services, replicated in any city seeking world status.[18] Steel and glass towers tend to be strangely opaque, despite all the glass, using surface design to redirect attention from the dealings which take place inside them. Widgery notes a similarity of design in the towers of Canary Wharf and the World Financial Center, New York (both designed by César Pelli), and compares work in the health service with the ethos of Canary Wharf:

> Proletarian decency over monetarist efficiency; one driven by compassion and the solidarities of work and neighbourhood, the other by the simpler calculation of profit and loss. There is no physical monument to what generations of decent working-class East Enders have created and given and made and suffered. But César Peli ... tells us that 'A skyscraper recognises that by virtue of its height it has acquired civic responsibilities. We expect it to have formal character-istics appropriate for this unique and socially charged role.' Now that would be interesting to see.[19]

Since the redevelopment of London Docklands in the 1980s, the rhetorical allusion to a civic sense has more or less disappeared. In Docklands, near the ExCeL event space and two chain hotels, a bronze sculpture, *Landed* by Les Johnson (2009), reduces the story of labour militancy and trade union organisation in the docks to the modelling of two day labourers under the foreman's eye. This is a successor to the naturalistic, bronze likenesses that proliferated in urban squares and parks in the late nineteenth century to remind citizens of the values they should espouse, represented mainly by white men of the ruling class. *Landed* is entirely competent and I have no wish to pick on it, yet I wonder what else could have been made to convey the histories of work and workers' solidarity which took place here.

With money comes mobility and a dissolution of allegiances. Bauman writes: 'If the new extraterritoriality of the elite feels like intoxicating freedom, the territoriality of the rest feels less like home ground, and ever more like prison ... more humiliating for the obtrusive sight of others' freedom to move.'[20] Planner Peter Hall argues that, 'less fortunate groups are likely to be increasingly damned up in the cities, where they will perhaps be housed after a fashion' but will 'find themselves in but not of the city'.[21] Bauman reads communication technologies as radically separating the mobile rich and the grounded poor: 'The database is an instrument of selection, separation and exclusion ... [which] washes out the locals.'[22] Meanwhile in far-away places, the mobile class plays. Sociologist Mimi Sheller writes that Caribbean islands have become a new Garden of Eden accessible by international flights, with inclusive holiday villages and the added frissons of piracy and marijuana.[23] The holiday brochures simulate the Land of Cockaigne,[24] yet these sites of far-away consumption offer only another imperative to work to pay for their exploration.

Similarly selective narratives were used to market London's Docklands redevelopment, with pictures of a sparkling Thames and water sports. For art historian Jon Bird, Docklands in the late 1980s was where multinationals swallowed up the generous offers of land available in enterprise zones to 'spew out' various types of architectural postmodernism and 'high-tech paroxysms of construction that are as incoherent as they are unregulated'.[25] The publicity material showed:

> harmony and coherence, a unity of places and functions not brutally differentiated into respective spheres of work, home and leisure, but woven together by the meandering course of the river into a spectacular architectural myth of liberal *civitas*. Canary Wharf is indeed a fantasy of community: a city within the City populated by a migrant army of executive, managerial and office staff serving the productive signifiers of postmodernity – microelectronics, telecommunications and international capital – along with the relevant support structures and lifestyle accoutrements, from food to culture …[26]

Bird also wrote on oppositional art in the form of changing billboards telling other stories of Docklands, produced by the art group The Art of Change.[27] The billboards soon disappeared while the imagery used for Docklands went global, as in the promotion of Gdańsk after the demise of state socialism (Figure 1.1). Bird summarises the familiarly strange scene, 'We look from a distance … each scene suffused with a gentle light which plays upon the towers and the water. Nothing is un-harmonious or out of place – these are viewpoints that allow us to possess the City in imagination.'[28] Looking in one direction along a redeveloped waterfront I might see iconic buildings: a skyline for the symbolic economy of city marketing; in another direction I might see zones of cultural consumption in the sites of redundant industries. These iconic towers and the designer bars and boutiques which cluster around the new art museums represent renewal, but perhaps they do this only for the elites who use them, or in ways which are more simulated than material. Sociologist Steven Miles remarks on the role of imagery in a consumer society as a new kind of social currency which, 'creates a demand for illusion which we pay others to produce for us'.[29] Citing Marc Augé,[30] he writes that: 'The non-place is the opposite of a utopia' since it has no organic social content but is defined economically and 'by a lack of community, a lack of unpredictability and a lack of difference'.[31] I suggest that something similar can be said of signature architecture.

Figure 1.1   Billboard for Gdańsk, Kraków, Poland

In a digital era, space is less important because people can operate anywhere that has a wifi connection, but images generate prestige. Journalist Aditya Chakrabortty writes of the Shard, by Renzo Piano, at 72 storeys London's highest building to date, that it, 'stalks Londoners everywhere they go'.[32] Visible from everywhere, it should be familiar. Close-up, it is evident that this structure with a seemingly broken tip is not an efficient use of space; its floors taper, wasting airspace but this does not matter: the prices are high enough. To take space here is super-conspicuous consumption: apartments cost £30–50 million. Chakrabortty reads the Shard as extending the ways in which London 'is becoming more unequal and dangerously dependent on hot money'.[33] He continues:

> This is a high-rise that has been imposed on London Bridge despite protests from residents, conservation groups and a warning from Unesco that it may compromise the world-heritage status of the nearby

Tower of London. What's more, its owners and occupiers will have very little to do with the area, which for all its centrality is also home to some of the worst deprivation and unemployment in the entire city. ... its developer ... talks of it as a virtual town, comprising a five-star hotel and Michelin-starred restaurants.[34]

He quotes a spokesperson for the property's agent who says that, since there are only 25 to 50 potential buyers globally in its price range, they can all be telephoned and advertising is not necessary.

Culture and redevelopment

In this divisive scenario, the arts play a role like that of design. Susan Buck-Morss writes,

> The artworld has flourished in the warm climate of the new globalisation. It is exemplary of the new business model, boasting a cultural universality that seizes on the market potential of a recently massified global elite. The new post-art ... is omnipresent, spilling out of museums and exhibitions, migrating in multimedia forms, its web-links advertised on multiple e-mails in your inbox.[35]

Broadly, at risk of over-generalising, there have been three overlapping strategies: the use of redundant industrial buildings for cultural institutions; the demarcation of inner-city cultural and heritage quarters; and the insertion in de-industrialised or inner-city districts of flagship institutions such as new museums of modern or contemporary art (or whole arts districts).

An example of the first strategy is Tate Liverpool, in a Victorian warehouse in Albert Dock. It is one of several museums on the site, such as the Museum of Slavery. Tate Liverpool opened in 1988, its interior re-designed by James Stirling. After refurbishment in 1998 the foyer was re-refurbished in 2006 by Arca, whose website describes 'a structured communication of the gallery's offering to people – shifting light platforms visible from across the dock ... a re-oriented reception area with a dramatic new desk. Educational areas were overlapped with hospitality suites.'[36] Tate Liverpool has always exhibited part of Tate's collection of modern art, but in the 1990s it evolved a community-based curating policy for temporary exhibitions. I always wondered if this was because Tate Liverpool was so far from London that it did not matter. The Baltic, Gateshead, is another example of an ex-industrial museum site, converted (again by Arca) from a flour mill on the Tyne. Elsewhere, nineteenth-century railway stations such as the Gare d'Orsay in Paris and the Hamburger Bahnhof in Berlin have been reused as major exhibition spaces, their train sheds transformed into high, light halls very suitable for the display of art.

An example of a cultural quarter is the Rope Walks in Liverpool, near the city centre. This was planned in 1997, and draws visitors into an area associated with popular music among old warehouses and small factories. Cultural historian Abigail Gilmore observes:

> It contained many of the right ingredients for regeneration as a quarter: built heritage assets, traces of its industrial past (the centre for rope making and supply to the shipping industry; merchant warehouses and residences), cheap (in some cases free) workspace for artists, musicians and other creative producers, licensed venues, pubs, clubs and bars that stretched back to Liverpool's musical past, secret spaces – courtyards, alleys and squares – and seeds of organic activity filling these places.[37]

Urbanist Graeme Evans remarks that while the sites designated for such quarters tend to be, as Gilmore says, activated organically, brought to prominence by individual intermediaries, institutionalised planning 'is less well-placed to capture this energy, which limits the viability of municipal or corporate cluster developments'.[38] This indicates a gap between production – artists moving into de-industrialised zones – and distribution – the cultural quarters as tourist attraction – where, as a quarter becomes recognised and rents rise, artists tend to be forced out. One of the first culturally recoded quarters was SoHo in New York, the garment district where artists moved into lofts in the 1970s. Sharon Zukin charted the conversion of this area from a mixed-use, organically developed quarter to a zone of boutiques, luxury chain stores and high-rent apartments.[39] In a later account she looks back,

> The district attracted an enormous amount of media attention in lifestyle magazines and art world journals.... Foot traffic swelled. By 1990 art galleries dominated the storefronts, joined by new, individually owned boutiques and professional services, while manufacturing visibly waned. SoHo was now known as an artists' district, but it was

also becoming an interesting place to shop for new art, trendy clothing and imported cheese. By 2000 art galleries began to be outnumbered by boutiques, and chain stores of every sort planted themselves on Broadway [nearby].... Only five years later, with rents dramatically rising, chain stores outnumbered boutiques.... By 2005 SoHo was no longer an artists' district; it was an urban shopping mall.[40]

Tate Modern is a reused industrial building and a flagship cultural institution inserted in a de-industrialised zone. It occupies a post-war brick power station designed by Giles Gilbert Scott which closed in 1981. The building was converted by architects Herzog and de Meuron, following a design completion in 1995. Its Turbine Hall – 35 metres high and 152 metres long – has become a quasi-public space and a temporary exhibition area; the permanent collection is displayed in the upper floors. Tate Modern has two shops, several food and drink outlets of different price levels, and a members' room. The collection was re-hung thematically for the opening, juxtaposing works from different periods and styles to engage visitors in a-historical ways. This has since been revised.

Architectural historian Simon Sadler writes that Tate Modern combines, 'absence and spatial excess' with a vertical circulation route that wends its way through, 'the cathedral-like multi-storey void of its emptied turbine hall'.[41] In 2012, three underground oil storage tanks were converted into additional live-art spaces; and a new ten-storey tower was constructed adjacent to the site (again designed by Herzog and de Meuron) to provide new gallery spaces and several floors of ultra-high-price apartments. Like SoHo, if more unevenly, the London Borough of Southwark has been changed by Tate insertion. Around it are new apartments, boutiques and bars. The waterside is popular with tourists but not quite gentrified. Nonetheless, despite the surviving signs of local culture in Southwark, Tate Modern is an engine of gentrification. It has remarkably moved the cultural hub of London out of the previously elite West End to the south side of the Thames; but it has achieved this – perhaps significantly – by constructing a new axis between Tate and the financial district via the Millennium Bridge in front of St Paul's Cathedral. Tate claims to generate '£100 million in economic benefits' for London,[42] and has received more than 40 million visitors. It is a great success, in sharp contrast to the Dome. Yet, for cultural theorist Esther Leslie, Tate has remade 'the space of cultural encounter' by being a 'simulacrum'.[43] Leslie continues:

Tate is a brand that niche-markets art experience. Its galleries are showrooms. However, this is still art and not just business. The commodity must not show too glossy a face. The reclamation of an industrial space ... lends the building a fashionably squatted aspect.... Tate Modern begins with a descent ... a former industrial site becomes home to the new-style accessibility rules culture industry.[44]

In 2012, the art group Liberate Tate tested Tate's claim to accessibility in *The Gift*, a live-art piece consisting of carrying a wind turbine blade into the Turbine Hall and offering it to the collection. In its form-follows-function way, and its pure whiteness, the blade might seem a quintessential modernist object, and hence an ideal addition to a collection of modern art. But although hundreds of Tate's members wrote in support of the attempted gift, it was declined by the museum's trustees. *The Gift*, however, was part of Liberate Tate's campaign to draw attention to the contradictions between Tate's sponsorship by the global oil industry and the humane ethos of modernism, and the ensuing publicity and documentation are as much part of the work as the turbine blade itself.[45]

Tate is versatile in other ways, however, including a summer show in 2009 of graffiti. This sign of what was once regarded as anti-social activity occupied Tate's exterior walls, with huge works commissioned from graffiti artists from several countries. This might seem an extreme version of a strategy to widen cultural inclusion except that graffiti-art is traded at international art auctions. Re-named street art (with a non-street-based derivative, urban art), it is collected by the new elite of the immaterial economy. The exhibition was sponsored by a Japanese car manufacturer and accompanied by guided walking tours in the East End to see graffiti in its old surroundings. The exotic is not confined, it seems, to far-away islands but is now encountered in the transitional zones of cities, between gentrified urban villages and residual streets of diverse occupation and, at times, anti-social activity.

To give a further example of a new arts zone, and how the strategy has spread to the ex-Eastern bloc after 1989, the new National Theatre and Ludwig Foundation buildings, a sculpture park and a terrace of bank headquarters mini-towers now occupy an ex-industrial riverside site in the Ferencváros district of Budapest. After the People's Theatre was blown up in 1965, a new site (then called Engels Square, now Erzsébet Square) was identified for the National Theatre in 1988. After delays and a false start to construction in 1998, building recommenced in 2000 using a design by

Mária Siklós. The design was (and remains) controversial, in terms both of how the commission was awarded and eclectic stylistic references of the design. In front of the theatre, by the river and the park, a ziggurat acts as an additional exhibition venue (Figure 1.2). Spending a day here during a contemporary art conference at the Ludwig a few years ago, I found the scene bizarre. Opposite the extreme geometry of the modernist Ludwig Forum and its glass façade, the National Theatre's exterior seemed a strange fusion of scales and details from different sources. The city looked a long way off from this end of a tram line, as if I had somehow landed in an art-world theme park, except that names such as Morgan Stanley on the mini-towers reminded me of the real relation between capital and high culture.

Figure 1.2   National Theatre and Ziggurat, Budapest, Mária Siklós

Barcelona

One of the best known city-wide strategies for culturally led urban renewal was that evolved in Barcelona after the death of General Franco in 1975. For sociologists Monica Degen and Marisol Garcia, Barcelona's model of urban regeneration has become a prominent example of cultural activity in redevelopment.[46] Other cities have sought to emulate it but differences in history, social conditions and climate mean that the experience is not transferable. Of these factors, climate is the least important. Barcelona has many outdoor cafés, yet there is seating outside cafés in Copenhagen, too, despite the cold: customers are simply given rugs as they sit out in the cold evenings. Perhaps they have hot drinks, too. Leaving that aside, differences in history and social conditions are more influential. Barcelona was one of the last sites of resistance to fascism in 1937, and the three chimneys of a power station at Besos, just beyond the city boundary, retain an association for local people with that resistance. In the cemetery high up on Montjuïc, there are memorials to those who were shot when the fascists took the city. Their names are carved in alphabetical order on rough stone pillars.

Urban regeneration began in part as a regeneration of governance, then, as much as of the city's slumped economy after Franco's death, contextualised by the wider move to social democracy in Spain. Degen and Garcia comment:

> In 1979 the newly elected socialist City Council rebuilt the city by drawing on strong civic ideals and, in a conscious political move, involved neighbourhood associations in the design of its urban policy. This involvement was the result of social and political pressure from the neighbourhood movement.... Barcelona's urban regeneration programme coincided with a wider programme of democratic citizenship construction in Spain, which involved the implementation of national welfare policies favouring education, training and health.[47]

Franco repressed the city's economy as punishment for its Left past, and prohibited use of the Catalan language (reproducing a repression which began in the eighteenth century).

Barcelona's independence was previously lost in 1714 when the city was besieged and fell to the Bourbons, at which point power moved to Madrid. The zone outside the city's walls was demarcated as a military zone, a free-fire zone, but its impact was mainly economic, limiting the scope for growth. Conditions within the walls deteriorated due to overcrowding, and production was limited due to cramped sites. Strikes occurred in the 1850s, as did several outbreaks of cholera. Permission was gained for the demolition of the walls in 1859, leading to a competition for a plan for the city's extension. Ildefons Cerdá, trained as a military engineer, produced a grid plan for what he called the city's urbanisation, or a rational re-ordering of space according to Enlightenment principles. I do not have the space to go into this but it was one of the most liberal of city plans ever formulated, with provision for decent housing for all social classes, green space, public transport, street lighting and seating, and the provision of half the width of streets for pedestrians. Its purpose was equally, however, to prevent revolt, a typical project of nineteenth-century liberal reformism. The plan represented a social contract: 'Between society and property as a social institution there cannot be and there is no diversity of interest ... nor any lineage of contradictions.'[48] More than a century later, Catalan nationalism reappeared, the language was rehabilitated, a cultural infrastructure was developed to support the emerging state and the city hosted the 1992 Olympic Games. In this period, cultural tourism was encouraged and its gains were fed back into the emerging cultural infrastructure for the benefit of local publics. In contrast to the redevelopment model of Britain and North America, the city led the process by investing in the refurbishment of the old port and the waterfront, leasing on sites to fund further schemes, while creating more than a hundred public spaces throughout the city (many in residential, not tourist, areas).

Information for cultural events was given in Catalan. Cultural planner Dianne Dodd remarks that even if tourists do not visit all the venues, simply knowing about them 'will encourage a return visit ... because these cultural elements are not built for tourist purposes, business or culturally educated tourists will be more interested in them, because they tend to search for authenticity'.[49] Authenticity is key. Cultural tourists think of themselves as intrepid travellers who seek out real places (even as they look for the sites in the brochures as well). But another factor specific to Barcelona was the contribution of local savings banks, which are committed to using profits to support culture. The Caixa Foundation, for example, funded by a bank in a disused textile factory, houses changing exhibitions of international contemporary art. In the end, the critical mass of attractions – art, fashion, food, obscure alleys and old bars as well as modernist buildings, the waterfront – enables Barcelona to attract repeat visitors, hooked on the authenticity of rubbing shoulders with artists, prostitutes and migrants in the city's old quarters, but equally happy to pay for contemporary comfort (and the safety of an art museum in a city increasingly identified with street crime).

Barcelona's public-sector-led policy shifted, however, in the preparations for the 2004 World Forum of Culture and redevelopment of El Raval, the old red-light district around the Museu d'Art Contemporani de Barcelona (MACBA) designed by Richard Meier (opened in 1995). There is a large open space in front, Plaça dels Angels, designed by F. Ramos Associates, which is appropriated by diverse groups through the day. Dog walkers arrive in the early morning, followed by tourists but also skateboarders in the afternoon. Different groups also have their own, informally claimed spaces: a guidebook says, 'outside, the spectacle is as intriguing as inside … skateboarders dominate the space south of the museum … you may well see … kids playing cricket in Plaça de Joan Coromines.'[50]

Several blocks of high-density nineteenth-century housing were cleared to make the site, as they were for the New Ramblas, designed by P. Cabrera i Massanés and J. Artigues i Vidal, constructed in the late 1990s. The difficulty is that the New Ramblas is sterile, in an area once particularly diverse. It is still partly so due to rent controls but refurbished apartments mean high service charges. The design of the New Ramblas, with rusting steel street lights which look like Richard Serra sculptures, reinforces a sense of alien affluence. The planners spoke of *esponjamiento*, a loosening of the weave of the urban fabric. Letting in the light by clearing space was seen, then, as the material side of an improvement ethos reflected, too, in the absence of the traditional street balconies in new, smooth-faced in-fill blocks.

Although neighbourhood associations participated in the early phase of plans, this declined, especially among young people, and such groups have little impact on the changes which re-shape Barcelona as a world city (a claim affirmed by its World Trade Centre, designed by I.M. Pei). The 2004 World Forum of Culture was a catalyst for further redevelopment; one site was leased at the outset to a North American developer for the largest mall in the Western Mediterranean. In the lead-in process to 2004, I attended a meeting addressed by the planners. Where the city's dissecting thoroughfare, Avenida Diagonal, meets the sea was described as empty, a waste space, hence ready for clearance. Looking at it, I found it consisted of working-class houses, small factories used as studio spaces by artists, and spatial appropriations by migrants. The site was discussed, nonetheless, by experts as a *design* problem managed by a development authority aiming to 'provide public access to a wide range of new spaces, improve the urban setting, and rezone neighbourhoods in the area.'[51] Re-zoning seems to be an understatement. Degen and Garcia conclude even-handedly:

Since the 1980s public investment has more than doubled in the cultural sphere … a strong cultural infrastructure has been provided in all districts of the city, reaching all sectors of the population. From a more cynical point of view ... [this] is deeply entrenched within Barcelona's place-marketing strategies.... culture has been given a legitimizing role to unite an increasingly socially heterogeneous society and is thus used as a tool to redefine an ambiguous notion of social cohesion.[52]

Bilbao

Comparing Barcelona's renewal to that of another frequently cited city, Bilbao, emphasises that Barcelona drew on its unique history to recreate a Catalan cultural infrastructure while Bilbao opted for a global brand of cultural experience in the shape of the Guggenheim, in a shining, spectacular, iconic (and so forth) building designed by Frank Gehry. I have not been to Bilbao, so rely here on published accounts.

Steven Miles remarks that, 'Effectively a franchising arrangement, the Guggenheim Museum would provide the focal point ... a "honey pot" at the centre of a much broader regenerative building programme.'[53] Apart from financing the building's construction after preparation of the site, the city is contracted to pay Guggenheim a seven-figure sum (in dollars) each year, indefinitely, for curatorial expertise. Despite the high curatorial fee it might be thought that the building is more spectacular than its contents, using titanium for a series of wild, curving, colliding surfaces (although there are more conventional, orthogonal stone-clad sections as well). But it is the shiny curves which are globally reproduced in colour images proclaiming the Bilbao effect. In a rather celebratory book, architectural critic Will Pryce writes:

It is the highly reflective titanium skin that gives these loose organic shapes a coherent visual image, one that contrasts very effectively with the dour industrial city around it. While the art inside is typical of corporate America, the juxtaposition of the building with its environment is the most striking since Pompidou [the Pompidou Centre, Paris] and achieved without the advantage of Paris as its backdrop.[54]

Pryce gives visitor figures of more than 5 million in the first three years. Steven Miles, however, states that the figure declined later, and that the Guggenheim generated 0.47 per cent of the Basque GNP (gross national product) in 1997.[55] Bilbao remains a shrinking city, its population falling from 429,797 in 1975 to 369,839 in 1991 and 358,875 in 1996.[56] In 2001, the Guggenheim hosted an Armani show for $12 million.

Beside this shiny corporate face, in context of the collapse of the city's old industries of ship-building and chemicals, there is also the matter of Basque nationalism. This periodically took a violent turn with bombings and shootings but Basque identity was then and remains now an emotive issue. According to the beholder's political position, Bilbao is either the primary city of a region or the capital of a yet to be recognised nation-state which is not Spain. Apart from that, Basque culture has its own organic organisation; by the 1980s, a network of local *casas de cultura* in Bilbao aimed to widen access to culture through local voluntary organisations and civic centres. The 1988 Plan General and 1989 Forum Bilbao on Urban Renewal sought to take the city into a post-industrial revival, learning from the experiences of other European cities (not necessarily Barcelona). One aim was to change the city's image in order to attract investment and cultural tourism but the strategy disregarded local voices, leading geographer Julia González to say, 'there has been an almost complete lack of communication ... so that economic regeneration and social regeneration appear as irreconcilable objectives'.[57] Perhaps the Guggenheim's attraction in some quarters was precisely that the global culture it purveys is not-Basque, hence not aligned to a separatism seen as unproductive for business. Indeed, for business elites looking to a global market, insertion of a globalised cultural brand on the city's skyline, and in its image in external perception, was a way to draw a line under history in the new time of spaces and flows and transnational regions of innovation, not delve into it for a renewed national identity.

Whether the Guggenheim has been successful is questionable. Economist Maria Sainz argues that for some, 'the city lacks the critical mass of attractions to take it from a provincial post-industrial town to a global cosmopolitan city.'[58] The spectacle dominates the city's image and design critic-curator Deyan Sudjic comments that the scheme has, 'stripped away a lot of the alibis for building museums, revealing the egotism and showmanship beneath the rhetoric of self-improvement and scholarship'.[59] That rhetoric began in the nineteenth century (see Chapter 5) but the egotism is recent. Murray Fraser and Joe Kerr claim that it was the Guggenheim which took Gehry from being a mere starchitect to the status of an international celebrity:

It would be hard to conceive a building project which so clearly exemplifies the workings of cultural imperialism, or the effects of global capitalism in this unholy alliance between an expansionist American institution and the regional government of a decayed heavy industrial area.[60]

Whatever else, the Guggenheim is global: the software used in its design was adapted from that used for French military aircraft; the titanium was mined in Australia, smelted in France, laminated in Pittsburgh, stripped in Britain and folded in Milan.[61] I do not have the data for its eco-footprint.

Is it over?

Perhaps the cultural turn epitomised by the Guggenheim, or the Bilbao effect, is turning. In 2012, Helsinki's City Board voted against a proposal for a new Guggenheim on its waterfront on the grounds of high cost and questionable governance. Culture Minister Paavo Arhinmäki asked why 'Finnish taxpayers should finance a rich, multinational foundation'.[62] At the same time, a poll carried out by the newspaper *Helsingin Sanomat* found 75 per cent of Helsinki residents were against the plan. But the issue is not closed; a redrafted proposal was submitted in 2013 at a lower cost to the city, on a different site, and involving the building of a permanent collection and a merger with one of the city's existing museums. A design competition was launched in 2014, with an international jury chaired by architectural theorist Mark Wigley.[63] A decision on whether or not to go ahead will be made only after the jury has deliberated, in June, 2015. I was in Helsinki for an academic conference a few days before finalising this book. I spent a morning at Kiasma, designed by Steven Holl and opened in 1998, the city's own museum of contemporary art which has become popular as a meeting place (Figure 1.3). I attended a reception at the City Hall where the Guggenheim was mentioned (nearly a thousand entries have been received for the design competition). I cannot see why Helsinki, with its existing architectural heritage and history of struggles for national independence, needs either the financial burden or the stardust sprinkle of this art brand.

Now, anyway, after the crash, the money has started to disappear. In 2011, a new arts centre designed by Oscar Niemeyer in Avilés, Spain closed after only six months. Journalist Giles Tremlett reported that, 'Several

Figure 1.3   Kiasma museum for contemporary art, Helsinki, Steven Holl

thousand people took to the streets ... in a display of support for an arts centre locals hoped would put the city on the global culture map.'[64] Bilbao shows that being on the culture map is not the same as regenerating local communities or economies after de-industrialisation, although it is not really a question of data but of qualitative change.

I wonder, then, if there is a credibility gap as capital's co-option of the arts begins to tarnish in a period of austerity and a widening divide between affluent and marginalised societies. It may be that some of the claims once made for culture as the lever of regeneration now seem unrealistic. There are successes, notably Tate Modern in terms of visitor numbers; and there are failures, too, including new museums which have closed shortly after opening (see Chapter 4). Meanwhile the regeneration sector, as it has become, turns more to property development (always its core business). It will be interesting to see what happens in Helsinki when a final decision is taken on the Guggenheim (which will be after this book's publication). Some of the new museums took strange forms, but estrangement is the general condition of the bleak, de-industrialised estate today. If the wasteland is to be really rehabilitated, it will be more by human warmth.

2

Creative Classes:
Aesthetics and Gentrification

In her novel *Cat's Eye*, published in 1989,[1] Canadian writer Margaret Atwood makes several references to the emerging arts district of Toronto. The references are incidental, background images for a story about an artist's attempt to retrieve memories of a childhood friend. Some of the memories turn out to be darker than she thought, or are irretrievable. The arts district of Toronto serves as a suitably ambivalent backdrop for her wanderings, offering traces of a past coloured by disquiet. Atwood's description of an arts district is fictional yet sufficiently credible to illuminate the localised impact of the cultural turn in urban strategies for renewal after de-industrialisation. Atwood sets her story in Toronto but similar scenarios have unfolded in other cities, adapted to their circumstances.

Atwood writes of 'tubular neon in cursive script' decorating the restored brick façades; she adds, 'and there's a lot of brass trim, a lot of real estate, a lot of money'.[2] Elaine Risley (the artist-protagonist) hates Toronto and has done so for as long as she can remember. It used to be just dull, she reflects, but now, 'you're supposed to say how much it's changed. *World-class city* is a phrase they use in magazines ... New York without the garbage and the muggings.'[3] People once went from Toronto to Buffalo for weekends but now the traffic is the other way. Looking at Toronto, she remarks, 'Every building I pass down here among the warehouses seems to cry *Renovate me! Renovate me!*'[4] Where wholesale clothing was once sold, 'the old Jewish delis are disappearing' and street signs say *Fashion District* under the names because everything is a district: 'There never used to be districts.'[5]

Elaine has a show at a small gallery called Sub-Versions. It is located in a transitional street, between a tattoo parlour and a restaurant-supply store:

'Both of these will go' because, as galleries move in, 'the handwriting's on the wall.'[6] Hand-writing suggests craft but older craft trades are displaced by this hand-writing. Sub-Versions is ambiguous, too: it could mean a subversion of bourgeois values, or the edgy quality of a fashionable subculture. The gallery appeals to collectors likely to be inner-city young professionals – bohos – and is a fire-ship for cultural recoding; it sails into the fleet of old trades and the properties in which they were housed, bringing disarray as scaffolding and skips.

Typically, in non-fictional cities, urban villages, cultural and heritage zones, designer bars with industrial light fittings and strange music emerge in such transitional zones. A district may be at its most interesting while in transition, before high capital ossifies it, but the script is written as soon as a gallery like Sub-Versions opens there. I am adding to Atwood's story, of course, but the picture is a process of estrangement which is all too familiar now. Reading the passage above again, Elaine's phrase 'the handwriting's on the wall'[7] may refer to the biblical story of Belshazzar's feast, when a mysterious hand wrote on the palace wall as the king feasted with his guests: 'Mene Mene Tekel Upharsin' (You have been weighed in the balance. Your days are numbered).[8]

Elaine does not like the arts district, and is disoriented by the changes. After the opening of her show, the curator calls Elaine: '"We" made the front page of a magazine ... "It's a real rave!" I shudder at her idea of a rave; and what does she mean by "we"?'[9] Elaine goes out to buy the magazine. She scans the beginning of the article and looks at the photographs:

> I suck in some coffee, skip to the last paragraph: the inevitable *eclectic*, the obligatory *post-feminist*, a *however* and a *despite*. Good old Toronto bet-hedging and qualification. A blistering attack would be preferable, some flying fur, a little fire and brimstone. That way I would know I'm still alive.
>
> I think savagely of the opening. Perhaps I should be deliberately provocative. Perhaps I should confirm their deepest suspicions ...[10]

Elaine remembers unhappy moments from childhood; she was disaffected by other children's power-plays, and now, as a mature artist, she remains caught in various binds, such as being the provider of the material which Sub-Versions needs to prosper in the new economy. Finally, Elaine returns to the West Coast.

Transitional zones

Geographer David Ley writes about (the real) Toronto as where the arts fuel gentrification as artists move into downtown areas despite the high rents: 'Artists must be enduring considerable sacrifices of both housing quality and affordability to maintain this residential habit.... their behaviour defies economic rationality, confirming that they are marching to a different drummer.'[11] The drummer is success. Its proof is visibility, getting known through shows and magazine reviews by well-known critics, and bought by collectors. The collectors, in turn, use loans to public museums to increase the value of the works they collect. This is complex: for artists (as producers) there is a balancing act between affordability and the need to be in a milieu and in reach of a critical mass of venues – outposts of an art world – where it is possible to make connections. Being an artist is both collaborative and competitive. But for cultural consumers such as tourists or visitors from the suburbs, the identity of an arts district as a place between past and future is part of the draw: an edginess and a sense of reassurance in a licensed mixing with other kinds of people in streets which require a constant negotiation of space. This is perceived as an authenticity, and artists are also attracted to it. Ley cites a sculptor:

> Artists need authentic locations. You know artists hate the suburbs. They're too confining. Every artist is an anthropologist, unveiling culture. It helps to get some distance on that culture in an environment that does not share all of its presuppositions, an old area, socially diverse, including poverty groups.[12]

As Ley notes, 'the suburbs and the shopping mall, emblems of a mass market and a failure of personal taste, are rejected.'[13] In Toronto there is an added layer of re-shaping the city. In the 1960s, Jane Jacobs celebrated the street in *The Death and Life of Great American Cities*; this informed the protection of older districts of Toronto against wholesale redevelopment so that, historian Christopher Klemek writes, 'Toronto became a reply to the urban crises south of the border.'[14]

New art districts are sites of continuous change. First small galleries move in and artists find low-cost live-in studios. Then other, more lucrative businesses move in as visitors are drawn to the area for its distinctly cultural feeling and the small designer bars, restaurants and shops which follow the galleries. At some point, property prices rise so that only successful artists can afford to stay unless there is rent control (as in some cases in New York's SoHo, one of the earliest arts districts in a redundant industrial neighbourhood). Then, as in SoHo, a range of up-market stores moves in, and bars and restaurants change to meet the needs of up-market customers: a second recoding occurs. Perhaps the sense of flux affirms the unfixed quality of the immaterial economy of media, communications, advertising and public relations which is also known as the creative sector or, critically, the culture industries. This is a sector in which values are produced through shifts of fashion and visibility in a loose but strong consensus of those wielding influence in the sector. For art, the network (or art world) comprises private-sector dealers, public-sector curators, critics, collectors and a few successful artists, or even an occasional public intellectual in countries which have them. The art world decides whose work is shown and whose is not. Its unwritten codes should not be transgressed. Sociologist Howard Becker notes, 'the conventional way of doing things in any art utilizes an existing cooperative network, which rewards those who manipulate the existing conventions appropriately in light of the associated aesthetic'.[15]

An example of this network in action is the maintenance of the category Contemporary Art. It is the informal, cooperative but also highly competitive network of dealers and others which determines what counts as the Contemporary. A small gallery succeeds if it finds new artists who are taken up by magazines and public museums, whose showing of such work adds value through the museum's supposedly objective judgement. But independent curators are junior players in the game, to whom more senior players out-source risk. The curators of a gallery like the fictional Sub-Versions are often self-employed. They are not on zero-hours contracts but their presence is negotiable. They need to be mobile, and to enjoy working in a flexible economy. The sense of impending instability of their predicament becomes addictive, especially in a big city where the atmosphere is already frenetic. They exemplify one part of work in the new economy, of which Richard Sennett writes that, 'rulers of the flexible realm' know that 'the great majority of those who toil in the flexible regime are left behind, and of course they regret it. But the flexibility they celebrate does not give ... any guidance for the conduct of an ordinary life.'[16] This implies that the art world, within the creative industries, shares the new economy's production of a feeling of permanent change as the new norm. This reminds me of Walter Benjamin's assertion, written in the 1930s, that the state of emergency 'is not the exception but the rule'.[17]

Art's flexible economy is destabilising, if masked by histories of continuous change in avant-gardism and revolutions of style. For dealers, it justifies decisions to dump artists whose work does not sell and promote others, whose work does sell, to senior status and higher prices in a retrospective show. Art is business, like derivatives; and the creative sector represents the soft power of capital's imperative to consume, recoding de-industrialised neighbourhoods as districts. As Elaine says, everywhere is a district now.

The processes of transition to an arts district tend to be uneven in pace and scope. They also depart from the model of transitional zones established in the inter-war period by Chicago sociologists E.W. Burgess, Louis Wirth and Robert Park. The Chicago School put emphasis on the conflicting claims to space produced by successive waves of migration into the city, and related urban conflicts to human nature. Although human nature is a contestable concept, the Chicago sociologists saw it as a mediation of both a biotic urge (a form of Darwinism, or the survival of the most adaptable species) and a cultural environment in which humans evolve mutual understandings, and communicate them to each other. The former leads to competition while the latter tends to cooperation and a shared moral order. Sociologist Mark Gottdiener summarises, 'Thus variation in the sectors of the city ... was produced by the overlay of moral orders through competitive-cooperation.'[18] To understand tensions between competition and cooperation, as between diverse groups within a specific city (Chicago being their model), Park investigated urban types – such as the hobo – whom they saw as typifying a transitional environment. Park had studied under Georg Simmel in Berlin, later utilising Simmel's theoretical sociology in observing the city's mixed publics in an attempt at a total understanding of 'the city',[19] and was one of the first sociologists to investigate the daily lives of urban African-Americans. He saw the introduction of playgrounds, sports facilities and municipal dance halls as aiding social cohesion by elevating the moral tone of a given neighbourhood.[20] Park and his colleagues were generally progressive, yet, as planner Peter Hall comments, the Chicago School was concerned with a transition from a pre-industrial to an industrialised city where exchange value replaced traditional values and class became a key differentiator,[21] not the shift from an industrial to a de-industrialised estate which might preoccupy sociologists today. There is a further issue, in that Burgess et al. saw the modern city as inherently unstable: 'the vast casual and mobile aggregations which constitute our urban populations are in a state of perpetual agitation, swept by every new wind of doctrine, subject to constant alarms' so that 'the community is in a chronic condition of crisis'.[22] This reflects their reading of Darwinism, and what they took to be a competitive aggression built into human nature (hence outside history, more or less inevitable). For them, the solution to a range of conflicts which they saw as always likely to arise (or which could not be prevented at source, given the constant flow of urban immigration) was the professional expertise of the planner and the sociologist.

To an extent, Burgess, Park and Wirth reiterated the dualism proposed in early sociology between the city as a zone of stress as well as a location of new forms of sociation, on the one hand, and rural settlements as stable, family-based and rooted in the land, on the other. In the 1920s and 1930s, this romantic view of the countryside translated into a biological lens through which to read city growth, as if it resembled plant growth. But biological metaphors, as noted above, put the problem of the city outside the realm of politics (a realm of conflict), thereby privileging the planner's quasi-scientific expertise and claim to an objectivity which can also be seen, in gendered terms, as a master-view (leading to the proliferation of master plans). In his study of urban street gangs, for instance, Burgess observed that gang members were often the children of migrants from rural areas in Europe who found the city an alien terrain where claims to space had to be fought for, affirming a view of conflict as an essential condition of expanding industrialised cities (and of rural life as a rose-tinted foil).

The Chicago sociologists remain influential, and Burgess's concentric ring diagram (based on Chicago's elevated railway around a central business district) is a model reproduced in many cities. Their research on ghettoes was flawed,[23] and their archetypal marginal person was the stereotyped 'culturally cosmopolitan emancipated Jew'.[24] But, by a marginal person they did not mean marginal in the sense of an outsider, more someone living between cultures, and perhaps a distant forerunner of the creative type introduced by the author of a more recent formula for understanding urban change, Richard Florida.

A creative class?

Florida sees the changes in urban conditions which have occurred since the 1950s as 'deeper and more pervasive' than those of the previous 50 years.[25] Identifying new technologies as a driving force, Florida does not accept what he says is a popular view: that such changes are imposed on people: 'Society is changing in large measure because we want it to.'[26] He does not say who constitutes the we in that sentence – everyone, everyone in North America, his friends or his employees ... – but goes on to identify a second driving force:

> The rise of human creativity [is] the key factor in our economy and society. Both at work and in other spheres of our lives, we value creativity more highly than ever, and cultivate it more intensely. The creative impulse – the attitude that distinguishes us, humans, from other species – is now being let loose on an unprecedented scale.
>
> ... creativity has come to be the most highly prized commodity in our economy – and yet it is not a commodity. Creativity comes from people. And while people can be hired and fired, their creative capacity cannot be bought and sold, or turned on and off at will. This is why ... we see the emergence of a new order in the workplace. Hiring for diversity, once a matter of legal compliance, has become a matter of economic survival because creativity comes in all colours, genders and personal preferences.[27]

This needs some unpacking. First, the narrative is universalising and all-inclusive. It includes all human life while, by inference, singling out North American affluent society as the site of creativity and economic development. Second, creativity is identified as a commodity but this status is then detached from its agents so that people take on the status of a human resource as their quasi-magical creativity floats free from exchange values. Creativity, that is, is bought or sold just as its possessors are hired and fired. His reference to a new workplace order may be accurate, however, if not quite as he intends.

Florida refers to diversity, no longer as compliance with equality legislation but now a matter of economic survival; this seems progressive but raises questions such as whether a diverse workforce is more creative as a product of cultural interfaces, or whether creative people are simply diverse in background. The latter might imply that arts education is a leveller, but the absent term in Florida's narrative is social class. It appears that Florida masks an erasure of class and class consciousness, that is, by coining the term creative class for people who work in the creative industries. The assertion seems to be that creative people are *déclassé*; this avoids asking to what extent they remain within older class structures or become a self-selected elite whose claim to status is based on a notion of creativity. I am not persuaded. It may be that the creative class, in as much as this is a useful category, constitutes a new elite inhabiting gated enclaves in post-industrial cities; yet this does not mean that members of this new elite are of a common outlook, nor that there is not a set of local distinctions within the creative class.

Another view is presented by Elizabeth Wilson in her book on bohemianism. On punk in the 1970s, she says that its 'howl of rage' was 'assimilated with surprising ease into the Reagan–Thatcher years of greed and brutal politics' because its cultural nihilism was 'adapted without too much difficulty to express the moral nihilism of capitalist economics'.[28] She says, further, that bohemianism was celebrated by 'a breathless flood of cultural material' as its adoption in mass culture affected public morality, too: 'The hippies of the 1960s, the Punks of the 1970s, 1980s New Romantics, fetish dressers and Queer Culture, were bohemians by another name. They provided a focus for dissidence and rebellion, yet were more rapidly marketed than ever.'[29] Sociologist Jim McGuigan cites Wilson's view of nineteenth-century bohemians as inhabiting an alternative world, and being, as he puts it, 'a marginal nuisance to respectable society'.[30] The mythical bohemian is, 'an ambiguous figure, caught up in countervailing forces, trying to live a life on the outside while looking in sceptically.... The bohemian wants to be authentic in an inauthentic world.'[31] Perhaps the creative class trades on such a myth of bohemianism subsumed in the mass media, which obscures real class divisions which remain in the de-industrialised estate produced by globalisation.

The superficiality of Florida's construction of a creative class is confirmed by his comments on what he calls the 'new labour market'.[32] Florida describes this new market for mainly hi-tech skills as horizontal, citing the case of a young professional immigrant from Belarus who moves from Norfolk, Virginia to Pittsburgh – Miami is too hot, New York is expensive – and from employment to self-employment and back again: 'people like this are ... navigating the new realities of the horizontal labour market'.[33] Florida alludes to increasing equality within firms, and to identification with a profession rather than a company. This reflects the demise of some large companies, no longer offering jobs for life, and a fluidity in employment which reflects the privilege attached to specialist knowledge in immaterial production. But when he alludes to the challenges, autonomy and satisfaction of the new economy, I read this as an unconvincing gloss on precarity. In contrast, commentator Guy Standing writes that, while 'some try to give the precariat a positive image, typifying a romantic free spirit who rejects the norms of the old working class', this is only part of the picture: 'there is nothing new in ... struggles against the dictates of subordinated labour'.[34] Rather than relaxing in the fabled delights of insecurity, then, the new precariat experience anger, anomie, anxiety and (as in the old economy) alienation.[35]

Florida claims that 'people bear more responsibility for every aspect of their careers' and that, as companies introduce large-scale redundancies as a result of shifts of production, there is not much reaction: 'no picket signs, no demonstrations, not a peep from the politicians'.[36] His perspective is blinkered by his rhetoric and, while he quotes an unemployed woman who accepts the situation 'as the way things are', this could suggest social disintegration. As he says, unwittingly, 'we are truly on our own'.[37] This accords with Zygmunt Bauman's view of the new world order of globalisation:

> Thrown into the vast open sea with no navigation charts and all the marker buoys sunk and barely visible, we have only two choices left: we may rejoice in the breath-taking vistas of new discoveries – or we may tremble out of fear of drowning. One option not really realistic is to claim sanctuary in a safe harbour ... what seems to be a tranquil haven today will be soon modernized, and a theme park, amusement promenade or crowded marine will replace the sedate boatsheds.[38]

The writing is on the wall. People put up with being adrift when they still have something to lose but, as Occupy demonstrated in the winter of 2011, there is a point when anger erupts.

Despite the weakness of his arguments – or because his assertions attract city managers and marketers for whom academic critique like mine is unhelpful – Florida has had a successful career as a consultant promoting the creative class in regenerating urban economies. Before moving on, I want to look at the de-politicisation which is integral to Florida's advocacy; and briefly at one aspect of a mentality which might exemplify the creative class.

Angela McRobbie suggests that, when work is multi-tasking and multi-sited, politics is left out. She adds, 'The necessity of speed and the velocity of transaction, along with the mobility and fluidity of individuals, throws into question a defining feature of this kind of work. This is its relation to the idea of reflexivity.'[39] Creative people are seen as being self-monitoring, reflexive, and self-motivating. Florida sees a horizontally structured workplace but McRobbie writes:

> If we ... consider reflexivity as a form of self-disciplining where subjects of the new enterprise culture are increasingly called upon to inspect themselves ... then reflexivity marks the space of self-responsibility, self blame. In this sense, it is a de-politicizing, de-socializing mechanism: Where have I gone wrong?[40]

McRobbie goes on to say that, sociology has made few inroads here as the media which covers the creative sector sees such disciplines as irrelevant; this is because neoliberalism is not only embedded in those media but also because they rubbish the political vocabulary 'associated with the left and with feminism' aligned to equality, anti-discrimination, workplace democracy and workers' representation.[41] McRobbie further states:

> In the cultural sector, with its emphasis on the creative and expressive, it might be imagined that this could be the right place for social minorities to succeed and for women to achieve equal participation. However it seems possible that quite the opposite is happening. What we see ... is the emergence of working practices which reproduce older patterns of marginalization ... while also disallowing any space or time for such issues to reach articulation. In this case the club culture question of 'are you on the guest list?' is extended to recruitment and personnel, so that getting an interview for contract creative work depends on informal knowledge and contacts, often friendships.[42]

So much for Florida's horizontal workplace and cuddly creativity which embraces diversity: the creative sector is a rat race. But who are the elite whose favours are sought? I refer, again, to the networks of dealers, curators, critics, collectors and successful artists who comprise an art world, and their equivalents in other fields.

Museum collections are organised as art-historical narratives so that individual works become episodes in a trajectory, but individual collecting is shaped by personal taste and narratives of the self. Sociologist Kevin Hetherington cites Benjamin that a collector is engaged in, 'removing things from their functional context' to put them 'in an imaginary and allegorical realm of constructed meaning'.[43] He adds, again from Benjamin:

Collecting is a form of singularization. [It] is all about trying to produce a stop or pause in the biography of an artefact and to transfigure its value by telling another story around it and its companion artifacts. It is about trying to fix the artefact within the flow of value and allow it to hold a position of significance. In effect, it is about trying to establish the qualities of eternity and of memorialized history on things that are transient and will eventually pass away.[44]

Hetherington's conclusion is that the museum is 'where the commodity comes to rest' as the bourgeois conception of the past is articulated in a set of objects.[45] Collectors who make their money in the new economy may have little regard for old bourgeois ideas. By buying new art they set themselves apart from the world of old money but they may still be trying to fix their image, if not in a lasting form, in a form which gains publicity. Art, as a commodity, does not come to rest but is part of a flow of added value, reflected in the re-branding of an inner-city neighbourhood as an arts district. The buildings are collected by designers and used as iconic images by developers; people are encouraged to move, and keep on moving creatively.

Symbolic economies

The function of the creative sector is to re-brand a city for a global market. Despite Florida's claim for diversity, re-branded cities tend to homogeneity. Sharon Zukin observes that when cities pursue such ends the outcome is 'an overbearing sameness' expressed in claims to have the tallest building, or the insertion of an art museum in a de-industrialised zone.[46] Allen Scott includes Toronto with Montreal, Barcelona, Amsterdam, Seoul, Hong Kong and Rio de Janeiro in a list of cities as, 'foci of important cultural production activities ... at a point in their development where they may well rapidly come to compete effectively with the top-ranked cities'.[47] Only New York and Los Angeles are top-ranked in Florida's scheme, with London, Paris, Milan and Tokyo as future contenders.

From another perspective based in global finance, Saskia Sassen defines New York, London and Tokyo as *the* global city; a single, geographically disbursed entity of enclaves connected by information technology. Continental Europe does badly in competition for global status, having only Frankfurt as a key financial centre, but the annual nomination of a European Community City or Capital of Culture creates a map based instead on heritage and contemporary culture. Among those designated, Liverpool (2008), Sibiu (2007), Patras (2006), Graz (2005) and Salamanca (2002) are major cultural but not economic hubs. Some major cities and national capitals have also been designated, such as Glasgow (1990), Dublin (1991), Madrid (1992), Lisbon (1994), Copenhagen (1996), Stockholm (1998) and Helsinki (2000). The EU (European Union) scheme goes against the grain of world cities by constructing an alternative measure based on culture and heritage, then, and foregrounds the divide between a European categorisation as a cultural or creative city, on the one hand, and, on the other, a range of definitions of the creative industries and the creative class mapped onto the (supposedly creative) cities they occupy.

Florida does not take the arts as *the* creative industry, however, and includes 'science and engineering, computers and mathematics, education, and the arts, design and entertainment' as sub-sectors of the creative industries.[48] Professionals in such areas comprise a super-creative core of a class which, more broadly, includes management, law, health, technology and marketing. In Florida's scheme, the working class and the service class play no role in the kinds of transition that he advocates beyond menial tasks. McRobbie argues (above) that the creative sector is de-politicised while the creative city is presented as conflict-free, shaped by creative solutions which are seen as politically neutral, as was planning expertise by the Chicago sociologists. The creative class may retreat from the unmediated signs of de-industrialisation in adjacent neighbourhoods,[49] or they may like the frisson of urban edginess; either way, they act to determine a dominant image of a city in which signs of conflict are erased in favour of the glitzy, spectacular and supposedly non-contentious signs of culture and innovation. In the symbolic economy by which cities compete for global recognition, images made for external perception freeze out those of everyday life.

Zukin argues that, while cities have always maintained symbolic economies of value – what should be visible, what is ordering – the post-industrial symbolic economy of place marketing and property development is qualitatively new. There is a 'traditional symbolic economy of city advocates and business elites' but there is also a new 'symbiosis of image and product ... the role of the symbolic economy in speaking for, or representing, the city'.[50] A city's image fixes its values rather than reflecting them; for Zukin, culture becomes 'a powerful means of controlling cities' by representing who participates in determining the dominant image.[51] For members of elites in the new economy, art offers opportunities for investment and an arena of influence through the networking opportunities available to members of a museum Board of Trustees. Meanwhile, art fuses with high finance. Zukin writes:

> The financial boom that lasted for most of the 1980s influenced sharp price rises in the real estate and art markets.... Regardless of aesthetics, investment in art, for prestige or speculation, represented a collective means of social mobility. At the same time, a collective belief in the growth of the symbolic economy of art represented belief in the growth of the city's economy. Visual representation became a means of financially re-presenting the city. By the 1990s, it seemed to be official policy that making a place for art in the city went along with establishing a marketable identity for the city as a whole.[52]

Geographer Andrew Harris charts a close, two-way relation between contemporary art and the financial services sector:

> It is likely that much of any new cultural activity over the next few years will again be branded and packaged as a willing partner in post-recessionary financial landscapes and new waves of economic expansion. This is particularly because ... the financial sector has not fallen but remains central to economic policy-making.... [The] crisis has instigated a financial coup against Western governments and a massive consolidation of the banking system. Likewise, there has been a major coup against critical art practice in countries such as the UK, with steep reduction in public subsidies for art, education and cultural institutions – despite attempted interventions from artists ...[53]

In other words, as the financial sector appropriates the public purse after a crisis caused by its own irrational behaviour up to the 2007 crash, and government becomes the facilitator rather than the regulator of capital's operations, cultural work which might otherwise criticise this state of affairs loses subsidies and venues, driving it into marginal spaces where its voice can be dismissed by the dominant elite as that of a *self-marginalising* profession.

The situation is not new. For sociologist Toby Miller, the creative sector discourse began in the 1960s with neoliberalism; he remarks:

the Global South similarly seeks secure streams of revenue from
intellectual property.... Harnessing the skills of the population is
meant to replace lost agricultural and manufacturing employment with
creative or cultural sector jobs in music, theatre, animation, recording,
radio, television, architecture, software design, toys, books, heritage,
tourism, advertising, fashion, crafts, photography, and cinema.[54]

Zukin observed in 1995 that, 'Every well-designed downtown has a
mixed-use shopping centre and a nearby artists' quarter ... every derelict
factory district or waterfront has been converted into one of those sites
of visual delectation – a themed shopping space ... restaurants, art
galleries.'[55] This has been replicated around the world as city after city
seeks sites of affluent, modish consumption where, 'the authority of art' is
joined to 'the cultural hegemony of a new financial elite and the politics
of public goods'.[56]

Consumption zones

In practice, the recoding of a zone as an arts district transforms it into
a zone of consumption comprising museum shops and cafés, boutiques
and bars, restaurants, and the place itself. If it has a waterfront vista,
developers are likely to be most interested. The museum becomes an
object of consumption too. Sociologist Grant McCracken argues that
consumer society has changed visitors' expectations of museums, leading
them to seek experiences that pull them towards 'a world of ... existential
mobility'.[57] And Florida sees the lifestyle of the creative class as a quest
for 'intense, high-quality, multidimensional experiences'.[58] Sociologist
Steven Miles argues instead that commodification normalises experience;
and that, 'consumption offers a new kind of citizenship ... that takes the
individual out of the political realm and prioritises the private-public one
instead'.[59] Hence, 'the world appears less finite than it was ... the debate
continues as to how schizophrenic identity becomes as a result'.[60]

The Enlightenment ideal of the city as *polis*, a political entity aspiring
to a state of *cosmopolis* (a heterogeneity unified by rationality, science and
language),[61] is replaced in this scenario by an ideal of market forces seen
as value-free and self-correcting. Paradoxically, the model of a self-correcting system derives from the self-contained systems of modern rationality,

found in the self-evident certainties of mathematics and geometry, while the 2007 crash demonstrates an inherent irrationality in capitalism.

Another form of hermetic containment is reflected in the white-walled modern art museum of which an archetypal case is the Museum of Modern Art (MoMA), New York, founded in 1929. MoMA does three things: it reconstructs the experience of a private collection for a general public, in rooms which are domestic in scale but linked in a selective narrative; it remakes art history as a narrative of progress, of which its collection is the defining model;[62] and uses the market's techniques to insert itself in the public mind and image of New York. Art historian Christoph Grunenberg writes of MoMA resembling, 'a business enterprise' which uses, 'the most up-to-date methods of distribution ... to shock and ... get its name in the newspapers and the public to visit its exhibitions'.[63] Within MoMA's white interior denoting a value-free space, then, a symbolic order is established in which artists, mainly white men, interpret the world. But this is a mid-twentieth-century view, overtaken by the exploits of artist-celebrities since the 1980s, who fit more easily into a definition of the creative class that does not privilege aesthetics.

The creative class brings new money which sustains a cappuccino lifestyle. Although neither the arts districts nor lifestyle consumption outlets put up keep-out notices there tends to be an air of affluence conveyed by arty design, which sends subliminal (or more overt) messages to outsiders who might drift in while attracting aspirational members of the less well-paid areas of the creative class to transitional-zone restaurants, designer bars and clubs, or shops which camouflage their trade (as in putting antiques in the window of a clothes shop). Customers here are likely to be served by members of what Florida calls the service class.

Playing a more instrumental role are cultural intermediaries: people in the creative sector, willing to take risks, image-making, dwelling in a creative flux, who, according to Justin O'Connor, 'interpret, package, transmit and manipulate symbols and knowledge in a way that produces new value'.[64] O'Connor did his research in Manchester, where clubs and popular music played a role in producing a 24-hour city, transforming the city's image in ways that planners and politicians could not. But there is evidence that consumers in redeveloped areas such as Castlefield in Manchester, near the universities, are active in occupying consumption spaces in their own ways, developing their own spatial practices.[65] This may not hinder gentrification, however. Consumers, like artists, may be harbingers of recoding and re-branding beyond their scope for determination.

Gentrification

The crudest view might be that gentrification is what happens when the creative class moves in. It happens in cities where the symbolic economy dominates, and spaces hitherto aligned to manufacturing or ordinary life are aestheticised to create urban villages and cultural quarters. The term was first used by Ruth Glass to describe conditions in inner-city districts where old working-class properties (typically nineteenth-century terraced houses) were occupied by middle-class incomers.[66] Examples in London include parts of Hackney, Dalston and parts of Battersea and Islington. Beck Road in Hackney, for instance, consists of terraces built for the working class which fell into partial dereliction in the post-war years, were adopted by an arts organisation for live-in artists' studios, then improved and bought out by many of the artists, sold on, and now house as many professionals in financial services as in the arts. Southwark, south of the Thames, is becoming another case, around Tate Modern. A nuance, however, is that in parts of Hackney, such as Stoke Newington, improvements are carried out through the agency of incoming middle-class home-owners rather than through external impetus, as in the insertion of high-profile cultural institutions and adjunct consumption sites.[67]

Gentrification, then denotes both renovation of houses of multiple (usually rented) occupation for single-owner occupation, or their division into high-rent apartments; and the conversion of de-industrialised sites (such as warehouses) to residential or mixed residential, arts and retail uses. The latter may be a vehicle for cultural recoding via the property market. It is a two-way street. Generally, gentrification produces a decrease in diversity in terms of income and class but possibly not of ethnicity (if I concede to Florida that young professionals tend to be ethnically diverse).

The pace may be uneven. Geographer Neil Smith writes of changes in inner-city districts in New York as interest rates and markets fluctuate to sometimes leave intrepid urban settlers marooned in a district which has failed to become a creative zone.[68] At the same time, the market looks more or less anywhere for the next hip zone. In 2004, *The New Yorker* carried a series of spoof predictions from characters such as Chip von Thurn and Taxis ('UnGeoWa is still more beachhead than neighbourhood') and Freddie Bullion of the Frick-Carnegie Homes ('The weed-choked rectangle of asphalt that they're calling BruBou is catching on fast with upper Manhattan's colourful bands of gypsies').[69] In reality, as Loretta Lees, Tom Slater and Elvin Wyly record, 2,000 tenants had to leave their homes in New York between 1999 and 2002 due to landlord harassment while 2,900 more were evicted. Meanwhile property prices in Manhattan rose by up to 225 per cent on the previous peak in the 1980s.[70]

After decades of a move to the suburbs by the managerial and professional class, especially in North America, and demonisation of the inner city as a crime zone, inner-city areas were rehabilitated by both economic and cultural factors. Young professionals found a non-suburban (or not family home) environment, and an edgy street scene as they resettled down-market sites. The new businesses which moved in afterwards met their consumption tastes. A rationalisation of this is the rent-gap model in which low-value properties begin to produce higher returns as they become fashionable (as in an arts district where artists may begin the process). If returns on suburban land are highest at first, as land values there rise so comparative returns decrease while those of inner-city areas increase, leading developers to invest there.[71] Another model is based on consumption rather than land values, and the spending power of the yuppies. John Rennie Short uses the terms 'yuppie' (young upwardly mobile professional) and 'yuffie' (young urban failure, the unemployed working class stranded in what have become marginal zones after de-industrialisation) to differentiate the winners and losers.[72] The yuppies drive gentrification, and are resented by members of what become residual publics. Ley's research looks mainly at this reading of gentrification, informed by Daniel Bell's characterisation of the post-industrial economy as entailing a shift from manufacturing to service sectors and the rise of a knowledge-economy, and new city-images in art.[73] Lees et al. summarise Ley's position:

> Ley argued that gentrification represented a new phase in urban development where consumption factors, taste, and a particular aesthetic outlook towards the city from an expanding middle class saw an 'imagineering of an alternative urbanism to suburbanization' which could not be captured by explanations of the process that privileged structural forces of production and housing market analysis.[74]

Ley puts the emphasis on qualitative factors, not on the quantitative economics of the housing market; and he is concerned as much with a mix of spatial uses as with residential property. A new qualitative factor was proposed in the 1980s by feminist geographer Damaris Rose, who identified the role of professional women – single mothers or women with working partners – in a reoccupation of the inner city. Lees et al. summarise, citing Rose's use of the term 'marginal gentrifier':

> [Rose] refers to the fact that marginally employed professionals, prominent among whom were women, single parents, and those receiving moderate incomes, were attracted to central-city neighbourhoods due to the range of support services they offered – which were unavailable in the suburbs. For example, the worry of precarious employment could be eased by networking and holding more than one job; and by minimizing space-time constraints, lone female parents could combine paid and unpaid (domestic) labour with greater ease than in suburban locations.[75]

This casts the gentrifier in a different light, as much coping with the negative effects of the new economy as capitalising on it, closer to McRobbie's concern with the negative effects of the new economy. Florida proposed that gay and lesbian publics lead gentrification by being members of the creative class, exemplifying its diversity, and by liberalising a district's social attitudes in ways that reduce barriers to incomers. He uses selective data of gay residence and the location of high-tech industry to generalise that, 'A place that welcomes a gay community welcomes all kinds of people.'[76] Lees et al. have little time for Florida, exposing various contradictions in his writing; they cite his 'bewildering set of indices ... to rank cities' creativity',[77] and quote geographer Jamie Peck that *The Rise of the Creative Class* contains, 'excruciating details of his [Florida's] biography, lifestyle and consumption habits' and 'less-than-analytical musings ... self-indulgent forms of amateur microsociology'.[78] I think that is enough said on Florida.

Cleaning up

For sociologist Monica Degen, 'metaphors of colonization permeate the official discourses' of urban regeneration.[79] Her comparative study of

Castlefield in Manchester and El Raval in Barcelona reveals that both neighbourhoods were transformed through improvements in aid of economic revival which aestheticise the spaces involved. But in El Raval (site of the Museu d'Art Contemporani de Barcelona – MACBA, see Chapter 1), a high-density, multi-ethnic neighbourhood of narrow streets lined by balconied eighteenth- and nineteenth-century apartment blocks which was once the red-light district, the aim was to sanitise the area. Degen quotes a city councillor that El Raval 'has had the function of receiving the residual activities of the city for many years'[80] while the grid plan and open spaces of the city's extension (planned by Ildefons Cerdá after demolition of the city's walls in the 1860s) is a model of orderliness; 'all regeneration ideas of the historic city … start from the basis of letting the values of the new city penetrate the values of the old city … [these are] hygiene, order, salubrious conditions, hierarchies and the specialization of functions.'[81] Degen sums up, 'The underlying assumption is that a regenerated public space, meaning here a purified space, will improve the social behaviour of its residents.'[82] She cites a local planner:

> [El Raval] was a place where the sun never shone, where there were no areas where children could play, and then of course they did other things.… Current urban changes have a lot to do with the social improvement of the area. It also helps other groups to enter. Before [the regeneration] few people would have settled down in the Old City and the very moment we change conditions people come back.[83]

The changes consisted in demolitions, the construction of a New Ramblas in the space of five blocks of old apartments, and some infill in which new buildings do not have balconies but smooth, white façades with, at most, decorative railings outside windows on the upper floors. The old Ramblas is one of the city's best known boulevards. It connects the city centre to the waterfront and the old port, with bars, kiosks and street performers, and is the site of the evening promenade. The New Ramblas connects residual alleys at each end, although it is not far from MACBA. The New Ramblas, too, has a wide, open space created by demolitions in front. But the colonisation works in two directions: the authorities carve out spaces and quarters on a model of urban ordering not far removed from, if more humane than, that used by Haussmann in Paris in the 1850s–60s to reduce the risk of mass revolt; but different groups use the space outside MACBA for their own diverse purposes. The skateboarders and bike-riders who occupy the site are not in revolt but do reassert a right to the city and may represent disorderliness in the eyes of the planners. But regeneration was not for them; it was meant to draw in other publics such as cultural tourists. For the authorities, recoding the area through spatial design encourages people to go there, to 'lose their fear and start entering its corners, its places'.[84] This assumes that the area was once a den of iniquity; indeed, it was to an extent once perceived as that, and tourists were advised to avoid it; but this drew them there precisely because cultural tourists think of themselves as intrepid travellers discovering the real city. El Raval was an adventure zone where they could rub shoulders with prostitutes, artists, migrants, dwellers for whom Barcelona remained an old Mediterranean sea-port, and (increasingly as cultural tourism grew) pickpockets and bag thieves. For the authorities, who both played on means to attract visitors and saw Mediterranean sea-ports as poor cities, the clean, pale façades of northern Europe denoted wealth, and were emulated in the façades of infill blocks without balconies. Demolition let in the light and the planners' gaze. Around the New Ramblas, in the new cultural quarter, blocks were refurbished. Degen continues:

> Making the area attractive also involved recoding the existing public spaces and surrounding buildings with new public amenities and cultural uses such as libraries, conference centres or exhibition spaces. The promotion of a cultural quarter was meant to demystify negative perceptions, promote alternative uses of space and attract a new public. Needless to say, these public facilities were designed for El Raval's transient population of Barcelona's citizens and tourists rather than the neighbourhood's local residents, and were expected to lead to 'a social change in the uses of the neighbourhood'.[85]

Degen adds that, although avoiding cynicism, she cannot ignore 'the commercial value that this central area ... has, once regenerated, for business, tourism and the property market'.[86] I agree.

There are two disturbing assumptions behind the rhetoric of regeneration (which, as Degen suspects, might really be property development). First, the sight of residual publics such as migrants, assumed to be abject rather than colourful, is taken as having a negative impact on the image and hence the market value of a redeveloped zone. Although the presence of artists as a transitional public is often a catalyst to such recoding, or adds to the frisson felt by cultural tourists, developers' images appeal to new professional elites seeking safe-but-exciting enclaves. The image of redevelopment is at odds with the creativity associated with artists as bohemians; but it is also at odds with the culture, in an anthropological sense, of the social groups who lived in the redeveloped zone prior to its redevelopment. In the place where the sun never shone it is assumed not only that people are abject, and probably inarticulate as well as disorderly, but also that they lack culture. They may indeed lack the high culture brought by contemporary art museums, but this does not mean that their ordinary lives do not consist of enactments of belief, allegiance and values such as mutual aid and solidarity. I do not want to romanticise this, nor to rely on a close alignment of community with place – many members of diverse and supposedly marginal publics have city-wide or global networks of communication – but the official rhetoric erases local cultures as a justification for urban clearances. In the process it tends to conflate high culture with vernacular cultures, introducing the pseudo-vernacular of an incoming, supposedly creative elite in place of that of residualised publics.

After the crash

After 2007, the young professionals in sectors such as financial services and advertising who comprise the creative class seemed less agents of urban regeneration than harbingers of crisis. While permanent instability is a normalised management strategy in the immaterial economy, or the culture of enterprise, designed to render employees insecure and conformist, willing to accept almost any deterioration in conditions to keep a livelihood, the system itself suddenly appeared insecure and irrational. Relying on unsustainable credit and driven by individualised greed while syphoning most of the world's wealth into the holdings of a new super-elite, the system of global capitalism seemed to lurch on the edge of a chasm. Through large subsidies from public expenditure, the banks were bailed out. Business-as-usual was quickly installed – officially to prevent financial meltdown – despite the obvious injustices and malfunctions of the system which was thus maintained. But urban redevelopment was not left unchanged, and shifted to a phase of urban clearances for which a cultural mask was no longer required in the aura of a crisis. Harris and fellow geographer Louis Moreno observe the end of the cultural turn:

> Arguably the creative city notion has flourished within the context of a long credit-fuelled boom in financial services and real estate. Policy-makers and cultural practitioners have often benefited from … new forms of upmarket consumption, corporate sponsorship and property-led regeneration … supported and supplemented by public investment in cultural facilities and urban renaissance programmes. The on-going economic downturn and political instigation of fiscal austerity therefore challenges many of the underlying assumptions which nurtured the new agenda of creativity.[87]

Central to those assumptions was the alignment of culture and creativity to universal benefit, as if a creative city was necessarily a good and beautiful place. At the same time, while cities adopted creative strategies and Florida proclaimed the need to attract the creative class, older, socially responsible policies – as articulated in the UK welfare state – were dismantled, and the public sector discredited in political hype as inefficient, boring and out-of-date. As public services declined, precarious employment conditions were normalised in the creative sector. McRobbie quotes the popular fashion/design magazine *i-D*: 'Fashion multi-taskers: suddenly they're everywhere…. And it's addictive. Once you've tried doing four jobs you'll never want anything else…. It's no longer necessary to be a full time anything to be successful and respected.'[88] Lees et al. suggest that, 'the worry of precarious employment could be eased by networking and holding more than one job',[89] but McRobbie's quote shows that this becomes excessive, linked to an imperative to be successful as a way to gain respect in a peer group. This may have parallels in Adorno's analysis of the authoritarian personality in the 1940s,[90] which identified conventional behaviour, routine submission to authority and cynicism as destructive to democracy.

The imperative to conform reappears in another guise in post-crash urban redevelopment, accompanied, or enabled, by clearances of residual publics from pockets of land, especially from post-war social housing blocks, to make way for designer-apartments for members of the creative class who have survived the crash. The rich get richer; the poor get poorer; the rich occupy refurbished, re-coded districts near their offices; the poor are peripheralised, sent out to wherever. I look at this scenario as a mask for a widening democratic deficit in Chapter 6.

On the wall

I end this chapter by asking whether the activities of artists resist or conform to the scenario of a post-crash creativity. The answer is both, according to which cases are investigated. But, after Charles Saatchi's patronage of the Young British Artists in the 1990s, and the rise to global prominence of London's Frieze Art Fair, it may be that a mainstream is emerging within the art world as a departure from the modernist concern with aesthetic value and a move towards celebrity culture.

To take a specific case, the conversion of a disused factory in Hoxton, London's newest arts district, into the Dirty House, designed by David Adjaye as a live-in studio for artists Tim Noble and Sue Webster in 2001–02, may illustrate a fusion of conformity and resistance within the cultural economy. This is pre-crash, but I wonder if it stands for a growing fusion of urban edge and the creative-class culture to which McRobbie alludes in her magazine quote (see p. 46). If it is, I suggest the outcome is an inverse chic, a high culture in the dirt (literally or by connotation), parallel to a view of Tate Modern advanced by cultural theorist Esther Leslie: 'The reclamation of an industrial space ... lends the building a fashionably squatted aspect.'[91]

Urbanist Ben Campkin describes the Dirty House as, 'blank and intriguing, anonymous yet highly idiosyncratic, plain and subtly decorative, unpretentious ... also ostentatious'.[92] It is an old factory, now three floors of studio and living space behind a blank wall. He cites the work *Dirty White Trash with Gulls* (1998) composed of rubbish collected from the streets, with two stuffed seagulls seemingly scavenging the heap; a spotlight throws the silhouette of a profile on the wall: the artists sitting back to back, one smoking while the other drinks: 'consuming and polluting their bodies with addictive toxins'.[93] Campkin observes:

> The work is abject in that someone else's domestic rubbish both repels and fascinates us, inviting us to construct a narrative about the identities of those who produced it ... the body of work these artists have produced can be read as a critique of consumerism; a politically neutral comment on the formation of identity, or the artists' identities

in relation to their waste products; or as a celebration of consumer capitalism and kitsch – bad taste aesthetics.[94]

The Dirty House is similarly ambiguous: its rough, dark façade seems to refuse conventional aesthetics, affirming industrial ordinariness; but its rough surface texture is a means to prevent fly-posting, bearing a special coating (made by a company called Clean Streets) to preserve the façade's pristine quality. The coating is mixed with crushed marble aggregates and is polluting, soon to be banned by EU law.[95] From the upper-floor living area there is 'a panoramic view to nearby skyscrapers in the … financial district', which offers 'surreptitious views to the street beneath, while preventing anyone on the street from seeing in'.[96] Here the art world fuses with the creative class in a post-industrial, de-politicised version of a Renaissance palace. Hoxton remains a transitional zone after gentrification was stalled by the crash; but the writing would be on the wall were it not for the protective coating.

3

Colliding Values:
Civic Hope and Capital's Bind

In April 2011 the Southbank Arts Centre, London, celebrated the sixtieth anniversary of the Festival of Britain. The original festival took place on the centenary of the Great Exhibition of 1851, which represented Britain as a nation of innovation in machinery and enterprise in manufacturing. It was a selective representation given the divide between wealth and poverty which marked British cities undergoing rapid industrialisation but the 1951 festival was a selective representation of another kind, proclaiming optimism as the antidote to post-war austerity. With bomb damage still ubiquitous in British cities (as elsewhere in Europe), and while food rationing remained in force, the need for an event of national reassurance was demonstrated by the fact that 150,000 people had emigrated from Britain to Canada between 1946 and 1948 looking for a better life.[1] The festival announced a future brightened by science, technology and culture, offering the best to everyone. But it was not only new; it was democratic and celebrated civic values as well. And it was fun.

I return to the festival itself below; first I look at the sixtieth anniversary event which, if by default, represented Britain in the midst of another regime of austerity following the financial services crisis of 2007. This pales, of course, beside rationing and bomb damage, but there are parallels in that both events occurred in periods of political change as well as austerity, and drew large attendances on the same site. *The Guardian* reported, 'To pay homage to the event that helped usher Britain out of the post-war doldrums, the Southbank Centre is hosting a four-month jamboree boasting everything from gardens sprouting from the concrete buildings to a museum chronicling the original festival.'[2] The reference to concrete alludes to more recent buildings on the site such as the National Theatre by Denys Lasdun, while the reference to gardens might suggest the green shoots of economic recovery.

In 2011, more than 3,000 visual and performing arts professionals contributed to the celebrations, including artist Tracey Emin, singer and song writer Billy Bragg, architect Zaha Hadid, conductor Colin Davis and veteran Labour orator Tony Benn. There were concerts, performances by 25 choirs, a street dance championship, a vintage festival, and 400 free events. Looking back on these events in September, 2011, Jude Kelly (Artistic Director of the Southbank Centre) was 'thrilled by the hugely enthusiastic response' of the thousands who contributed to the celebrations, 'from world-class artists to community groups and schools around the country – and enjoyed by [2.8] millions of visitors'.[3] Seeing the event as 'a precedent for our future aspirations as a year-round festival site', she also thanked the sponsor, a global credit card company.[4] Again, the inferences are clear: festivals have become a common element in the symbolic economies of cities – Edinburgh has them more or less permanently – and no major arts event takes place without corporate sponsorship. A map of the 2011 festival shows the locations of 33 sights, including a carousel, a funfair, a row of beach huts designed by artists, a Mobile Gull Appreciation Unit in the form of a giant seagull, a 70-metre urban beach with deckchairs and boards showing replica 1950s railways posters (Figure 3.1) and a giant straw fox. There were also 21 eating and drinking places, mostly franchises offering pizza, all-day breakfasts, burgers or sushi. There was a museum

Figure 3.1   The beach at the Southbank Centre, 2011

of the 1951 festival exhibiting memorabilia, art and photographs, but no attempt to reconstruct the Skylon, the iconic sculpture of the 1951 festival.

Journalist Sam Jones writes of the fox, named Susan, by Alex Rinsler, that she 'is keeping a vigil over Waterloo Bridge. Her glare, enough to chill the dreams of the capital's pet rabbits, is softened by the sounds of piped birdsong and the distant giggles of toddlers playing on the sandy beach by the Thames'; he adds:

> On the way up to a new garden on the roof of the Queen Elizabeth Hall, where a band plays English Country Garden, visitors come to an al fresco gallery known as Helmand. Staring down from its walls are the dusty faces of British service personnel in Afghanistan. In one photograph, a union flag-draped coffin waits to be loaded onto a transport plane at an airfield far from the Thames.[5]

After a million people had marched through London against the Iraq war in 2003 and were disregarded by the Blair regime, a photograph of a coffin may have seemed a brave inclusion in an event which relied as much on sponsorship as on the use of its public-sector site.

A more ambivalent contribution to the event was Tom Lynham's language architecture, a number of phrases in large red letters on yellow fabric mounted throughout the site. On the railings by the river were SANDY SANDWICHES, WALK THE PLANK and FISH AND CHIPS. Elsewhere, visitors were invited to FIND YOURSELF, or reminded of MAD DOGS AND ENGLISHMEN. WISH YOU WERE HERE occupied four separate banners. Nearby was TWIST OF FATE. Collaborating with Steve Smith, Michael Marriott and Andrew Lock, Lynham saw these phrases as, 'evangelical, heroic, and infectious', echoing 'the happenstance that occurs when millions of people converge on a public space'.[6] He continues:

> The story was all about British-ness: how could this be defined with our mongrel cultural mix, and could our creative output clarify who we are? ...
>
> Southbank is so porous ... we decided the words should run like ribbons throughout the site, signalling the contents and prompting visitors to tell us their own stories. High visibility beacons carrying the Festival's graphic identity provided context, meeting points and maps. Thousands of metres of printed fabric wrapped around the architecture provided the beginnings of conversations. The collateral linked the

new rooftop garden, surprise fountains, pop-up restaurants, a Festival museum, poets in residence, book readings, concerts, fairgrounds ...[7]

Defining Britishness was a preoccupation in the 2000s, pervading the Millennium Dome and Antony Gormley's project *One & Other* in Trafalgar Square, London in the summer of 2009. I discuss both below but the inference is that such efforts demonstrated the impossibility of the task in a city and a country which is increasingly multicultural, and where the division between rich and poor is widening as pressures for devolution collide with globalisation. By a series of photographs of British citizens on the South Bank, a placard asked, 'Who are you? Were you born on these islands? What do you look like? What do you believe in? How do others see you?' Visitor Niki Seth-Smith recalled that one question was missing: 'Do you see yourself as British?' while 'the British political classes are digesting, or perhaps trying not to digest, the astounding outcome of the Scottish elections'.[8] At those elections, the Scottish National Party became a devolved government. Since then, a referendum has been held on full independence. I could ask what price Britishness now but, while a valid question, this would re-direct attention from a deeper issue: whether united or devolved, what values do the societies and publics of these islands claim or enact? Culture, with its association in classical thought with universal beauty, goodness and truth, is another means to direct critical attention away from values – especially in the white-walled, value-free spaces of the modern art museum – towards a more limited aesthetic of style and mode. Culture's limits and capacity to contain variety within a single ethos clash, here, with the recognition of difference which shapes the urban environment today.

Lynham's reference to a mongrel cultural mix (above) echoes Leonie Sandercock's argument for a multi-ethnic sense of society. Writing in 2006, citing Richard Sennett and geographers James Donald and Ash Amin, she advocates a focus on neighbourhood-scale institutions and spaces conducive to inter-cultural exchange, and an agonistic politics encouraging a, 'broad social participation in the never completed process of making meanings and creating values'.[9] This means the end of dominant cultures to which those seen as others must assimilate, and a 'perpetual contestation over what is or might become common ground'.[10] The most obvious sign of agonistic spatiality at the Southbank Centre today is the display of skills by skateboarders in a residual space between subways below the site, decorated (or recoded) with graffiti and much photographed by tourists.

1951

In 1951, the war had been over for six years but the nation had been more or less bankrupted by it and was still recovering economically, as new social pressures emerged. Historian David Kynaston notes, 'The end of the 1940s – decade of war and austerity – signalled no immediate passage into the sunlit uplands.'[11] He cites Dan Jacobson, who arrived in London from South Africa in 1950:

> The public buildings were filthy, pitted with shrapnel scars, running with pigeon dung ... eminent statesmen and dead kings of stone looked out upon the world with soot-blackened faces ... bus tickets and torn newspapers blew down the streets or lay in white heaps in the parks; cats bred in the bomb-sites, where people flung old shoes, tin cans, and cardboard boxes; whole suburbs of private houses were peeling, cracking, crazing, their windows unwashed, their steps unswept, their gardens untended; innumerable little cafés reeked of chips frying in stale fat ...[12]

Gladys Langford, a Census collector in north London, wrote, 'The climbing of steps, the squalor of some of the households, the inability to get a reply and the knowledge that I should have to retread the streets again and again, reduced me to near hysteria.'[13] These and other accounts from the period indicate a Britain still showing the signs of war damage, lacking the resources to rebuild, and retaining the largely class-based deprivations of the pre-war years. For instance, the Census revealed that 4.8 million homes (of 12.4 million) had no bathroom and 2.8 million had only shared access to a lavatory; there was a shortage of at least 700,000 houses, and many people lived in small, shared lodgings. Bread was rationed. A black market flourished. One grocer remarked in 1948, 'Black market dealings pervade every sphere of life and every commodity.'[14] Shortages were initially a result of enemy action during the war, as ships bringing vital supplies were torpedoed, but rationing in 1951 was more a consequence of Britain's efforts to finance a continuing world role – with naval fleets in the Atlantic, the Mediterranean and the Indian Ocean, a large army and 100 air force squadrons sited around the globe – at the same time as dismantling its empire. Historian Tony Judt comments that the only way Britain could pay its way was by 'unprecedented conditions of restraint and voluntary penury.... Everything was rationed, restricted, controlled.'[15] This does not at all deny the achievements of the post-war Labour government, however, which can be read in context of a Europe-wide imperative to repair identities on which Judt remarks, 'The post-1945 urge for change went well beyond welfare. The years following World War Two were a sort of foreshortened Age of Reform ... long-pressing problems were belatedly addressed.'[16] But the imposition of austerity after six years of war may have undermined efforts to foster feelings of national well-being so that the Festival of Britain was an antidote intended to rally the nation despite its predicament.

Writer Barry Turner reads the festival's role as shaping public culture by 'exposing fresh ideas to an unsophisticated audience in a language they could understand'.[17] In 1851, the Great Exhibition had been intended to 'improve the taste of the middle classes' while informing manufacturers about 'mechanical improvements' and morally educating the working class.[18] In 1951, the Festival of Britain was intended to interpret a principle of equality in terms of free access to the best of science, technology and culture.

The festival was a nationwide series of events through the summer. It was initially proposed by the Royal Society of Arts in 1943, developed by a committee set up in 1945 and organised in the post-war Labour years by Herbert Morrison, the party's deputy leader. It comprised 2,000 events, including a Pageant of Wales and St Fagan's Folk Festival in Cardiff, an arts festival in Liverpool, the exhibition The Living Tradition in Edinburgh, and the Ulster Farm and Factory Exhibition, Belfast; a touring Land exhibition in Manchester, Leeds, Birmingham and Nottingham; and a 1943 aircraft carrier, Campania, repainted white and re-fitted as a touring exhibition venue, which visited Southampton, Dundee, Hull, Newcastle, Plymouth, Bristol, Cardiff, Belfast, Birkenhead and Glasgow. The Campania's exhibition had three themes: the Land of Britain, Discovery and People at Home. The British Film Institute commissioned documentaries, though not on controversial topics; among those made, Waters of Time, by Basil Wright, depicted the progress of the ship Highland Princess from The Nore, where the Thames meets the North Sea, to London Docks and back again.

It is important not to overlook how many events took place outside London. Turner recalls the programme in Bury St Edmunds: 'The emphasis was on amateur performance, starting with an afternoon of song and dance by local schools.'[19] The festival's impresario, Gerald Barry, visited many events outside London and recorded his experiences, among them *The Story of Liverpool*:

> It told in a remarkably clear and vivid way the historical, sociological and commercial development of the city from a 12th-century village to the great seaport and industrial centre of today. Nothing was sidestepped, neither slave trade, slums nor the devastation of the blitz. What made it more remarkable was the fact that it was almost entirely the voluntary work of art students.[20]

And in the city:

> Huge processions progressed through the streets rather in the style of Venetian pageants ... All the dresses and the devices carried in the procession were made by amateur enterprise and the most striking use was made of colour. When the procession ended and gathered under the portico of St George's Hall, it was already dusk and Bengal Lights flared up behind the columns of the portico, first red then green. But the river itself became the scene of the most spectacular pageantry. What were probably the biggest fireworks displays in the world were held on the river with fire boats passing up and down stream and the spectacle culminating with the firing of 2,000 rockets. Half a million people turned out each time to enjoy this tremendous show.[21]

In London, Turner notes, 'As seen from Downing Street, the Festival was the only bright spot in a bleak year.'[22] In the 1950 election, Clement Attlee's government saw a majority of 146 cut to five. By the end of 1951 the government which had created the welfare state and put on the festival had been defeated. Even before that, at official ceremonies, Attlee, a modest man (as Winston Churchill frequently emphasised) was overshadowed by Churchill. Heavy rain accompanied the opening ceremony, when Attlee was made to walk from the entrance while Churchill's car was waved through; and the royal party took a wrong turn and 'saw the whole thing back to front'.[23]

Apart from the Festival Hall, key sites on the South Bank were the Dome of Discovery and the Skylon. The Dome, designed by Ralph Tubbs and, at 365 feet wide and 93 feet high the largest dome in the world, contained themed exhibitions: Land; Earth; Polar; Sea; Sky; Outer Space; Living World; and Physical World. These had an educational role, while exhibitions in a Downstream Circuit of pavilions explored themes likely to reassure people and to draw attention to post-war achievements: The People of Britain; Homes and Gardens; New Schools; Health; Sport; The Seaside; and The Lion and Unicorn. By the riverside was a row of different types of street lamp, one of which folded to allow the bulb to be changed; and a demonstration of making ice cream wafers. The Lion and Unicorn pavilion had a whimsical feeling: a flight of plaster doves flew from a wicker cage, texts from Shakespeare and the Bible were displayed on a blackboard, and various eccentricities related to *Alice Through the Looking Glass* were depicted. The title, 'The Lion and the Unicorn' is, coincidentally, that of an essay by George Orwell, subtitled 'Socialism and the English Genius', in which he praises the English preference for improvisation while arguing for socialism because capitalism 'does not work'.[24] Among the items on his agenda are the nationalisation of mines, transport, land and the banks, the first two of which were realised by the Labour government, and a maximum income no more than ten times that of the lowest paid. Orwell saw these as serious policy proposals (as they might remain now).

The Skylon, meanwhile, defied gravity and the functionalism of modern architecture. Turner comments, 'in a utilitarian age when nothing was wasted, few could bring themselves to believe that this extraordinary structure had no practical use whatever. Pointing towards the unknown, it was for many a symbol of hope.'[25] Designed by Hidalgo Moya, Phillip Powell and Felix Samuely, it consisted of six cables, three rods and a central, vertical steel form held in place by tensegrity (all parts are in uniaxial compression or tension). The name fuses pylon, sky and nylon. Shortly before the official unveiling, Phillip Gordon, a student at Birkbeck College, attached a London University Air Squadron scarf to it (removed before the ceremony). After the festival, the Conservative government cleared the site and both the Skylon and the Dome were broken up and sold for scrap: a potent symbol of hope's wreck, like the later demolition of modernist tower blocks.

The Skylon afforded moments of wonder as it seemed to soar free from the force of gravity, a metaphor for hopes damned up in wartime and restricted by austerity. And it brought the potentially distanced realm of science and technology into human orbit, mysterious but material.

In 1947 a Mass Observation survey asked people if they thought that humans had progressed, gaining a 49 per cent positive and 30 per cent negative response, with 21 per cent undecided.[26] Among the ways in which humans progressed (if they had), science was identified by 40 per cent of men and 18 per cent of women, above social improvements (19 per cent and 23 per cent) and education (17 per cent and 11 per cent).[27] Among those who thought humanity had not progressed, 48 per cent identified war and abuses of science as the cause. Many, too, thought science was progressing too fast or was a tool of violence. For example, 'the war's pulled us up and made us stop and think in what a senseless way we're using all the best of the world's brains and money'.[28] This was two years after Hiroshima and Nagasaki had been destroyed by atomic bombs. Four years after the survey, in 1951, wartime memories were mediated by economic and social preoccupations but the Skylon reminded its publics that technology need not be harnessed to a war machine; indeed, it could be as useless as art. The Skylon, then, expressed the optimism of the festival. But the event was not only an opportunity for wonder; it was an instrumentalist attempt by government to revive and re-shape public confidence while renewing a sense of national identity as the empire waned and migrations began to make British cities multi-ethnic.

Nonetheless, I discuss the Festival of Britain here because it clearly emerged from the values on which, too, the welfare state was founded (and which produced the Arts Council as the vehicle for re-shaping cultural provision in the post-war years), and enacts those values in a democratic, optimistic way. The messages expressed in the festival's exhibitions may have been paternalistic, or at least relied on professional expertise, just as its organisation was more top-down than based on vernacular, tacit knowledges; but its core aim was to improve the lot of ordinary citizens and show what that might mean. I wonder whether that idea is now encapsulated in an unrecoverable past, discarded like wreckage floating in the sea by today's entrepreneurialism.

An Arts Council

One aspect of imagining a better world took the form of state support for the arts, as in the commissioning of paintings and sculptures by John Piper, Henry Moore, Barbara Hepworth and Jacob Epstein, among others, for the festival; and an outdoor sculpture show in Battersea Park. In this context, and integral to the ideology of the welfare state, the Arts Council was established following the precedent of the Council for the Encouragement of Music and the Arts during the war. At the re-opening of the Tate Gallery in 1946, Foreign Secretary Ernest Bevin said to an audience of 4,000 people: 'the people of this country love form and beauty … they need them for the complete fulfilment of their lives, and after what they have been through in the last six or seven years, they deserve them'.[29] During the war, morale had been maintained in London by lunchtime concerts and Picture of the Month exhibitions at the National Gallery.[30] Cinemas stayed defiantly open during air raids. After the war, maintaining national morale transposed into constructing a national culture.

In 1946, the Arts Council's charter stated its purpose as, 'developing a greater knowledge, understanding and practice of the fine arts' and increasing 'the accessibility of the fine arts to the public' while improving 'the standard of execution of the fine arts'.[31] I am not sure what improving production standards in art means but it was clear that increasing public access to the arts meant access to the best of art, however defined. Cultural provision was located in a wider provision of social benefits such as education, transport, energy, water and health (all public services by the end of the 1940s). There are nuances: including the arts in the welfare state followed a trajectory of improvements in the conditions of the lower classes in the previous century (Chapter 5) which constituted a humanitarian project *and* a means of social ordering. Added to this in the post-war period was a desire for a public culture which linked the arts to democracy and socialism, and a debate as to what art was.

The art critic Herbert Read, for instance, argued for a crafts revival in which ordinary, useful objects could be well-made and treated as artworks. Asking whether a chair could be a work of art he wrote:

> If an object is made of appropriate materials to an appropriate design and perfectly fulfils its function, then we need not worry any more about its aesthetic value: it is *automatically* a work of art. Fitness for function is the modern definition of the eternal quality we call beauty, and this fitness for function is the inevitable result of an economy directed to use and not to profit.[32]

This was published in 1941, when paper was rationed and government approval was required for new books. He continued, 'we may note that when the profit system has to place function before profit' as in the manufacture of aeroplanes, a work of art also follows.[33] Otherwise the profit motive means 'the capitalist must put chairs on the market to suit every kind of purse ... [and since] it must cost as little as possible ... the capitalist must progressively lower the quality of the materials ... cheap wood and little of it, cheap springs and cheap upholstery'.[34] Read was an anarchist and saw no role for cultural elites, nor for a division between the artist and the lay person; instead, he argued that 'the worker has as much latent sensibility as any human being, but that sensibility can only be awakened when meaning is restored to his daily work, and he is allowed to create his own culture'.[35] In the new society he envisaged, culture 'will come as naturally as the fruit to the well-planted tree'.[36] He celebrated modern industry but his project for 'new values in art, literature, music and science'[37] was framed by a radical, democratic socialism in which the division between art and life is (or will be) dissolved.

Read influenced the spread of art education in schools through his book *Education Through Art*,[38] again for progressive purposes: to produce 'better people and better communities'.[39] A degree of paternalism pervades this post-war hope, shared by an Arts Council which saw its role as not unlike that of a colonial administrator spreading benign civilisation, but the Arts Council's role was not to require artists to follow, nor publics to seek, any specific kind of art. This was a reaction against Socialist Realism in the Soviet Union but also a rejection of a national style. Economist John Maynard Keynes was instrumental in establishing the Arts Council and regarded state support for the arts as stimulating 'any societies or bodies which are striving with serious purpose and a reasonable prospect of success to present for public enjoyment the arts of drama, music and painting'.[40]

The Arts Council operated at arms-length from government yet it tended to affirm the status of an informal consensus among art-world elites. Art historian Brandon Taylor remarks that the council favoured 'modern and foreign art', while its profile was 'of a self-electing system of committees that caused Raymond Williams later to characterise it as "persons of experience and goodwill" who made up an "informal ruling class".'[41] In 1967, art historian John Willett wrote that policy makers felt 'a genuine concern with high artistic standards, which private patronage alone would not be able to maintain'.[42] Again, the question of what constitutes high standards remains problematic, 'decided neither by academic (or other) principles nor by public feeling but by taste: the taste prevailing among dealers and critics and virtually the whole official art world outside a

few bodies labelled Royal'.[43] Sociologist Nicholas Pearson notes that
there has been a tendency to privilege a metropolitan view and adhere
to a 'notion of art and culture as a received tradition within the ideas of
excellence', informed in turn by a view of the nation which 'was not the
sum of the nation's parts, but related more to an abstract understanding
of a tradition that was and is separate from the developing practice of art
within Britain'.[44] That developing practice, if called the art of today, would
include art in evening classes and local art societies, amateur photography,
home movies, and the plethora of quasi-artistic practices distributed by
social media now. In contrast, Contemporary Art is a narrow stream of
cultural production, distinct also from the cultural work of artists working
for change, or as provocateurs (Chapter 7).

One thing has changed since the 1950s: improvements in, and widening
public access to, the arts were not seen then as having an economic role
but as social improvement or moral education. Since the 1980s, the arts
have been realigned to the symbolic economies by which cities compete
globally for investment and cultural tourism; this shift is epitomised by
a new terminology: no longer *arts administration* in service of a public
interest but *arts management* on a business model. Allowing the notion of
excellence to retain a rhetorical status which is useful when denying funds
to competing arts organisations, a regime of efficiency, private-sector
sponsorship, and business methods of management and publicity –
combined with a progressive if often mechanistic requirement to address
diversity – has replaced the vision of public service which shaped the Arts
Council in the 1940s. It is in this context of a value shift that the arts have
been aligned to urban redevelopment schemes, producing the cultural turn
which this book critiques, and the growth of new art museums discussed
in the next chapter. It has not produced a future vision equivalent to that of
the Festival of Britain, however much that vision was embedded in older,
stereotypical notions of what constituted Britishness. In 1951, the question
was more about ideology in the period of a democratic socialist state.

As I look back (having been born in 1950), the Festival of Britain was
a moment of hope for a genuinely better world to be achieved through
science, technology and culture within the welfare state. In 2011, the
sixtieth anniversary event was not uninteresting, and contained some
questioning images (like those from Afghanistan). Yet my feeling, walking
around the site, was that this was a nostalgic event which borrowed the
visual appearances of the 1951 festival but did not recreate its spirit, as
commercial sponsorship and consumption dominated retro messages of

a good life in a good society. People were invited to eat, drink and spend money more than to think again about what the festival had represented to the post-war generation. But perhaps that message of hope was already lost. If the festival attempted a unifying national narrative, the Millennium Dome in 2000 and Antony Gormley's *One & Other* in 2009 demonstrated that this is not viable now.

A national void?

The Millennium Dome, designed by Richard Rogers, sited on the south bank of the Thames east of the Festival Hall, is an easy target. On the opening night there were long queues when the privatised security state met VIP status; ordinary people (as they were called) watched the spectacle on television but journalists (VIPs for the night) wrote about their irritation at being made to queue for hours. Jim McGuigan cites an article by Polly Toynbee which was recycled from the liberal-Left *Guardian* to the populist Right *Daily Mail* under the title of 'I Paid Up, I Queued Up, and Now I'm Thoroughly Fed Up' and then 'The £758 Million Disaster Zone'.[45] Owen Hatherley sums up a widely held view in retrospect:

> The Dome's exhibition turned out to house a vast McDonalds and array of corporate advertisement, holding it up to a public ridicule that has only recently subsided [in 2010]. Within a few years, the area had taken on a definite identity, albeit not the one that was in the original brochure, and for most of the 2000s this was the place London forgot; a desolate landscape, one that was fascinatingly *wrong*, given the ecological and social-democratic ideas that had initially been thrown around in relation to it. A holding pen for Canary Wharf, yet somehow so much weirder than the usual Thames-side developments that they inhabit.[46]

Part of the difficulty was that the Dome's contents were decided relatively late in the project, more attention going to its material structure and a need to raise corporate sponsorship. But another part of the difficulty was that excessive claims were made for the project. McGuigan quotes Tony Blair: 'It will bring the nation together in common purpose.... It will unite the nation. It will be a meeting point of people from all backgrounds ... to lift our horizons ... to imagine our futures.'[47] These claims around nation and history were always at odds with the emphasis on (transnational) corporate sponsorship but also echo the speculative tone of the claims made for culture as a driving force of economic development, transmuting here to what may have been a conscious echo of the 1951 agenda contradicted by New Labour's first efforts to dismantle the welfare state.

The Dome was coated in Teflon but built on a reclaimed toxic site. Despite its identification with New Labour, it began as a Conservative project promoted by John Major and Michael Heseltine (the government minister who went to Liverpool after the Toxteth disturbances of July 1981 to inaugurate a national programme of garden festivals aimed at regeneration). Heseltine foresaw millions of foreign visitors who would be 'deeply impressed' and aware of the City of London's pre-eminence as a financial centre as well as of Britain's technological prowess, its innovative genius and its excellent companies; without evident irony, he ended his remarks, 'It is about selling ourselves and our country.'[48] Yes, I suppose it was. In the run up to the opening, however, it was about selling space in the Dome's themed zones. These were grouped under three headings: Who We Are (Body, Mind, Faith, Self-Portrait); What We Do (Work; Learning; Rest; Play; Talk; Money; Journey); and Where We Are (Shared Ground; Living Island; Home Planet). The three meta-themes resembled a corporate version of the questions asked in Paul Gauguin's painting *Where Do We Come From? What Are We? Where Are We Going?* (1897, Boston, Museum of Fine Arts). Gauguin saw this canvas as his greatest work, biblical in its scale and questioning of European civilisation when he sought to live as a native in French Polynesia.[49] His questions were rhetorical, and the central figure in the composition (although male) seems to reference images of Eve plucking an apple in the Garden of Eden. It was a composition made for a European public to which Gauguin showed himself as, colloquially, having gone native in protest against the market values of European society. I doubt such a claim could be made for the Dome's 14 themed zones, which affirm rather than protest against a structure of values incorporating elements of liberal humanism (the sense of individual self) in a spatial approximation of a corporate brochure.

An obvious comparison should be made, nonetheless, between the Dome's themed areas and those of the Festival of Britain. To reiterate, the *Campania*'s sea-borne exhibitions presented the Land of Britain, Discovery, and People at Home. The Dome of Discovery – a precedent for the

Millennium Dome – exhibited Land; Earth; Polar; Sea; Sky; Outer Space; Living World; and Physical World; the pavilions outside it showed The People of Britain; Homes and Gardens; New Schools; Health; Sport; The Seaside; and The Lion and Unicorn. At first glance, the festival's themes suggest a nation-state advertising itself, too, in a period of uncertainties. But the uncertainties then were related to material circumstances in a nation damaged by the war, not to self-doubt or to a project of modernisation which, under New Labour, undid much of the progressive work of the Atlee government. Themes such as Land, Sea, Sky and so forth relate, as well, to educational intentions; those of New Schools, Health and Sport were intended to celebrate the achievements of the welfare state which was at the time under construction. In 2000, all this was in disarray, and the public sector was dismissed as outdated and inefficient, a burden beginning to be replaced by public–private partnerships (in which the public sector made the major investment and carried the risk while maximising opportunities for private profit). Characteristically, the private sector was not prepared to take the risk of managing the Dome, which had to be taken on by a non-departmental public body overseen by a government minister. From 1997 to 1998 it was Peter Mandelson, grandson of Herbert Morrison. Sponsors raised managerial issues, but I think the real difficulty was that the project of representing a united nation, or telling a national story, was no longer viable in Britain in 2000. Some of the reasons can be read as positive: Britain is a reasonably well-integrated multi-ethnic country with a multiplicity of stories grounded in different cultures; to this is added the pressure of devolution. But as Scottish, Welsh and Irish identities secede from Britishness, it is unclear what English identity is left. The 1951 constructs of Homes and Gardens or People at Home have a cloying middle-class homeliness, but a display of old seaside postcards in the Dome simply reproduced this, as if Britain could do no more than fall back into its rather patch-and-mend and slightly sordid past.

Seeing the Dome's metaphorical location in a waste-ground between a lost past and a future of uncertain shape, architectural historian Simon Sadler writes of the Dome's failure to tell the story of time signified by its site on the Greenwich meridian:

> The Dome's visitors were offered neither a nostalgic affirmation of their British nationhood nor a futuristic vision of a reordered world. The Dome's putative general theme of Time suspended its visitors in

a present threatened by change, without bearings in work, place, or belief. The Millennium Experience failed to direct its visitors' attention toward anything; it failed to structure consciousness because it was embarrassed by a tacit ideological programme of 'reskilling' devised to satisfy its sponsors' demand for flexible labour and the state's unease about the loss of traditional industries.[50]

Nation-building, a colonial activity, meets neoliberalism in Docklands (Figure 3.2). Sadler speculates that late capitalism is beyond representation but sees the Dome as evoking postmodern sublimity while a 'disconnect of scales that exemplified postmodern life' is felt more in daily life than in exhibitions. Sadler also sees a pervasive de-territorialisation reproduced in the Dome, to an understandably negative reception;[51] and a failure to design a structure for a post-industrial space of flows of which the icons are leisure centres, computer networks, logistics depots, airports, and music festivals.'[52] He continues, 'Images are the mainstay of the spectacle, and the Millennium Dome had many images, arrayed through montages and electronic displays ... offering little in the way of a window onto an alternative reality.'[53] Sadler contrasts this to the future conveyed through objects at the Festival of Britain: the largest sheet of glass in the world; big new railway engines; the Skylon.

Figure 3.2   The Millennium Dome and Canary Wharf

Inside the container

I do not want to go on about the Dome's failure, which would be too easy. But I want to add a further dimension to its critique, which I cited in the book's Introduction: Peter Sloterdijk argues in *In the Interior World of Capital*[54] that the project of capital is the total containment of all human life, the whole world. He begins with the invention of the geographer's globe in the late fifteenth century as a means to represent a round Earth; this enables a masterful gaze which slips easily from seeing to controlling. But more to the point is that Sloterdijk takes the 1851 Great Exhibition as a metaphor for this containment of the whole world, citing Fyodor Dostoyevsky's contemporary account in *Notes from the Underground* (1864).

Dostoyevsky visited London in 1862, after the relocation of the Crystal Palace which housed the Great Exhibition to the suburb named after it; but he saw the International Exhibition in South Kensington, which was intended to surpass even the Great Exhibition. In the next year or so he read Nikolay Chernyshevsky's *What Is to Be Done?* (1863),[55] in which a new type of human is announced who, Sloterdijk summarises, 'having found the technological solution to the social question, would live with its kind in a communal palace of glass and metal – the archetype of living communities in the East and West'.[56] Sloterdijk comments:

> Chernyshevsky's culture palace had been designed as a climatized luxury shell in which there would be an eternal spring of consensus. Here the sun of good intentions would shine day and night, and the peaceful coexistence of all with all could be taken for granted. Boundless sentimentality would characterize the internal climate, and an overstretched humanitarian domestic morality would result in a spontaneous empathy of all with the fates of all. For Dostoyevsky, the image of the whole of society moving into the palace of civilization symbolized the will of the Western branch of humanity to conclude the initiative it had started – to make the world happy and achieve mutual understanding between peoples – in a post-historical relaxed state....
>
> Here a new doctrine of Last Things is formulated as a dogmatics of consumption.[57]

Sloterdijk cites Walter Benjamin's critique of the arcades of Paris (iron and glass structures taken as precedent for Charles Fourier's ideal community's housing in Phalansteries as well as by Chernyshervsky),[58] suggesting that

Benjamin's approach to space and technology can be re-formulated for the architecture of consumerism (as in the mall). He concludes,

> As for capitalism, we can only now say that it always meant more than the relations of production; its shaping power had always gone much further than can be encapsulated in the thought figure of the global market. It implies the project of placing the entire working life, wish life and expressive life of the people it affected within the immanence of spending power.[59]

Herbert Marcuse argued similarly in his critique of consumerism, *One-Dimensional Man* (1964).[60] Sloterdijk also, coincidentally, echoes sociologist Conrad Lodziak's argument that consumerism produces new human needs (or wants experienced as needs) to compensate for the alienation and exhaustion of work.[61] Consumers' agency is limited to the choices offered within consumerism, or 'a form of active passivity'.[62] This is the context for an appropriation of a need for freedom: 'In the ideology of consumerism, consumer choices reflect the interpretive freedom of the individual ... harnessed to the project of creating a self-identity.'[63] Meanwhile, freedom is privatised as public services are replaced by private-sector service provision represented as offering new choices to people supported by the state who are regarded as clients or quasi-customers. Perhaps the Dome offered a similar array of narrative services from which visitors could construct their own national stories, as the latest enclosure in which to unify the world and, in neoliberal 2000, unify it as a world of corporate rule even though much of the cost came from the National Lottery via the Millennium Commission. The Teflon-coated tent contained everything in its themed zones yet failed to say that there was no longer a story to tell.

That was not quite the end of the non-story: almost as an answer to the Dome, *One & Other* attempted to give a 'composite picture of the nation'[64] when 2,400 people selected by a national ballot occupied the empty plinth in London's Trafalgar Square for an hour each, to do as they liked. It was not easy to see the plinthers (as they were called) from the ground but the day's activities were screened nightly on a private-sector television channel. Some plinthers used their hour to gain publicity for a cause or charity; some took photographs; some danced, sang or played musical instruments; others seemed at a loss to know how to fill their hour. I have written elsewhere on *One & Other* as a reinvention of the form of the public monument,[65] and here will say simply that a random collection of people's antics is diverse but cannot convey a national story because, emphatically, there is no such story to tell. Zygmunt Bauman writes that, 'Everything is down to the individual' in the realm of consumption while 'freedom to become anybody' has a bitter after-taste of anxiety when 'its opposite brings no unadulterated pleasure either, since it forecloses what freedom needs to stay open'.[66] In order to contain everything under one roof, capital requires a structure of social relations which renders them empty, like the abandoned state: atomism. This is useful in dealing with dissent, redirecting it to a realm of individual choice rather than the shared experiences of common life; and runs parallel to the appropriation of the outward forms of dissent, such as graffiti, in a popularised rather than democratised public culture. And it runs parallel to the anomie which, Guy Standing argues in context of the flexible economy, is 'a listlessness associated with sustained defeat, compounded by the condemnation lobbed at many in the precariat by politicians and middle-class commentators'.[67]

Cool: containment and void

McGuigan begins *Cool Capitalism*, a critique of late capitalism's incorporation of areas of disaffection, by saying that cool is, 'the front region of capitalism today for those who are seduced by its cultural appeal'.[68] Citing a public relations survey in China in 2004, he notes,

> The market research evidence showed that Chinese students value 'cool', whatever that means, and they associated it with leading Western or Westernised brand companies, most notably Nike, Sony, Adidas, BMW, Microsoft, Coca-Cola, IBM, Nokia, Samsung, Ferrari and Christian Dior. Cool has travelled a long way, from the West coast of Africa to the Americas and around the whole world – as far, in fact, as 'Communist' China.[69]

The reference to West Africa follows art historian Robert Farris Thompson's tracing of the attitudes denoted by cool to the Yoruba concept of *itutu* (composure) and a sense of vitality and personal power in body language. The brands listed are associated with a narrow range of consumption – trainers and sports clothing, IT, cars, fizzy drinks and perfume – which stand for identity. McGuigan, citing researcher Thomas Frank, uses 'cool' to describe a trend which began in 1960s counter-culture and refreshed 'the culture and political economy of corporate America' by integrating into it a rebel ideology, breaking with '1950s conformity, the robotic American way of life that critics, humanistic and social-scientific, had incessantly attacked'.[70] The trend affected management before it reached consumers but centred on the consumer's subjectivity:

> Consumer subjectivity became the object of attention for this new school of management. It was assumed that the customer had become 'hip', in a quaint old term, to what was going on in this forerunner of the cool business discourse.... At the same time, business became 'funky', having shed its reputation for bureaucratic conformity. Simultaneously, the longing for another world has diminished for the young, to be replaced by the longing for cool commodities and their fetishistic properties.[71]

Sharon Zukin observes a later phase of cool as control, based on research in New York after the culturally coded redevelopment of SoHo. Taking the Disney Company's activities, from film to real estate, she comments that the symbolic economy unifies finance, labour, the arts and design in a common pursuit and production of a new language to deal with difference:

> Styles that develop on the streets are cycled through mass media ... where, divorced from their social context, they become images of cool. On urban billboards advertising designer perfumes or jeans, they are recycled to the streets, where they become a provocation, breeding imitation and even violence. The beachheads of designer stores ... are fiercely parodied for the props of fashion-conscious teenagers in inner-city ghettos. The cacophony of demands for justice is translated into a coherent demand for jeans. Claims for public space by culture industries inspire the counterpolitics of display in late-20th-century urban riots.[72]

That coincides with McGuigan's argument, which he extends by reference to a new form of excess in celebrity culture. It is not that star-status is new but that it is now available to more people – he cites attributed celebrities: 'people who are famous simply for being famous'[73] – so that consumers can introject the stardust. This is another form of the scenario in which statues in a public square reminded citizens of the values they were required to emulate, but stardust and celebrity status are as nebulous as notions of innovation and excellence in the arts, and I wonder if creativity is taken similarly to mean almost anything when a positive sounding spin is required for something.

The claims made for creativity are vague or undemonstrable, as were those for New Labour's short-lived re-branding of Britain as Cool Britannia in 1997. Sadler reads Cool Britannia as attempting, 'to recapture, update, and re-thermostat for the 1990s the White Heat creative energy' of the 1960s promoted by the Wilson government.[74] The term originated in 1967 in a song by the Bonzo Dog Doo Dah Band, but is associated with the manufacture of optimism around New Labour's election victory in 1997. It might (or might not) be epitomised by singer Geri Halliwell's wearing a Union Jack dress at the Brit Awards in London that year. By 1998, commentators were questioning its validity. It was always rubbish but I mention it because the notion of a cool nation associated with the surface characteristics of popular music, fashion, art, architecture and design could have arisen only in the context of a cultural turn in policy and a generalised if undefined investment in creativity as key to renewal after de-industrialisation. Another fruit on this dubious plant was the notion of the creative city.

The creative city

Richard Florida's notion of a creative class (Chapter 2) instantiates the cultural turn in one way; the construct of a creative city proposed by arts consultant Charles Landry does so in another.[75] Like the Dome, the creative city is an easy target, so I will be brief. It has in any case been superseded by a more brutal phase of redevelopment – postcode clearance in the post-crash era – which I discuss in Chapter 6. I see, nonetheless, how the notion of a creative city was attractive to city authorities, offering them a less costly alternative to infrastructure renewal, building houses, improving health and so forth, within a general rhetoric of cultural regeneration. As such it masks failures in other policy areas by producing bright new images which promise transformation in a period of resource constraint.

Landry calls his book a toolkit for urban innovators, noting that he put forward ideas which often were not at first implemented but succeeded, 'when I found creative implementers able ... to link cultural industries to job creation and spatial regeneration'.[76] He does not cite the cultural class – Florida is not listed in the index – but defines creative people qualitatively as good communicators and listeners, team players, diplomats and networkers. These traits can be found in people in any profession or trade, operating locally, regionally or globally, which is probably preferable (or less divisive) than Florida's class of young professionals. Landry asserts that thinking creatively about cities means thinking about all aspects of their running and redevelopment, which needs a creative milieu and creative organisations.[77] This puts the accent on the dynamics of city authorities and arts organisations in what might be regarded as a cultural turn in planning associated with (but not limited to) links to the cultural industries. Yet Landry admits that creativity cannot be defined: 'it eluded me'.[78] There are aspects of creativity in business, and to a lesser extent in local government, while a broader notion of a social creativity is 'undervalued and not seen as innovation', even though new social institutions are key to urban renewal.[79] Landry is, I am sure, well-intentioned but I cannot help reading statements of this kind – while accurate in a way – as part of the apparatus of social inclusion introduced by New Labour after 1997. To be clear, I have no problem with non-privileged publics having access to all aspects of the social body, quite the opposite; but the category of social inclusion rests on that of social exclusion in a dualism produced by a dismissive rather than empathetic attitude. This occurred when urban redevelopment policies promoted cultural flagships to drive the gentrification of inner-cities and de-industrialised zones, producing centres which, in turn, rendered adjacent areas as margins and their populations as residual publics. Among those and other sundry publics, as it were, social exclusion gave a respectable gloss to earlier notions of an (anarchistic, destructive and obviously idle) underclass.

Perhaps the creative city was constructed in an ambience of the universal benefit associated in classical thought with culture. In keeping with the new economy of immaterial production and image, culturally led redevelopment tends to affirm the status quo. Or, as geographer Paul Chatterton writes:

> The creative city is little more than a rhetorical device which can placate the hearts and minds of local councillors and politicians that

they are actually doing something whilst doing hardly anything at all. In practice, it is part of a broader shift towards new forms of entre-preneurial urban management used to boost the image of ailing cities and persuade highly mobile global capital and professional and service classes that urban areas are interesting and sage places to live.[80]

For the most part, Landry's book is episodic, a list of projects in which he has been involved, from renting a granny in Berlin[81] to using hawks to control pigeons in Woking[82] and recycling spaces in Karlsruhe.[83] I pick these randomly, but none are specifically about the arts. Again, I have no problem there: there is no shortage of arts advocacy, while art does not reduce crime or poverty, or make trains run on time. If it contributes to place identity it often reflects reductive and elite scenarios. Leaving that aside, the non-contentious projects profiled in *The Creative City* are unlikely to change anything politically. If they are contained by a rhetoric of social inclusion, however, they should be evaluated in such terms.

Ruth Levitas argues that social exclusion is subordinated to a neoliberal discourse of market imperatives;[84] urbanist Rob Atkinson argues, citing Levitas, that 'attention is largely focused upon those living in the margins of society who display socially unacceptable forms of behaviour ... a simplistic and reductive model is created'.[85] He adds that the terms 'social cohesion' and 'integration' are problematic and 'tend to be presented in neutral terms', while exclusion 'is located within a particular social and economic discourse (social conservatism and economic neoliberalism).[86]

Exclusion from the labour market, however, may not be for some the problem it is deemed to be by those for whom productivity is a norm. Little seems to have changed since nineteenth-century statues proclaimed the virtues in which citizens should believe, and bountiful people brought art and good manners to the masses. This is where I depart from Landry, who writes that cultural heritage has, 'provided a worldwide focus for urban renewal' through inspiration from 'the buildings, artefacts, traditions, values and skills of the past. Culture helps us to adapt to change by anchoring our sense of being' and building confidence to face the future.'[87] It might for some, but culture becomes a moral commodity, making people feel good about the conditions in which they live, which means de-indus-trialisation and global capital's total containment. Catherine Belsey defines culture instead as codes determining a vocabulary of action, specifying 'the meanings we set out to inhabit or repudiate, the values we make efforts to live by or protest against, and the protest is also cultural'.[88] I prefer that. It accepts the limit of culture as an inescapable condition (like language, without which I cannot say anything); but it opens a possibility for continuous negotiation.

4

New Cool:
England's New Art Museums

Following a shift from a civic model of arts administration exemplified by the Festival of Britain to a model of arts management in the 1980s, New Labour's re-branding of Britain as Cool Britannia, and the success of one of its two flagships, Tate Modern (in contrast to the ill-received Millennium Dome), new art museums proliferated in English provincial cities through the 1990s and 2000s. Often funded by the National Lottery, the new museums were intended to drive urban redevelopment although most have adopted outreach and education strategies to widen access to culture in a civic spirit. But, without detracting from the efforts of museum staff and volunteers, the *proliferation* of new venues in de-industrialised zones appears in retrospect as both a re-branding via culture and, probably, a cosmetic solution to the problems caused by de-industrialisation. Before describing the new art museums I visited in 2014, I want to outline a few points from the critical literature.

Museologist Jennifer Barrett writes of a post-museum based on, 'notions of cultural diversity, accessibility, engagement and the use of objects, rather than the continued accumulation of objects'.[1] In postcolonial contexts this can mean returning objects to the communities from whom they were acquired; otherwise it means emphasising experience over appreciation so that the museum, 'becomes more like a cultural centre'.[2] There are also questions of how a museum's public is constituted. In 1989, arts consultant Philip Wright wrote that because museums serve 'fragmented publics who want to learn and do different things at different speeds', the methods used to address the issue of imparting knowledge will be 'continually undermined by frustrating compromises which will rarely … be satisfactorily resolved'.[3]

Art historian Peter Vergo identifies the idea that a museum should offer interpretations of its holdings as distinctly modern, citing an eighteenth-century visitor to the British Museum who, asking what an object was, was informed that such explanations were, 'not the function of the museum's staff'.[4] He concludes that only from the nineteenth century onwards, notably from the founding of the Victoria and Albert Museum in South Kensington, museum going was 'not to be equated with mindless gawping' but a process of self-education in which even the most private response to art is 'a broadening of our intellectual horizons, a deepening and enriching of our experience … our education'.[5]

In the late twentieth century, the idea of self-education was democratised in the eco-museum, no longer a guardian of cultural treasures for those in possession of a suitable education but a decentred institution attuned to cultural empowerment and recognition of the cultures of everyday lives. Museologist Nancy Fuller explains:

> Ecomuseums are based on the belief that museums and communities should be related to the whole of life. They are concerned with integrating the family home with other aspects of the community, such as the natural environment, economics, and social relationships. Ecomuseums are community learning centres that link the past with the present as a strategy to deal with the future needs of that particular society.[6]

That sounds like praxis: the gaining of insights on past conditions as a means to understand present and future possibilities for change. The concept arose in France in the afterlife of the uprising of May 1968. For Fuller, the eco-museum is a change-agent 'that links education, culture, and power', rather than assimilating public understandings of culture to a dominant narrative.[7] As such, it can be anywhere, in a neighbourhood or street, possibly not in a temple of art. Since then – Fuller wrote in the early 1990s – there have been experiments within and outside institutions. I do not have scope here to go into this material, but ideas of community and empowerment have been absorbed at least by museum education departments while the residual function of display is accompanied by more ardent efforts at interpretation. Still, museums are, for the most part, institutions of high culture, obliged since the 1980s to meld 'residually public-spirited good intentions' with market realism.[8]

Square circles

Jim McGuigan writes:

> State-funded cultural goods have become *marketized* to such an extent
> that their circulation resembles that of the non-state sector, the
> private market of cultural commodities. [This is] a strand in the larger
> process of commodification, whereby all value is ultimately reduced to
> exchange value.[9]

Now, to enter an art museum is not to be made to look at anything but to
be invited into a gift shop, café, designer-bar or restaurant, and selective
displays of information. Activities, thematic displays and interactive
devices seek engagement but may substitute the interpretation (or
selective representation) of art for its contemplation (and the gaining
of knowledge not only of the art but also the self who observes it). But
that is an explicitly modernist attitude. In any case, the argument around
interpretation and interaction was overtaken in the 1990s by the move
of star architects into museum design. The Guggenheim in Bilbao is an
obvious case (Chapter 1).

Citing a 'prescient' essay by Rosalind Krauss (in which Krauss, in 1990,
foresees a euphoria of space overwhelming that of art in museums of
contemporary art), art historian Claire Bishop writes that the spread of
such museums was accompanied by an 'increased scale and proximity to
big business' in a shift from the patrician institution to 'a populist temple
of leisure and entertainment'.[10] Many new art museums outside Europe
have been private-sector enterprises, mounting blockbuster shows to
attract cultural tourists (including those from within various art worlds)
and staging the now ubiquitous biennales and triennales. Echoing Krauss,
Bishop adds, 'the visual expression' of contemporary art's privatization is,
'the triumph of starchitecture', so that 'the museum's external wrapper
has become more important than its contents ... leaving art with the
option of looking ever more lost inside gigantic post-industrial hangars, or
supersizing to compete with its envelope'.[11] I would suggest, too, that the
museum's external wrapper becomes the wrapper of the city hosting it, as
a symbolic icon. Geographers Ash Amin and Nigel Thrift write that what
they call the naming of cities happens in ways which 'confirm or subvert
stereotypes', while 'a narrative of the city is constructed, and over the
years the city comes to be memorialized in detail'.[12] They pin this making

of a city to specific spatial attachments: a particular street or corner or building which, once it is familiar, creates a form of access to a city, or it might be an art museum, or where a pub or cheap café used to be. I leave that open; the next part of the chapter follows my visits to some of the new art museums. I do not claim an authoritative view: I was a day-tripper by train.

Baltic

The Newcastle side of the Tyne quayside is occupied by hotels, restaurants and bars, a short walk from the city centre. On the south side, in Gateshead, are two iconic cultural spaces: Baltic Centre for Contemporary Art, designed by Dominic Williams, converted from a flour mill, and the Sage Music Centre, designed by Spencer de Grey of Foster and Partners. The two banks are joined by the Millennium Bridge designed by Wilkinson Eyre.

Baltic opened a minute after midnight on 13 July 2002. Five thousand people queued to enter the space, which aims to be where artists interact with the public, participating in the institution's review of 'all the ways of creating, displaying and collecting the art of our time' in the context of 'a transparent culture of collaboration and a focus on creative practice'.[13] That brings together various buzz-words but the reference to 'the art of our time' departs from the rhetoric of the contemporary. Internationally known and regional artists (some of whom are both) have exhibited (one of the most memorable for me was by the painter James Hugonin in 2006) in a programme which is thematic and linked to international trends.

Owen Hatherley reads Baltic and the Sage as 'quintessentially Urban Renaissance', and although he sees Baltic as 'undeniably aimed at tourists' also says 'the exhibitions and the public spaces are of a very high standard and I suspect that at least some arty young Geordies are pleased it exists'.[14] No doubt they are. I am, too. Hatherley notes that on his visit the exterior of the building displayed a reproduction of a miners' banner from a show by photographer Martin Parr: 'Victory to the Miners. Victory to the Working Class'.[15] On one of my previous visits it supported an image of dancing girls (Figure 4.1).

I have heard arguments that Baltic is too provincial, or does not attract enough people; I have also heard arguments to the opposite effect. I am not a local so I cannot speak beyond my limited experience as a visitor.

Figure 4.1   Baltic, Gateshead

The range of exhibitions, several at once on different floors, seems broad, and I am more interested in the quality of reception and engagement than in visitor numbers. In 2014, Baltic hosted an event on the Jetty Project by sculptor Wolfgang Weileder and urbanist Simon Guy, based on the conservation of Dunstan Staiths, a wooden industrial structure on the Tyne, where trains once brought coal for loading onto boats (when there was a coal industry). The form of the project was open, to be determined in part through the day's small-group discussions with local residents, artists, architects and academics. Writing in 2003, Keith McIntyre supposed that 'audiences new to contemporary art will inevitably view art with suspicion … elitist and esoteric'.[16] This event suggests otherwise: people spoke with feeling and confidence, shared personal memories and, especially, seemed at ease with the location.

Outside Baltic, the Millennium Bridge (Figure 4.2) seems an equivalent of the Skylon (Chapter 3), its six hydraulic rams enabling it to rotate by 40 degrees on its bearings to open and allow boats through. This has become a regularly observed spectacle. The bridge was lifted into place in November 2000, opened in September 2002, and won the 2002 Stirling Prize. In contrast to the lumpy form of the Millennium Bridge opposite Tate Modern in London, this appears so elegantly simple, spare and economic in the best modernist spirit.

Figure 4.2   The Millennium Bridge, Newcastle-Gateshead

The New Art Gallery, Walsall

If the Millennium Bridge across the Tyne is like the Skylon, my impression of the New Art Gallery, Walsall, by Caruso St John, is that it has some of the qualities of the Festival Hall, especially in the interior (Figure 4.3). The attention paid to detailing, and high quality of materials – wood and leather (a local industry) – plus a feeling of generous spaces says that the best that design can do is offered to the publics of a provincial city in a de-industriaised region (the Black Country). A few changes have been made since the gallery opened in 2000, such as converting the fourth-floor restaurant into additional gallery space for temporary shows.

An early statement from the architects reads: '[we] are interested in urbanism that responds to real situations ... with spaces of democracy and difference, and with the inherently loose and broken character of English urban fabric'.[17] In the gallery this translates into an emphasis on a domestic-scale (a precedent set in 1929 by the Museum of Modern Art, New York)[18] and the cladding of interior walls in Douglas Fir. The New Art Gallery houses the Garman Ryan collection, previously housed elsewhere in Walsall, which contains works by Monet, Dufy, Epstein, Gaudier-Brzeska, Modigliani and Freud, as well as artefacts from India, China

Figure 4.3   The New Art Gallery, Walsall, interior

and Egypt, and works by Blake and Reynolds. These rooms are 'intended to be like a house: an intimate setting' for the collection, in contrast to 6-metre high walls and clerestory on floor 3.[19] Floor 4, for shows by regional artists, has 8-metre high walls. The mission is, 'to present, collect and interpret historic and contemporary art in innovative and challenging ways that encourage the engagement and enjoyment of existing and future audiences'.[20] The gallery's purpose is, 'to provide a cultural and educational service of the very highest quality and to act as a forum for civic pride and community identity for the people of Walsall and the region'.[21]

From outside, the building's pale cladding shimmers and the slit windows state allegiance to postmodernism. The streets leading to the gallery are busier than when I went there ten years ago. There is a new bar and a new hotel across the rectangular pool outside; but other spaces are yet to be redeveloped. It is the interior and the experience of visiting the gallery which linger in my mind: the use of visibly rich, well-maintained, high-specification materials imparts civic values which bear out the institution's mission statement; my encounters with staff – one of whom previously worked in financial services – were friendly and helpful, and imparted a sense of belonging to a team; and, in the café talking to the director, Stephen Snoddy, we were approached by a man asserting that most people in Walsall never go to the New Art Gallery. This might not be what museum directors want to be told in front of visitors but a conversation ensued in which both parties argued strongly but with mutual respect about the gallery's relation to its communities. In fact, some exhibitions have concerned the Black Country, and attendance figures are relatively good. But this encounter was another case of civic values enacted in a cultural venue regardless of pressures to meet commercial targets or reiterate global trends.

The Hepworth, Wakefield

The taxi driver who drove me from the station asked me what I thought about some buildings we passed. He described their construction method with some knowledge; at the Hepworth he pointed to a derelict mill, saying the town had been promised regeneration years ago but was still waiting. I reserved my judgement on the gallery, although I needed to ask him where to find the way in. Inside, I found a lot of people enjoying themselves, and friendly staff and volunteers. I was pleased that admission was free, and (as I later found out) that there is a free bus service from the Hepworth to the station.

Designed by David Chipperfield, the Hepworth opened in 2011. It attracted 100,000 visitors in its first five weeks and remains busy. The building contains ten trapezoid halls. Natural light on the upper level maximises the view over the Calder with its derelict mills and boats (Figure 4.4). The galleries contain more than 40 wood and plaster working models by Barabara Hepworth, some bronzes, and changing exhibitions. Its intimacy with the river separates the Hepworth from the rest of Wakefield but echoes Chipperfield's first gallery commission, the River and Rowing Museum on a meadow by the Thames. There, spaces on pilotis are clad in horizontal strips of green oak while glazing brings the landscape into the museum's lower level.[22]

The Hepworth can be described as a pale grey shed, its interior designed not to interfere with reception of its content. But the distinctive style is more than functional; it makes a statement about what design can do: 'Cool Construction can make one pause. It … demands patience and scrutiny, but that reveals in return a slow and unparalleled beauty.'[23] That takes me back to the empty museums of modern art I used to enjoy; but here there were crowds. Still, this is not a case of a wrapper dominating

Figure 4.4   The Hepworth, Wakefield

the contents but, more, protecting them from the weather (although the weather, colloquially, includes the climate of dereliction which remains evident outside).

The Turner Contemporary, Margate

I saw the Turner Contemporary from the station, far off, through a wire fence around some roadworks. Before me was a seafront of amusement arcades and bars, and the defunct Dreamland amusement park.[24] Then I found the old town: Regency terraces and narrow streets becoming gentrified, a boutique hotel. Near the Turner was an early-nineteenth-century building in process of conversion, I suppose to flats, not the only site with scaffolding and a skip. On the jetty, shed doors are painted in bright pink and orange: vernacular culture biting back.

Like the Hepworth, the Turner was designed by Chipperfield; and, again like the Hepworth, it is a set of halls within a pale cladding with extensive glazing (Figure 4.5). The view of the sea is amazing but I had the same problem that I have at Tate St Ives: the view is better than most of the art displayed. Looking at a Helen Frankenthaler exhibition, I remembered I used to like that kind of art. An interpreter was at work, trying to engage people individually. I escaped to the nice café, wondering if the cool-clad shed was an architectural equivalent, now, of the attempt at timeless art in the 1960s (which became so dated), but the museum commemorates J.M.W. Turner, who spent time in Margate in the 1820s and 1830s. Chipperfield's shed was not, however, the building first proposed in 2001 when a design competition was launched. Two practices, Snøhetta and Spence, collaborated on a building to be located off the Harbour Arm, but 'people were sceptical that the proposed building would ever be built, in part because of the location but perhaps more significantly because the town felt it had been promised much over the years which had never materialised'.[25] In 2006 it was ditched. Temporary shows and events had begun to create a public for new art, nonetheless, in collaboration with the Museum of Modern Art, Oxford. A second design competition was launched. Chipperfield won with a design for six rectangular, interlocking halls on a plinth, accepting that local interests would have a say in its function. He hopes the Turner will be, 'where people can meet, be inspired, inspire one another and feel somehow uplifted'.[26] I was uplifted looking at the sea. I wonder if Margate will be gentrified, or if people will visit from London and go straight home.

Figure 4.5   The Turner Contemporary, Margate

The Jerwood Gallery, Hastings

My abiding memory of the Jerwood is dual: first, the excellent collection of modern British painting it houses; second, the vernacular architectural forms of the fishermen's net stores on the shingle beach outside, stretching beyond. And there were two posters, one on a white van behind the gallery, another on a wall opposite, protesting against the gallery.

Hastings still has a fishing fleet and the boats in bright colours stand along the beach. In the evening, a golden light lit the shingle, the huts and the Jerwood's tile cladding. The tiles are pewter-glazed; in an ordinary light they have a charcoal hue and oily iridescence but in the sunset they were magical. Designed by Hana Loftus and Tom Grieve of HAT Projects, the Jerwood is smaller than most new art museums, at a fraction of the cost of the Turner. It is untypical, too, in being funded not by the National Lottery but by the philanthropic Jerwood Foundation. The building is an example of sustainable design: solar panels, ground-source probes providing 60 per cent of the heating and most of the cooling, and natural ventilation (Figure 4.6). Built on the Stade (the shingle beach) on the site of a local authority coach park, the gallery aroused opposition from the fishing community, and from people who feared that losing the coach park would reduce the number of visitors. Perhaps this masks a deeper resentment at high culture in its chic cladding, heightened by the attempt to visually (but not socially) mimic the vernacular of the fishermen's stores (Figure 4.7). The architects undertook another scheme in London – the conversion of multiple-occupancy housing into offices – which could be seen as gentrifying; yet I doubt the Jerwood will lead to gentrification in Hastings. Across the road from the gallery, a block of unfinished flats crudely appropriating the black, pitched roofs of the fishermen's stores, remains unfinished because the properties failed to sell from plan. If Hastings property prices are rising (I was told) it is because people are moving from London, not to weekend cottages, but to permanent homes which are what they can afford as London prices reach further unreal heights.

The Jerwood does not bring in many visitors: I was the only person in the galleries apart from two volunteers and a couple in the café with its view over the beach and the boats. There is an entry fee; and the café is the wrong side of the ticket desk. A volunteer said they hoped more people would come but it was too far from London. In fact, the journey time is the same as for Margate, but Margate has a high-speed train and more hype. I shall go again, equally for the collection and the walk along the beach.

Figure 4.6   The Jerwood Gallery, Hastings

Figure 4.7   Fishermen's stores on the Stade, Hastings

Middlesbrough Institute of Modern Art (MIMA)

Apart from the permanent collection at the Jerwood, the best exhibition I saw was at MIMA: *Art and Optimism in 1950s Britain* curated by Alix Collingwood, with works by Auerbach, Bacon, Freud, Pasmore and Paolozzi; documentaries from the period with their clipped BBC English; examples of post-war design; and a re-creation of a 1950s sitting room. The show brought international art to Middlesbrough and commemorated the founding of the Friends of Middlesbrough Art Gallery in 1950.

MIMA was designed by Erick van Egeraat, from Rotterdam, following a design competition in 2002. It opened in 2007 and has attracted more than 1 million visitors, and 50,000 participants in education events. The design is unlike the cool-clad Hepworth or Turner, with a glass façade and a 16-metre high foyer in which the reception morphs into the shop, leading to a small café. The building is vertically layered, glass on one side, pale limestone on the other, with a staircase dramatically dissecting the foyer. The exhibition rooms are artificially lit, at the back, almost like an afterthought.

MIMA looks out over a green space with fountains which rise and fall in cycles (Figure 4.8), and a sculpture, *Bottle of Notes* (1995) by Claes Oldenburg and Coosje van Bruggen. With new County and Magistrates court buildings and a Registry Office, the site resembles a colonial administrative district, set well apart from the commercial streets and residential areas. The County Court was the first element in this public-sector redevelopment scheme, with *Bottle of Notes* set in what was then a residual site, commemorating the locally born Captain Cook. It is a blue and white painted steel lattice of writing taken from Cook's notebooks, shaped like a bottle with a message inside as if it had somehow washed up in Middlesbrough. When the sculpture was unveiled, art critic Richard Cork reviewed it for *Modern Painters*, relating it to the modernism of Umberto Boccioni and Vladimir Tatlin. He praised the local authority for being so brave in commissioning it. The review appeared under the heading Art and Travel, at the back of the magazine.

MIMA is only a few minutes' walk from the recently refurbished railway station but it feels like a world on its own. Middlesbrough, however, has changed. In the 1990s, everything was worn out. Now the shopping centre is busy; a pound-shop dominates the central square but a row of colourful banners proclaim that Middlesbrough feels like a city (from a failed attempt to gain city status). The renewal is uneven but it exists. I

Figure 4.8   Middlesbrough Institute of Modern Art

doubt that MIMA has brought in many tourists, but the local authority's attempt to regain a sense of civic values is admirable, while the exhibition *Art and Optimism* suggested a reclamation of the values celebrated in 1951 at the Festival of Britain. MIMA became part of Teesside University in 2014. Perhaps this will enable curating which challenges the tired notions of a creative class and a creative city in favour of an idea of the cultural venue as politicised space. Or is that naïve?

Epilogues

Not all the new museums which were funded in the 2000s survived, largely for two reasons. First, Lottery funding applied only to capital expenditure, not running costs; institutions were expected to operate on a business model. Second, the arts consultants employed to draft bids exaggerated projected visitor numbers and spin-off employment. A third factor may be that an economic case for the arts predominated over civic values and local needs, and was not realistic. McGuigan sees a crisis 'concerning assumptions of aesthetic authority' in the 1960s, whereby 'public support for the arts as a set of superior values to mass-marketed

culture was no longer regarded as self-evidently justified',[27] followed
in the 1980s by a shift to economic benefit as *the* criterion for public
arts investment, informed by John Myerscough's report *The Economic
Importance of the Arts in Britain*.[28] McGuigan adds, 'Public subsidy to the
arts was not a luxury … but had an instrumental value beyond the arts
themselves.'[29] This extended to claims that the arts could deal with social
exclusion but evidence was recorded unevenly, if at all, and mechanisti-
cally. Arts consultant François Matarasso tried to undertake qualitative
research[30] but was accused of failing to match his conclusions to his data.[31]
McGuigan says this is not important because such reports are rhetorical
anyway as, 'an elementary apparatus of empiricism is used to justify a
reductive politics of measurable impact'.[32] I agree. In any case, all this
was overtaken by demands from the Treasury to see the evidence. At that
point, the Arts Council did not have even a list of commissions funded
within Lottery projects. At the same time, academic discussion of cultural
policy has been returning to aesthetic and even metaphysical arguments
for the arts.[33]

A shift in policy emerged when UK Secretary of State for Culture,
Media and Sport, Tessa Jowell addressed arts managers in London in 2005.
She praised the diversity and originality of the arts, stating, 'I've been
making speeches on the arts for the last four years and my message has
been consistent: what the arts do that only the arts do is most important.'[34]
Citing attendance figures in passing, she reiterated, 'What we must now
do is to find a way of focusing on what the arts can do in themselves … a
more rounded definition of what we are about in funding the arts.'[35] This
is a reversion to intrinsic value or the autonomy claimed for modern art,
its advantage being that it cannot be measured. The argument did not turn
quite full circle, in that instrumentalism remains part of the discourse, but
reductions in the arts budget after 2007 have meant that there is less to
argue about.

In that context, because capital projects take years to deliver, the
proliferation of new cultural venues continued into the 2000s but has
probably come to an end. Arts funding lost out to the 2012 London
Olympics, and a cynic might assert that British cities are full up when
it comes to new arts buildings. The Turner Contemporary and the
Hepworth may be the last of a genre, characteristically cool in a grey,
shed-like sublimity.

As I said above, not all the new arts venues remain open. I do not want
to dwell on failure so look only briefly at two cases, plus one environmental

centre: the National Centre for Popular Music in Sheffield (designed by Nigel Coates); The Public in West Bromwich (by Will Alsop and Julian Flannery); and the Earth Centre at Conisbrough, near Doncaster, South Yorkshire.

The Public was a spectacular building with irregular, pink-edged blobby windows scattered on its dark cladding but the technology of the interior was over-ambitious, leading to some negative press coverage. Between its opening in 2009 and closure in 2013, The Public housed 30 arts organisations and saw more than a million visitors. Its website states:

> The Public set out to be a force for the better in the community, a place where the arts could be used to raise aspirations, to bring the world to West Bromwich and to show the world all the exciting and inspiring work carried out in West Bromwich. The Public opened its doors to a very diverse community and provided opportunities which could not have existed without it.[36]

Not enough people went there, and the problem was bigger than The Public: a letter in the press asserted that a road scheme isolated the town centre, 'making this once busy hub a hole in a doughnut'.[37] There were 'thriving shops, a beautiful Victorian and Edwardian heritage … the cinema and the gorgeous Dartmouth Park', but now 'all that could be seen was endless dilapidated junk-food shops, charity shops and nail bars … the tattiest market'.[38] The letter ends, 'Did councillors ever consider a new cinema or baths, or renovating the park? No, they spent [£Nm] on an arts centre.'[39] In 2013, low revenue led Sandwell Metropolitan Borough Council to withdraw funding as local government expenditure became a casualty of the austerity regime.

The National Centre for Popular Music opened in March 1999 and closed in June 2000. The building consisted of four stainless steel drums alluding to the city's main industry, arranged around a central atrium. The cladding is as shiny as the Guggenheim Museum in Bilbao; this is a landmark building near the city centre. The lower level contained a shop, café, bar, temporary exhibition space and offices; the museum was on the upper level, requiring an entry fee. One criticism was that the exhibits were not interesting enough while the admission price was too high. One visitor put comments online, from which I quote (which may be unrepresentative):

I left the museum disappointed, thinking be populist but at least have
something of a local nature.... Apart from an exhibition with pictures
of the closed Corporation and Fiesta clubs [in Manchester] I left feeling
a little empty handed. It didn't know whether it wanted to be a music
theme park or crèche, or a scholarly museum.... In 1999 Sheffield was
probably 10 years behind Manchester and Liverpool in being a world
renowned tourist destination.[40]

Visitor projections were 400,000 a year, revised down to 150,000 after
just over 104,000 had visited in the first seven months. In 2001 the centre
became a live music venue, and in 2003 it was sold to Sheffield Hallam
University, whose Students' Union it now houses.

The Earth Centre, funded by the National Lottery as a Millennium
project, was a particularly sad failure because, although in design
terms it was unspectacular, it was a good educational project on
environmental issues before they rose on the international agenda. It
employed ex-mine workers who, despite their commitment to the project
– I had conversations with some of them on two visits in 1999 – were
made redundant again when the project failed to attract the projected
number of paying visitors rather than the school groups who came for
free. The preponderance of school groups was a sign of success for an
educational project, of course, but not compatible with a business model
based on consultants' fantasies. The centre's entrance was directly from
Conisbrough station, a short distance from Doncaster, and people arriving
by rail received a discount on the entrance fee. This is not a tourist area but
perhaps there was confusion as to whether the Earth Centre was a theme
park or an educational facility. The main gallery, Planet Earth Experience,
exhibited images of earth, air, fire and water projected through a series
of moving panels suggesting, in a semi-abstract way, life forms such as
fish, birds and people. There was a water cleansing system using reeds
and papyrus, which processed all waste liquid on the site for re-use in
irrigation, and gardens designed for different climate zones. There were
colourful sculptures, and the café provided locally sourced organic food. I
found enough to interest me for the day, and went again, but I was already
interested in green issues and found quiet places to sit in the 400-acre site
by the Don. I did not seek activities. I simply liked it there and enjoyed
watching the reed-bed water system.

The Earth Centre sought to enact green values; its stated aim was to
'provide inspiration and access to people and organisations that can help

individuals make decisions … that will make a significant and positive impact on our future'.[41] This, again, suggests civic values and public service as celebrated in the post-war years, mapped now onto environmental concerns. It closed in 2004; the site was sold for development in 2010.

Looking back …

Perhaps it is easier in the regions, out of sight of a metropolitan elite who imagine that trains only arrive in London, to create a distinct feeling, not of place but of collaboration. There is a precedent: the Museum of Neo-Realism, Vila Franca de Xira, by Alcino Soutinho. This is a museum of Portuguese Socialist culture, collecting work by Neo-Realist writers, dramatists, artists, performers and composers from the Left from the 1920s to the 1960s. Portugal was a fascist state until 1974 in which culture was a location of resistant stories. The museum grew from a project for a documentation centre, and has temporary exhibitions as well as research facilities. It is supported by the local authority, in a region known for labour militancy. This is a case of a reinvention of the museum's traditional function of collecting and archiving, to tell stories from the grassroots not the elite; and an articulation of a politicised image of, not place as in the regeneration rhetoric, but time (the time of resistance in the time when what was resisted has been overthrown). It is a contrast to the co-option of culture to the regeneration industry, and to examples cited by Bishop of numerous new showcase museums designed to suit the symbolic economies of cities in Asia, Latin America and the Middle East (such as the M+ in Hong Kong, due to open in 2015).[42] There are other exceptions as well: Bishop cites the van Abbemuseum in Eindhoven, Netherlands, using its permanent collection, 'as a temporary exhibition' curated in different ways to constitute a critique of museum display and reception. Bishop cites the director, Charles Esche, who says that a museum's task is to 'take a position, because relativism is the dominant narrative of the market, where everything is equalized by exchange value'.[43] For instance, some presentations have concerned the legacy of state socialism and the possibilities for its future reactivation.[44]

Bishop also cites the Museo Nacional Centro de Arte Reina Sofía, Madrid, not for the uses of its public concourse (which, like Tate Modern's lower floor, remains institutional rather than public space), but for the content articulated in its exhibitions through juxtapositions. For instance, the section titled 'From Revolt to Pre-moderrnity, 1962–82' contains Agnès Varda's photographic series *Cuba Is Not Congo* (1963), Alain Resnais' film on African art, *Statues Also Die* (1953), Gillo Pontecorvo's anti-colonial film *The Battle of Algiers*, and books by Albert Camus and Jean-Paul Sartre. Leaving aside juxtapositions of media, the content is articulated as anti colonialism.[45]

Bishop writes:

Neoliberalism's subordination of culture to economic value denigrates not only museums but the humanities more broadly, whose own systems of assessment increasingly have to justify themselves according to metrics…. We seem hopelessly unable to devise an alternative value system: technocracy unwittingly abetted by post-structuralism has dismantled much of the vocabulary in which the significance of culture and the humanities was previously couched, making the task of persuasively defining this in non-economic terms ever more pressing.[46]

Without a vocabulary nothing can be said that can be shared. Perhaps, now, an emerging role for museums is to recreate possibilities for politicised and civic vocabularies of imagination, not through interactive devices or received notions of populism, but through provocation and a partisan approach.

Back in Middlesbrough, journalist Jon Ronson reports another approach to regeneration. On a visit to an abandoned ship once used as a nightclub in Newcastle, he looks at 'an expanse of flattened nothingness' that previously housed a close-knit if violent community; a local man, John Coates, explains, 'So they levelled the place. They had to really.'[47] The ship is a wreck, past re-use; all the electrical cables (which John helped install) have been stolen. In 2004, plans were announced to transform Middlesbrough with money from Dubai: a primary school like a spelling block, a cinema like a Rubik's cube, blocks of flats inspired by Prada, a new art college and an Anish Kapoor sculpture.[48] The scheme was launched at the Venice Biennale but a condition of the deal was that the ship had to go. There is a Kapoor sculpture and a new art college now. What used to be the wrong side of the railway has been redeveloped: bright-coloured postmodern blocks constituting, as Hatherley observes, a Pop Art District: 'It's perhaps the most outrageous and demented of all the boom's schemes … based essentially on gambling … on a super-casino.'[49] One of the new blocks says Bohaus (Figure 4.9), conjuring memories of a previous Left culture in the guise of postmodern eclecticism. But Bohaus is not Bauhaus.

Hatherley notes that in Teesside the public sector has tried to 'resuscitate' the private sector via 'regeneration companies and the sell-off of public assets to prompt property development, a new University to stimulate the knowledge economy, the building of art galleries to attract creative capital and of shopping malls to inculcate consumerism'.[50] This failed because the infrastructure was inadequate, and because faith was put in the notion of a creative class who produce money by being there. In the new district, Middlehaven, there is a BoHo Zone, 'a new neo-modernist building to house arts organizations. It's the veritable front line of urban cool … next to the new police station.'[51] Perhaps regeneration fails because it is a simplistic as well as a mechanistic approach, relying on instrumental interventions and a mysterious assumption that one thing always leads to another regardless of local or changing conditions.

Figure 4.9   Middlesbrough: Bohouse

Amin and Thrift write that philosophies of becoming tend to have characteristics including the idea of tools as 'a vital element of knowing, not as simply a passive means of representing the known', and a consideration of 'other modes of subjectivity than consciousness'.[52] Time is not a simple advance, either; and 'becoming is discontinuous'.[53]Art offers access to modes of subjectivity and the expression of values as well as visual impressions, but when its institutions are co-opted to redevelopment, which means global imperatives of productivity, consumption and profit generation, this overlooks the – almost naïve – idea that cultural provision can both meet local needs and introduce international art which speaks of another world, a dimension in which everything is possible, a world turned upside down, as in the fracturing, radical and utopian content of some of the art exhibited in the new museums and national collections. As to a new architectural sublime: I am unsure.

5

New Codes:
Culture as Social Ordering

In the late 1860s, Matthew Arnold – a public intellectual in today's terms, a man of letters in nineteenth-century terms – perceived a crisis of national cohesion following a fracturing of allegiance to the established church. Anglicanism reflected the interests of the landed gentry whose members occupied most of its offices, while Methodism, Baptism and other churches protesting against its mystique appealed to non-privileged people, after a history of radical dissent going back to groups such as the Quakers in the English Revolution in the 1640s. To give an example of how the established church became elitist: church organs were introduced in the eighteenth century, requiring trained players in place of the village fiddlers who used to play at services. Arnold saw such divisions as damaging religion's role as a guardian of social unity when social cohesion was already threatened by political unrest. In these circumstances, culture was the remaining means to engender the cohesion which religion no longer offered.

Arnold's book *Culture and Anarchy* was published in 1869. In 1867 to 1869, civil unrest occurred in Birmingham and Lancashire, provoked by the Irish Protestant extremist Patrick Murphy (who regaled crowds with familiar tales of sodomy in the monastery, seduction at the confessional, and nuns walled up alive). Historian Bernard Porter summarises that, from the 1850s on, the main reasons for civil unrest were 'starvation ... the Catholic Church and the Irish'.[1] There were bread riots in Liverpool, the Midlands and London in 1855, when a crowd ransacked shops in Mayfair. In the 1860s, there were strikes – machines were sabotaged and black-legs (strike breakers) attacked – contextualised by a struggle for parliamentary reform after the 1832 Reform Act only partially widened voting rights.[2] A key force here, until the 1850s, was Chartism. In 1819, a peaceful Chartist demonstration outside St Peter's church in Manchester was charged by the militia (a private force drawn from the gentry, providing their own horses and sabres). Eleven demonstrators were killed, more than 400 wounded, and the spectre of the Peterloo Massacre haunted liberal opinion while enhancing fears of future insurrection. Yet the Chartists were constitutional. In the late 1840s, the Chartist Land Company sought to widen the vote by widening property ownership, buying agricultural land and building model villages (as at Minster Lovell in Oxfordshire, where the houses and one-acre plots still exist). The scheme failed and damaged Chartism, which was replaced on the radical Left, Porter says, 'by a vacuum' giving rise to dozens of riots and disturbances,[3] such as a demonstration in Hyde Park on 23 July 1866 when railings were torn up and the crowd moved to streets housing London's gentlemen's clubs. Troops were called in but Porter reads these events as contained:

> The ruling classes … could afford to tolerate a certain amount of riot, so long as … it did not threaten the basis their system rested on. Even the 1866 riots did not really do that: extending the franchise, slowly, was a policy that came well within the bounds of conventional liberal ideology.… When, in 1867, a Reform bill was passed, the trouble stopped. The other occasions for disturbances were less worrying. There was no way in which the state, the monarchy or liberal capitalism were ever going to be toppled.… To the mid-Victorian mind it was not a political but a criminal problem, whose potential political sting would be drawn when poverty was eradicated by growing prosperity, and by a few discriminating measures of social reform.[4]

Although Porter's interest is in the emergence of a secret police, this gives a succinct picture of liberalism as a political-economic philosophy in tension between reform and repression.

Still, there were continuing protests at food shortages and welfare cuts, as in Stalybridge in 1863, when the houses and shops of members of the local relief committee responsible for the cuts were attacked.[5] In 1867 – as Arnold worked on *Culture and Anarchy* – Irish nationalists detonated a bomb at Clerkenwell police station, killing 12 people. This is tangential to a discussion of cultural policy but is the context for Arnold's genuine fear that social cohesion was at risk, so that culture was the last defence against social breakdown.

Added to the fear of internal unrest was a fear that revolution in Europe might be contagious. Although dissidents from the Paris Commune of

1871 came to London, the authorities felt it inappropriate to police their activities closely unless they threatened the British state. Again, that left culture as a form of soft policing, along with improvements in the material conditions of the lower classes, such as housing. Widening access to culture and education worked in two ways, however: a rise in adult literacy meant that working-class people could read radical literature, just as it created access to high culture as a means of moral reform.

Culture or anarchy?

Elected Oxford Professor of Poetry in 1857, Arnold was the first holder of the post to give his lectures in English not Latin. Apart from classical authors, several of whom he translated, one of the poets whose work Arnold admired was William Wordsworth, whose ballads employed ordinary language to appeal to a wide audience while retaining poetry's role of imparting moral insights. Like Wordsworth (who died in 1851), Arnold evolved a position which was rational and religious, reading the Christian pantheon as not unlike that of classical myth. He sought rational means to social stability, which included the cultivation of sensibility. Culture, he wrote, 'shows its single-minded love of perfection, its desire simply to make reason and the will of God prevail, its freedom from fanaticism ...'[6] He refers to machinery – a term which he uses broadly for institutions such as industrialism, athletics or political organisation, which I think means mechanistic approaches – before cautioning against extremes:

> But the flexibility which sweetness and light give, and which is one of the rewards of culture pursued in good faith, enables a man [sic] to see that a tendency may be necessary ... salutary, and yet that the generations or individuals who obey this tendency are sacrificed to it, that they fall short of the hope of perfection by following it.[7]

This is a warning against being captured by sentiment (as perhaps he thought the Evangelical wing of Anglicanism had been).

In the following passage in *Culture and Anarchy*, Arnold targets wealth accumulation: 'culture admits the necessity of the movement towards fortune-making and exaggerated industrialism ... but insists ... that the passing generations of industrialists, forming, for the most part, the stout main body of Philistinism, are sacrificed to it.'[8] Arnold introduces three terms here: culture as the reasonable pursuit of perfection; sweetness and light as culture's reward; and Philistinism as the wilful refusal of such cultivation. Arnold was critical of an interpretation of being free as doing what one likes, arguing that the Victorian middle class echoed the claims of the eighteenth-century gentry: 'Our middle class, our great representative of trade and Dissent', with its individualism in business and religion, 'dreads a powerful administration which might somehow interfere with it'.[9] And in the working class he saw a similar lack of public consciousness: 'Our masses are quite as raw and uncultivated as the French; so far from their having the idea of public duty and of discipline' that, for instance, they would rather 'flee to the mines' than join the army during the Crimean War.[10] This leads into a tirade against mass political self-interest:

> this and that man, and this and that body of men, all over the country, are beginning to assert and put in practice an Englishman's right to do what he likes; his right to march where he likes, meet where he likes, enter where he likes, hoot as he likes, threaten as he likes, smash as he likes. All this, I say, tends to anarchy; and though a number of excellent people, and particularly my friends of the Liberal or progressive party … are kind enough to reassure us by saying that these are trifles.[11]

This is coincidentally echoed in Porter's summary, and Arnold is as critical of trade unions as of shop-keepers and Liberals who settle for utilitarian reform.

Arnold's social ideal was represented by the educated middle class, within Anglicanism but critical of dogma, politically aware but neither extremist nor pragmatic. This class within a class alone could uphold just law and build, 'anything precious and lasting now, or … for the future'.[12] Against a tide of social and moral-philosophical disintegration, 'culture is the most resolute enemy of anarchy, because of the great hopes and designs for the State which culture teaches us to nourish'.[13] No better case could be made for art museums as the glue of social cohesion, and the sentiment remains in the post-war provision of culture as civic benefit.

Temples of art and sites of abjection

From the 1870s onwards, a proliferation of public monuments occurred across Europe and the Americas. In new nations such as Germany and Italy, or the United States after civil war in the 1860s, monuments borrowed the look of classical or gothic pasts to bestow a sense of timelessness on manufactured identities; or naturalism to bestow a more homely certainty. In France after its defeat at Sedan in 1870, Austria-Hungary in its decline, and Britain after the 1860s, the threat of revolt was addressed by the manufacture of national identities trading on invented pasts. Representations of kings, colonialists and mythological figures, like the stone and bronze in which they were made, lent monuments an aura of inevitability as if to say that to challenge the power they represented would be futile, while naturalistic likenesses of public figures in public squares and urban parks imparted normality. And there were museums and exhibitions, from the Great Exhibition in 1851 and the founding of a public museum district in South Kensington, London, to the opening of the Tate Gallery at Millbank, on the site of a crumbling women's prison in 1897.

Art historian Carol Duncan writes that art museums 'have always been compared to older ceremonial monuments such as palaces or temples.... they were deliberately designed to resemble them.'[14] Visitors gazed at the classical colonnades and porticos; flights of steps to the museum entrance made them look up to culture. Inside, the exhibits were categorised, catalogued and cleaned, arranged as selective narratives. In ethnographic museums, this illustrated the assumed superiority of European civilisations;[15] in art museums it followed chronology and national schools, informed by the emergence of the nation-state. To visit a museum was to be reminded of certain legacies, to reaffirm membership of the society which upheld them, and belong to a realm of, as Arnold put it, sweetness and light. Duncan adds, 'To control a museum means precisely to control the representation of a community and its highest values and truths ... the power to define the relative standing of individuals within that community.'[16] In the late nineteenth century, the standing of classes was a matter of conjecture. For historian Eric Hobsbawm, this is when a recognisable English working class emerged in a period of rapid industrialisation and urban expansion, with highly differentiated skills, and able to develop tactics such as the strike and the national agreement.[17]

Hobsbawm identifies three particular changes in conditions from 1873 to 1896 (a period of economic downturn): a 'dramatic fall' in living costs; the rise of the domestic mass market in processed goods; and new housing, which 'created so much of the environment of working-class life, the rows of terraced houses outside the old town centres'.[18] If Arnold's advocacy of culture inflected intellectual life in the late nineteenth century – *Culture and Anarchy* was re-published in a popular edition at 7 shillings in 1889 – these changes were as influential in shaping the material conditions in which the Tate Gallery was proposed as a home for Henry Tate's pictures, also in 1889 (when, too, an opera house opened in Blackpool).

The widening of access to culture was enabled by laws such as the Act for Encouraging the Establishment of Museums in Large Towns (1845) and the Public Libraries Act (1850). The new museums were financed through local taxation and initially covered design and the natural sciences. Art museums followed, with art schools in Brighton, Exeter, Nottingham, Liverpool and Wolverhampton, among other places. Art historian Brandon Taylor reads the opening of the Tate Gallery as a matter of both art and social ordering. Much was made of the museum's site on that of a prison: the Prince of Wales said at the opening ceremony, 'I am glad to think that in place [of the prison] we have this beautiful temple of art.'[19] And the *Norwood Press* reported, 'many working men and women were to be seen wandering through the rooms and gazing with much interest at the pictures ... the residents there are not going to neglect the beautiful art gallery which had been placed so close to their doors'.[20] But other reports stressed an alignment of lower-class publics to a need for moral tales, or simply mused on what the lower orders would make of it:

Carriage folk [middle-class visitors] were there in considerable numbers, but the majority of the visitors came from the immediate neighbourhood.... Where once stood a building the inside of which no one wished to see, another has arisen ... whose cool fountain courts and cheerful galleries invite the reposeful contemplation of things of beauty. And so the crowd, nothing loth, entered yesterday into possession of their new palace of art, gazed in curious admiration at the fountain with its goldfish, wondered at the clean tessellated floor, and having thoroughly appreciated both, tried to understand the pictures, in which lay a new world of romance and mystery, mingled with the world they know better: on the one hand the allegories of Watts, on the other the realism of Frith.[21]

One correspondent wrote, after asking an attendant whether 'these people' could understand the pictures and being told that they do after a few visits, 'whatever doubt might have been in my mind before ... I came to the conclusion that so far as I had been able to judge, this was the only successful rival I had found to the public-house'.[22]

The need for behavioural improvement was linked to productivity, and in this context art museums were deemed likely to improve social attitudes; to this end, museums were also established in working-class areas such as Bethnal Green in the East End of London, their moral underpinning evident in popular illustrations juxtaposing afternoons spent in a picture gallery and a gin palace.[23] Together with an 'obsession with cleanliness and healthy living', attitudes to art museums rested on a commitment to 'civic order and moral superiority' aligned to middle-class values.[24] Picture galleries in working-class areas were seen as *instrumental* in social improvement when the expectation was that such areas of a city would be scenes of grime and physical malformation. As Taylor argues:

> Such rhetorical practices served to assemble the population of the capital around art and a national tradition.... The gallery must have constituted a splendid symbol of national unity.... Yet the place of an urban working class within the scenario of elevated culture ... remained chronically unresolved.[25]

Those who received charity were required to be productive and know their place. Hobsbawm notes a 'growing residential segregation' in an exodus of the middle and lower-middle classes from formerly mixed areas, and in 'the construction of new and *de facto* single-class urban quarters and suburbs.'[26] In the 1850s, British Prime Minister Lord Palmerston asserted that discontent produced disorder; hence, 'Britain's security lay in the fact that her people were contented.' In Europe, 'Successful revolutions needed revolution-fodder ... engendered by governing tyrannically', as Porter notes, adding, 'Some mid-Victorians defined tyranny very broadly.'[27] The solution was prosperity and, Porter continues, 'prosperity would come automatically, as a result of the natural dynamism of Britain's free market economy, whose benefits eventually would filter down to everyone who worked.'[28] This was supported by wealth extraction in the colonies. Tate derived his money from the sugar cube, sourced by plantations in the West Indies which relied on slave labour until liberal reformism abolished the trade throughout the Empire in the 1830s.

Taylor finds 'an almost unquestioned belief in the efficacy of picture galleries' as part of the explanation for Tate's offer to donate his large collection of 'contemporary' British art to the nation.[29] But he also cites a, 'declining imperialism and the beginning of the end of the old European order that would eventuate in the war of 1914'.[30] Taylor reads Tate's taste in art as informed by his Unitarian religious belief: 'The most general technical character of the works he admired was a high-polish illusionistic naturalism ... [a] preference for pictorial illusions of moral situations and scenes'.[31] Naturalism offered historical information, and images with which lay viewers could readily engage, although Tate's collection included realists as well as pre-Raphaelites and scene painters. Tate offered his collection to the National Gallery, but it required more space than could be provided there. The site eventually agreed, the redundant penitentiary, was separated from the museums in South Kensington but near the government in Whitehall; and Millbank was perceived as a dangerous area ripe for improvement, being 'excluded from the civilized society and heavily associated with dirt, inaccessibility and crime'.[32] The site was described in the *Daily News* as unsuitable for a gallery, 'full in the face of half-a-dozen manufactories ...a dirty spot ... blue mould and green damp are the prevalent conditions of the region'.[33] The building inserted to cleanse the site was designed by Sidney R.J. Smith, commissioned by Tate, in an Italianate style with a cupola and a pedimented colonnade, faced in Portland stone. It was described as 'Gorgonesque' in *The Spectator*.[34] Around the temple of art there was to be a housing development for deserving artisans.

During the period of the gallery's planning, design and construction, a Royal Commission whose members included the Prince of Wales reviewed the housing conditions of the poor. It reported in 1885 that, if there had been improvements, 'the evils of overcrowding, especially in London, were a public scandal, and were becoming in certain localities more serious that they ever were', while legislation previously passed to address this was not enforced.[35] A pamphlet by the clergyman Andrew Mearns, *The Bitter Cry of Outcast London*, drew attention to the plight of the working poor, describing walls and ceilings, 'black with the accretions of filth which have gathered upon them through long years of neglect' and filth 'running down the walls', while in tenement blocks each room housed a family and, in some cases, animals as well.[36] This was taken up by the press: the *Pall Mall Gazette* called for an official inquiry, as did the more conservative *Times*. The Royal Commission followed Victoria's intervention.

The problem, however, was older. The move to urban areas began in the eighteenth century with the introduction of machines to replace labourers on farms, and the drift of rural families to hiring fairs and, not infrequently, workhouses. In cities the work was often no less seasonal than on the land; one kind of poverty was exchanged for another in the informal settlements which spread along the railway lines. Friedrich Engels saw this in Manchester in 1844:

> Immediately under the railway bridge there stands a court the filth and horrors of which surpass all the others by far, just because it was hitherto so cut off, so secluded that the way to it could never be found.... Passing along a rough bank, among stakes and washing lines, one penetrates into this chaos of small, one-storied, one-roomed huts, in most of which there is no artificial floor; kitchen, living and sleeping-room all in one. In such a hole ... I found two beds ... which, with a staircase and chimney-place, exactly fitted the room. In several others I found absolutely nothing, while the door stood open, and the inhabitants leaned against it. Everywhere before the doors, refuse and offal; that any sort of pavement lay underneath could not be seen but only felt, here and there, with the feet.[37]

While reformers saw such conditions as a sickness to be cured, James Donald explains that Engels saw them as, 'an inevitable consequence of the forms of production that produce this spatial organisation'.[38] By the 1880s and 1890s, the pity felt by middle-class reformers who visited the poor in their terrible housing was not confined to their material conditions but also included their morals. For such people, crime was a viable means to a living – a child thief brought in the same as the wages for making 56 gross of boxes of matches – and morality an alien code. Mearns wrote that few among this class cared whether couples were married; incest was common and 'no form of vice and sensuality causes surprise or attracts attention.... The vilest practices are looked upon with the most matter-of-fact indifference.'[39] This may reflect expectations, as in East London (above), but Peter Hall remarks that 'For the Victorian middle class, this was perhaps the most shocking feature of all.'[40]

The poor continued not to have any money, and unrest did not go away. As said above, the 1880s was a period of economic depression which questioned Britain's competitiveness in world markets. Hall writes that, 'During the 1880s ... throughout London, there was a spirit of cataclysmic, even violent, change in the air.'[41] The fabled mob might erupt from the East End and destroy the city. This produced new insights: looking back in 1926, Beatrice Webb wrote of a, 'growing uneasiness, amounting to conviction, that the industrial organism, which had yielded rent, interest and profit on a stupendous scale, had failed to provide a decent livelihood and tolerable conditions' for most people in Britain.[42] In large cities, gangs attacked people in the street and stole from shops. Court sentences were draconian, including hard labour and flogging, yet this did not allay 'the real terror among the middle classes' as Hall puts it,[43] that there would be a revolution. On 8 February 1886, the Commissioner of the Metropolitan Police was forced to resign when a force of 600 men failed to prevent a crowd of 3,000 from breaking windows and looting shops in Pall Mall. On 23 October 1887, people gathered under a red flag in Trafalgar Square, moved down Whitehall and interrupted a service in Westminster Abbey. Also in 1887, Charles Booth, a Liverpool ship-owner, presented a report to the Royal Statistical Society on poverty in the East End. Booth differentiated a semi-criminal element, mainly young men, from a larger group of people in chronic want, 'shiftless, hand-to-mouth, pleasure loving, and always poor', including many widows, unmarried women, and children.[44] Above that group was another, afflicted by the slump; and a fourth, at the top of the socio-economic scale, of people in work but with low earnings, who 'live hard times very patiently'.[45] These were the deserving poor, who might be expected to go to art museums on Sundays.

The Tate Gallery was opened by the Prince of Wales on 21 July 1897 and provided, Taylor says, 'the connection between art, the nation and the gradual eradication of crime'.[46] The site, after the demolition of the prison by ex-dock workers and builders unemployed in the slump, was (as said above) marked for new workers' housing before 1897, with a school and public laundry to emphasise the connections to learning and cleanliness as self-improvement. The *Daily News* carried a proposal that 'clerks and others of a similar standing' should live in a new 'residential colony of a class somewhat superior to the "artisan" neighbourhood, and a little more in keeping with ... the vicinity of this splendid national institution'.[47] The new blocks were named after British artists. Taylor writes,

> Such rhetorical practices served to assemble the population of the capital around art and a national tradition.... The gallery must have constituted a splendid symbol of national unity towards the end of Queen Victoria's reign. Yet the place of the urban working class within the scenario of elevated culture ... remained chronically unresolved. In Whitechapel the crowds were expected to be destitute and the pictures could be interpreted accordingly – that is, moralistically. But Millbank was not the East End. In a region close to the very heart of London the

constitution of a class audience, and with it the balance of moral and artistic concerns, was more uncertain still.[48]

A mask of access

Before returning to the present, I want to go back to Georgian London. Using a geological metaphor, this is the strata beneath that of the art museum as a means of social ordering. If culture answered dereliction in the 1890s, before that it reflected a widening gap between rich and poor while new cultural forms, notably the pleasure garden, only *seemed* to widen access to the cultural scene.

Georgian England was a place of new commercial ventures, new wealth, new towns and new social divisions. The division between land owners and agricultural labourers, merchants and hired hands, or ship-owners and hired crews, was there before; but throughout the eighteenth century, expressions of wealth grew more ostentatious. George III was perceived as shaping a British identity aligned to prudence and domestic virtue, but this did not prevent displays of wealth by the upper class as commerce took the place of land as the main source of wealth. Historian Hannah Greig writes that the royal court was pivotal in social and political life, 'as a resort of formal and informal sociability … one of numerous extra-parliamentary spheres of political activity, and home to the type of social politics now widely identified with the coffee house, theatre, private residence, and other venues'.[49] Admission to court required specific (and already anachronistic) forms of dress: embroidered gowns and lace for women; a tail-coat, waistcoat, breeches and silk stockings for men. Hence, 'Personal bills and household accounts reveal the staggering expense that could be incurred to equip a person for regular attendance at court.'[50]

Through the eighteenth century, coffee houses were replaced as meeting sites by the more selective gentlemen's clubs, in which windows onto the street allowed the display of privilege shielded from the interference but not the gaze of passers-by. Jane Rendell notes that clubs consolidated differentiations between genders, and between men of different status: 'the careful protection of subscription and gambling rooms and their physical remoteness from the street, suggest that exclusivity operates around notions of secrecy'.[51] Meanwhile, Georgian London saw a shift from the sobriety of the early eighteenth century to ostentation, and the extensive development of property. Richard Sennett writes, 'From the building of the first Bloomsbury squares ... urban development in London consistently razed housing and shops inhabited by the very poor to create homes for the middle class or the rich.'[52] Some squares dated to the 1720s–30s, but new garden squares and terraces were built on green sites around what is now Regent's Park. Regent Street, in contrast, was the result of clearance of a zone of high-density lower-class housing in the 1820s. The habitations cleared were regarded as sites of iniquity and disease, but did not evince the pity of Victorian times. The white, colonnaded, stucco-fronted terraces founded a new city on the site of the old, with little trace of the former state. It was decidedly modern, constructing sober certainties. The façades of houses in the garden squares were rational in proportion (although the backs were whatever the builder made them) but Greig notes that inside was another matter: citing the gilded 1750s music room of Norfolk House and the red-glass drawing room of Northumberland House, she finds 'the architectural ostentation and drama that lay behind seemingly uniform and relatively modest exteriors'.[53] This was the setting for events which enabled the Beau Monde – 'the cohort of privileged individuals who enjoyed public prominence within the framework of the London season'[54] – to stage appearances to itself.

The season was when the aristocracy left their estates and came to London. By the 1800s it was also a migration of the aspirant upper middle class from country estates or provincial houses to London, or to take the waters at a spa. Participation in the season's events allowed a temporary and contingent suspension of status. Greig remarks that if being in fashion was a matter of 'credentials other than inherited wealth and rank', newspaper reports still focused on title; for instance, *Bell's Weekly Messenger* carried a column headed 'Fashionables' in which (in 1796 to 1798) 68 per cent of those cited were 'members of the royal family or members of the peerage, their wives, or heirs', while a further 24 per cent were 'younger sons with close peerage connections, often MPs ... or office-holders in the military, church, and legal professions'.[55] My purpose is not to write a social history of Georgian London, of course, but the question is whether a period of apparent blurring of class boundaries through marriages between aristocrats and merchants' daughters (or merchants and aristocrats' daughters) was in reality a period of cultural opening up, or one of a covert consolidation of divisions.

This can be observed in the seemingly open pleasure gardens at Vauxhall, Marylebone and Ranelagh in London, which were accessed by ticket, either for the evening or by a season ticket. The tickets were affordable for the middle classes, although further expenditure was required once inside, especially for food and drink. There were tree-lined promenades, a central bandstand at Vauxhall and musicians' enclosures at the other gardens, sculptures, artificial lakes, illuminations and colourful pavilions. At Ranelagh, which charged a higher price and aimed at gentility, there was a central rotunda which housed stalls in a gilded interior. There were masquerades: 'visual displays of conspicuous consumption on a massive scale', which adapted the form of carnival from Venice, with masked dancing, to a northern liminality in which, 'pleasure is permitted, but in a controlled and legitimate manner'.[56] But, as Rendell adds, there was also, at least in eighteenth-century literary accounts of the pleasure gardens, 'intrigue, seduction, adultery, rape and perversion'.[57]

The anonymity of a masquerade might subvert rigid social ordering. Rendell argues that, in the way pleasure gardens and the masquerades they hosted are described in the literature of rambling – 'an urban activity generated through the pursuit of pleasure [which] involved visits to places of leisure ... [mainly by] young, single, heterosexual and upper-class men'[58] – wearing the obligatory costume and mask disguised identities in terms of, 'surface, artifice, travesty, self-alienation and phantasmagoria'.[59] Costumes might be androgynous, or enable cross-dressing, or disguise class origin (in contrast to its exhibition at court). Drinking, dancing and gambling were collective acts, yet had their own forms of social distinction. Some of the scope for transgression offered by masquerades in late Georgian times was eliminated later in the less risky form of the masked ball but, while they lasted, masquerades facilitated an apparent subversion which Rendell reads as, 'threatening to public patriarchal order, particularly to relations of looking between the sexes'.[60] This is an important argument around licensed disorder, and I do not discount it. However, I would see beside that a way in which pleasure gardens maintained social codes. Greig writes:

For historians, much of the importance of the pleasure gardens lies in the fact that tickets not titles secured admission to their entertainments. Much has also been made of their affordability. At a shilling a go (comparable to cheap seats in the theatre), Vauxhall was theoretically accessible to those of modest means.... Cultural historians have thus emphasized the pleasure gardens' significance as stages for fluidity and social mixing. Furthermore, the pleasure gardens were apparently places where social norms and identities were suspended, and where reality was blurred by artifice.... Here, if anywhere, it was believed that the prostitute could present herself as a peeress and the rake as a respectable man.[61]

The gardens, then, were one place where privilege was presented visually and in other ways to a mass public, as the proprietors encouraged attendance by the aristocracy as a magnet, to appropriate their status as an, 'implicit suggestion that fashionable society was somehow knowable and identifiable'.[62] The illustrator Thomas Rowlandson depicts exactly this in *A View of Vauxhall Gardens* (1784, reprinted in 1809). In the centre foreground there are two elegantly dressed women who have been surrounded by spectators.[63] They are probably Georgiana, Duchess of Devonshire and her sister, Lady Duncannon. Among the spectators, Grieg identifies three newspaper editors. She notes, 'the distinctiveness of the fashionable company, and the role of the press and public in monitoring that social differentiation'.[64] The fashionable elite bought season tickets; those who wanted to watch them bought tickets for the evening, hoping to be lucky and listening to rumours as to who planned to be where. But when the stars appeared, they tried to avoid mingling with such aspirants:

Whilst topographical perspectives show criss-crossed walks that seem designed to encourage spontaneous encounters, first-person descriptions hint at a more carefully choreographed use of space. Opportunities for chance encounters appear to have been rare rather than the norm. At Vauxhall ... instead of roaming the grounds at whim, the fashionable society more often remained sequestered for lengthy stretches in their supper boxes. When the Duchess of Devonshire was spotted ... it was with a large party, noisily supping and facing the orchestra ...[65]

Appearances at the theatre were similarly class-differentiated according to where people sat and whom they could see, watching the audience tending to overshadow the play. It was not until the late nineteenth century that August Strindberg required the lights to be switched off during a performance of one of his plays in Paris; before that the audience was part of the show. As Greig concludes, 'the primary function of participating in these occasions [at the gardens, theatre or opera] was the rich, complex, and inward-looking articulation of group identity'.[66] In the gaze of aspiring publics, the Beau Monde paraded their elite status rather than took part in the informal or unplanned mixing which (Chapter 6) has sometimes been assumed to occur in open, urban spaces.

Instead of informality and social mixing, however, 'The appearance of public togetherness disguised a reality wherein the titled lady dismissed the wife of a city merchant, and a wealthy Yorkshire gentleman rarely conversed with a lord.'[67] Social distinctions were observed in the nineteenth century as well, but liberal opinion felt a need to ameliorate the divide between wealth and deprivation while Georgian England had limited its pursuit of emancipation to abolishing the slave trade and securing political rights for the commercial class (or bourgeoisie).

In the post-war reconstruction of Europe, there was a widely perceived need to do something about divisions, particularly those between nationalities in the aftermath of war, and between races after the Holocaust; and there was an articulation of civic values, evident in the Festival of Britain (Chapter 3). Through the 1980s and 1990s, these values were eroded, replaced by a free market ethos resembling that of the eighteenth century prior to liberal reformism. After the 2007 crash, I think the resumption of *laissez-faire* reconstructs urban policies (or the lack of them in de-regulation) closer to a Georgian attitude of clearance and ignorance of suffering as the poor, again, are peripheralised. A difference, however, which might be ironic, is that the art collected by the new rich who inhabit the gated compounds and urban villages of post-gentrification cities, and consume conspicuously in designer bars and art museums, includes street art derived from graffiti, recoded by another name and dressed up for the market. I do not know what social order this portends except that it is evidence of capital's containment of more or less everything, as acted out in the art market, a sub-sector of the cultural and creative industries.

Art's institutions and social ordering

I want to end by looking briefly at the beginning of public art collections in the Georgian period, and bring the argument back to the present as analogies appear. These are loose, but I hope this chapter begins to establish that cultural forms which may seem open yet retain the apparatus of privilege, as in the pleasure gardens and press reports of the Tate Gallery in 1897; and that, in Victorian London, art museums were part of a wider social ordering, instruments of stability and a desired cohesion. It could be asked, after the erasure of civic values which occurred in the 1980s to the 2000s, whether that remains valid or whether ventures such as the Millennium Dome and Tate Modern (Chapter 3) were instruments of cohesion which were as anachronistic as Georgian court dress, residual efforts at a national identity when the reality had fled, no-one in power really cared, and the power of the state was itself waning.

In Georgian England, the gentry liked landscapes which reminded them of their estates, and dogs, horses and pictures of their children. They could cope with a little classicisation, as in the pastoral scenes of figures-in-landscape painted by Claude Lorrain. Kings and princes collected paintings which reflected their status in the grandeur of the settings and the heroic stances of the figures depicted, and portraits of themselves in fancy clothes. Joshua Reynolds earned the equivalent of a banker's salary today by painting historical portraits, a category fusing the aristocratic status of subjects from classical myth and history with settings such as the grounds of a country house, for those who wanted to look grand and could pay. The establishment of a Royal Academy brought England into line with European powers, if reluctantly, and introduced a public view of art in annual shows but, for the most part, art was in private collections, accessed only by invitation.

Taylor notes, for instance, 'The fine British collection of Sir John Leicester in Hill Street, Mayfair was made available in 1818, by admission card obtainable only by those known to the owner or his friends,' on some Thursdays during the season.[68] The visitors included 'the crowd of beauty and fashion, the chief nobility and gentry, the distinguished members of the legislature and of the learned profession, the taste and educated mind of England'.[69] Like Tate later, Leicester collected British art, as did Sir Walter Fawkes, whose collection was on view to selected visitors in 1819. Elsewhere a proliferation of dioramas and waxworks appealed to a mass public. Taylor argues that:

> It was precisely the gap between the two available forms of public pleasure – the traditional aristocratic pleasure of beholding valuable paintings, and the delights of marvelling at the painted commercial illusions and street exotica – that must have been striking in late Hanoverian and early Victorian London. The popular shows underscored the appetite for exhibitions; yet they remained commercial rather than fine art. For all these reasons it seemed to reforming

politicians that a national gallery in the centre of London could bring popular appetite and elevated pleasure into conjunction.[70]

This is close to the sentiment which informed the opening of the Tate Gallery as a temple of art for all classes. After a preliminary effort in Pall Mall in the 1820s, following the Whig victory in the 1830 elections, it was decided to open a purpose-built gallery. Taylor writes that the siting of the National Gallery in Trafalgar Square was part of a defining process of reform for London, and hence for the nation: 'a legitimation and a perpetuation of the larger social and psychic divisions of the city'.[71] National institutions were planned to line the square, and the poor housing to the north and east was cleared. Taylor concludes that while it gave access to all parts of the city, the new road layout radiating from the square, 'divided neighbouring districts from each other' while perpetuating, 'a social geography of difference within the metropolitan fabric, at the same time as symbolically unifying its disparate parts'.[72]

Like the pleasure gardens but more instrumental, this constructed a new centre and with it new margins, separating abjection from wealth. Attitudes to otherness later softened, mainly through charity, and a gradual widening of suffrage introduced new agendas to politics; but perhaps it was literacy which most changed the situation. Raymond Williams sees the same divide here between high and popular literature. He cites Arnold's bewailing of, 'cheap literature, hideous of ignoble aspect, like the tawdry novels which flare in the bookshelves of our railway stations, and which seem designed ... for people with a low standard of life'.[73] Arnold's problem, he suggests, was that the middle classes needed to lift themselves out of low taste. From the extracts of *Culture and Anarchy* cited above, social breakdown was to be avoided through the presence of an *educated* middle class, which required institutions such as a national gallery and a museum of British art to enhance its educational provision. The question as to how far working-class people could join them in their flights of wonder remained open to conjecture. High culture was a means to assimilate the skilled working class into middle-class attitudes; but the relations of wealth and power by which they were allowed into the temples of art reinforced social distinctions.

In 1994, a new museum of modern art opened in San Francisco – SFMOMA – in a purpose-designed, spectacular building designed by Mario Botta. Lisa Jardine reports that SFMOMA was financed entirely by donors, whose art also lined its walls. She writes,

Not everyone felt comfortable with such a close relationship between dynastic money and the Bay Area's landmark building and art collection. There were muttered fears that exhibitions and events would effectively be controlled by the small group of rich and powerful individuals who had personally underwritten SFMOMA. There were suggestions that the collection was in any case idiosyncratic and unrepresentative of what was truly best in American art, since it had largely been accumulated ... as gifts from the same sort of wealthy art-amateur who had purchased without real expertise.[74]

She points out that, given the large scale of much of the art, donating it to a museum was a reasonable way to house it. She likens the building to a cathedral in its 'insistent grandeur' and 'awestruck reverence'.[75] One part of the museum's holdings is the collection of Albert M. Bender, an Irish migrant who arrived in San Francisco in 1879 to become a leading insurance broker in the 1890s. He donated 36 pictures at the museum's founding (on a previous site) in 1935. 'Everything', Jardine reflects, about SFMOMA:

ensures that we approach the art with a sense of wonder, in a state of spiritual elevation. The light-filled atrium, the soaring spaces tell us that what we encounter ... is endowed with transcendent meaning and profound significance – that we will find here the secular equivalent of spiritual enlightenment.[76]

No tawdry novels here; just plaques displaying the donor's names to visitors, and Perspex panels at the entrance which list the donors in order of the size of their gift. The aristocratic pleasure of beholding valuable paintings has been radically separated from the delights of marvelling at ... signs of wealth and privilege.

6

New Air: Urban Spaces and Democratic Deficits

In his novel *Lilac and Flag*, John Berger describes a public space called Alexanderplatz. There is a real place called that in Berlin, but Berger's Alexanderplatz is in every city:

> It was a mystery why there were always so many people on Alexanderplatz. There was the bus station, but this couldn't explain the crowds at night. Perhaps people were there simply because it was so big. Perhaps the bare, empty space, which was not like that of a park, compelled crowds to gather there.... All cities have one such space, where victories are celebrated, where crowds dance at the new year, where political marches begin and end, a space that belongs to the people, just as the buildings with pillars and carvings belong to the rich. When you cross it, it's like crossing a stage. On this stage, in times of summary justice, tyrants and traitors are hanged from lamp posts. The eternal audience are the poor, all the poor of the past and all the poor of the future ...[1]

This fictional description conveys several aspects of public spaces in modern cities: they are crowded, and this attracts people; their use is performative, whether for the display of power, for revolt, or for trade; the audience is the poor (joined now by tourists looking at a human zoo); and the space is framed, literally, by grandiose buildings belonging to past or present elites. Tyrants may fall in effigy in such places, like Napoleon Bonaparte in Paris in 1871 or Stalin in Budapest in 1956; social distinctions are suspended on special occasions like New Year or even upended in resistant re-creations of Carnival but this is as artificial as the suspension of disbelief in a theatre, lasting for the duration of the show.

I use a fictional text to introduce a chapter on urban spaces and public life because while both public space and the life it houses allude to a public sphere (as the real-metaphorical location of a society's determination of its values and modes of organisation for itself), I doubt that there has been such a sphere in European urban history. The concept remains valuable as an aspiration, a horizon for future action, but it lacks a really-existing status. This does not limit allusions to mythicised pasts in the literature, usually involving the Greek city state (*polis*) and the *agora* of classical Athens. Urbanist Ali Madanipour notes that today's public spaces have lost some of their past functions: although, 'a high degree of socio-spatial concentration' gave public spaces 'an overarching significance', the activity by which they were animated has migrated to spaces which 'may not find any degree of significance at all, particularly in marginal areas, where fewer people and activities are concentrated'.[2] I take that activity to be politics, the determination of the *polis*. But Madanipour revalidates public spaces today by taking the *agora* of Athens as 'the best known public space of all time' and 'the meeting place of the town'.[3] He expands:

> The agora was more than a marketplace; it also served as a place of assembly for the town's people and a setting in which ceremonies and spectacles were performed alongside each other, acting as an integrative platform for the social life of the city.... Originally, the agora was just an open space.... With specialization of activities and spaces, various public buildings grew around it, such as the meeting place of the city council, the offices of magistrates, temples and altars, fountain houses, law courts, and covered halls for the use of citizens and merchants.... the agora remained the heart of the city and its civic activities.[4]

This is not inaccurate inasmuch as an open space for buying and selling was, over a period, formalised and contained by city offices and temples; but civic life is harder to pin down in specific sites. It is too easy to idealise the *agora* as an archetypal spatial form to which future squares should correspond, as if the form is timeless. This is to project an idea onto a history which is sufficiently remote to bear almost any inscription, when the image inscribed on this as-if-blank screen is a mask for a present democratic deficit and not an accurate picture of a specific past. Most public spaces are given over to consumption today, of goods and services in adjacent food and drink outlets, or as the place itself in tourism (trying to find the places in the brochure to photograph them, often disappointed when the results are less interesting than prior expectations).[5] Sometimes open spaces are repossessed by publics in a self-organising performance of the everyday – which could mean skateboarding but just as appropriately the way people sit on public steps to look at the view or eat their sandwiches – which is more or less what Henri Lefebvre meant by representational spaces, or the informal occupation of the space produced in plans (the space of representation).[6] Another way to put that is as lived and conceived space, respectively. Occupation and adaptation never erase the space of plans; but when the authorities intervene, similarly, occupations may be ended but linger in the minds of those who were there, never quite erased in personal consciousness.

Public spaces might affirm a notion that cities are free places inasmuch as people do have free access to them, but this is a recent idea. The *agora* was a market space to which the rich sent their servants. It was a space of social mixing to some extent, but association was limited by distinctions of status and gender in Athens. Richard Sennett notes:

> most of the ceremonial and political events that occurred here were out of bounds to the immense population of slaves and foreigners who supported the economy ... the number of citizens in Attica during the fourth century B.C. [was] 20,000–30,000 out of a population of 150,000 to 250,000.[7]

Activities such as eating and drinking, making deals, and religious observances took place in buildings along the sides of the *agora*, and discussion between citizens in a colonnaded space (the *stoa*) on the north side. But the citizens who participated there had the leisure to do so, as a non-working elite (from which the denigration of trade – siting the tradesman's entrance at the back of a grand house – emanates). For Sennett, being seen was being accountable; but he takes speech rather than action as the defining act of citizenship. For Hannah Arendt, a major influence on Sennett, to be political meant that, 'everything was decided through words and persuasion and not through force and violence'.[8] Arendt explains that for women, slaves and strangers, the right of speech was withheld (as it was for Jews in Germany in the 1930s). And domestic life was constructed as a twilight zone because, simply, it lacked the bright light of the political.

For whatever reason, and it may be not much more than an academic equivalent of looking for the places in the tourist brochure, the *agora* of

Athens remains an iconic public space in modern urbanism. But another layer has been overlaid on this historical bedrock: the assertion that cities create freedom. Sennett cites the inscription '*Stadt Luft macht frei* (city air makes one free)'[9] from the gates of cities in the Hanseatic League, a network of guilds trading across the North and Baltic Seas, rather than of cities, from the twelfth century. The League managed to shift political power from princes to burghers as, together, the merchants (who later became the bourgeoisie) could negotiate trading privileges and become the social group from which officials – burghers – were chosen. Sennett goes on to say, echoing early sociology, that cities gave freedom from ties to the land and afforded individual rights to property.[10] In the eighteenth century, such a protection of private wealth from the emerging entity of the national state was a bourgeois preoccupation; in the nineteenth-century climate of reform, increasing regulation redirected some of that wealth to public services, a trajectory which reached its highest point in the post-war welfare state.

Private wealth and private houses were in tension with the state, notionally representing all of a society's publics; but there were other tensions as well. Sennett argues that the rise of cities is contextualised by the growth of Humanism and the teachings of Thomas Aquinas. That is, the religious revival following Aquinas' *Imitation of Christ* was a source of new 'practices of charity'[11] as religious communities admitted travellers, the sick, foundlings and the insane.[12] Hospitality was at odds with the pursuit of private wealth:

> Medieval economic and religious developments pushed the sense of place in opposite directions, a dissonance which echoes down in our own times. The economy of the city gave people a freedom of individual action … [but] the religion of the city made places where people cared about each other. '*Stadt Luft macht frei*' opposed 'the Imitation of Christ.' This great tension between economy and religion produced the first signs of the duality which marks the modern city … the desire to cut free of communal bonds in the name of individual liberty … [and] the desire to find a place in which people care about each other.[13]

Later in *Flesh and Stone*, Sennett describes the ghetto in Venice. As a trading city, Venice was a city of strangers who had no more political rights than foreigners in classical Athens had them, and were required to lodge in designated places – ghettoes – the gates and doors of which were locked at night. Venice was cosmopolitan in trade but, 'the right to do business in the city did not bring a more general freedom'.[14] Nor did it protect minorities, such as Jews, from attacks or from accusations of contagion.

Transitional zones

The above brief history indicates tensions in public space between the display of power and social mixing. But social mixing does not guarantee that those who mix do so on equal terms or have common aims which they can articulate coherently, or can resolve their differences in demands. Social mixing occurred in the pleasure gardens of Georgian London (Chapter 5) but distinctions between elites and non-privileged groups were affirmed rather than diluted. The issue is complicated by neoliberal attacks on public space, such as the attempted clearance of street people from Grand Central station, New York, in 1988. For Mayor Koch, stations were for transportation not loitering. Art theorist Rosalyn Deutsche objected, 'Such a statement makes it seem that individual locations ... and the spatial organisation of the city as a whole contain an inherent meaning determined by the imperative to fulfil needs that are supposed to be natural, simply practical.'[15] A presumption for social ordering of this kind underpins the rise of Business Improvement Districts (BIDs) in New York, by which businesses adopted responsibility for improving public spaces near their buildings. Sharon Zukin links this to a rise in evictions while, too, parks became camping grounds for mental patients ejected from hospitals with more or less no support.[16] It was also an aspect of the rise of corporatism. The BIDs can tax themselves to pay for improvements, and make good declining provision such as street cleaning; and they can frame regulations which sanitise sites. Zukin asserts that if it is known who defines this image of the city, the question of occupation is open. She adds that city authorities approve BIDs' plans, 'because the property owners ... are powerful and their projects promise to create revenue'.[17] The early modern tension between charity and wealth resurfaces here as the symbolic economies designed for external perception which are put in place by elites erase the presence of poor people as a prerequisite, not for the eradication of poverty, but for the maintenance of a dominant image. BIDs adopt public spaces such as urban parks and plazas, making them nice and safe but masking the democratic deficit of what is in effect privatised management, as highly visible improvements limit the invisible performative practices of public determination and diverse lives.

Besides, radical social change happens only rarely in public places. Occupations may have a symbolic quality (as if occupying the city) but shifts of power usually happen elsewhere. For example, the storming of the Winter Palace in the Bolshevik Revolution was a military act; it took over the building so that the ministers of the Provisional Government *inside* the palace could be arrested and cast, as Leon Trotsky put it, into the dustbin of history. There were no crowds with banners, no onlookers. Restaurants remained open; the trams continued to run as normal. The decision to undertake the attack was taken at a meeting of the Bolshevik Central Committee, to which Lenin arrived late, disguised in a wig, inside the Smolny Institute.[18] The re-enactment in 1920 *was* a public spectacle,[19] and a reaffirmation of the shift of power to the people (although now less the people in the soviets, more as represented by the Party).

Revolutions in public places are rare now, although they do occur. For example, in Lisbon in April 1974, people placed carnations in the barrels of soldiers' guns, ending the fascist period; but the army had already decided at its own meetings (mainly of officers) that it would not intervene, while the dead dictator had left no successor. As in Petrograd, revolutions are most often planned in meetings in hired rooms, in transitional spaces such as the café, or in domestic spaces beyond surveillance. Some of the conversations which led to the Egyptian Revolution of 1952 took place among younger army officers in a Cairo tea house.

In seventeenth-century England, newspapers and political pamphlets circulated in coffee houses. They were gendered, but the men who gathered there were of equal status for the moment, in another temporary suspension of rank. As Sennett describes, once a man had entered and paid a penny for his coffee, he joined the company and the conversation at the table; commerce needed information, and for that:

> distinctions of rank were temporarily suspended; anyone sitting in the coffeehouse had a right to talk to anyone else, to enter into any conversation ... It was bad form even to touch on the social origins of other persons ... the free flow of talk might then be impeded.[20]

Social distinctions were evident in clothing, gesture and accent, of course, but a *commercial* need for news constituted coffee houses, in this commercial era, as where opinions on literature and art, politics and trade were formed and exchanged among people of temporary equality. Jürgen Habermas argues that coffee houses gave access to power and 'embraced the wider strata of the middle class, including craftsmen and shopkeepers'.[21] Later, in London, exclusivity returned in gentlemen's clubs, but these were still transitional spaces between public and private life. Jane Rendell observes that clubs can be claimed as public spaces, but as proprietor-owned spaces with specific rules of membership they are also private (cited in Chapter 5).[22] Sennett admits that 'the coffeehouse is a romanticised and overidealised institution',[23] although that may follow from the glimpse of a public sphere which coffee houses offer, which has not otherwise been realised in European history. In retrospect, then, I do not deny the role of public spaces in a democracy, nor condone their privatisation; but I wonder if they are the sites of unplanned social mixing which they are sometimes held to be.

Parks and public (as opposed to private, garden) squares indicate that a city has enough wealth to allocate space for non-productive purposes, but it is in streets that people mix both routinely and unexpectedly according to circumstances; and it is mainly in workplaces and associations based on common interest (like an art society or a single-issue political campaign), which tend to occur indoors, that they find common cause. In modern cities, the street may be more regulated in its uses than a park. This can be progressive, as in Ildefons Cerdá's plan for the northern extension of Barcelona (1859),[24] in which half the street was for pedestrians, with a presumption of decent housing for all classes, green spaces and public transport. Still, this was liberalism, and the underlying aim was to prevent insurrection and non-productivity after strikes and outbreaks of cholera in the 1850s. Each block had a central garden, perhaps a formalised equivalent of balconies over the street in the old city: both are transitional spaces where residents mix informally but not with strangers. Unplanned social mixing would imply that strangers were encountered too, but it tends to be only in crisis situations that unplanned association occurs in otherwise regulated sites. Perhaps there is a more casual possibility for acquaintanceship in urban parks, in a situation of ease. Crisis and ease are, after all, situations in which the rules of behaviour and the codes of social distinction may sometimes be relaxed, yet usually within socially agreed (if historically specific and thus changing) limits.

Nice places

Central Park, New York was planned in the 1850s, advocated by elites who saw the lack of a park as a sign of backwardness compared to European cities, which inhibited trade.[25] In 1857, a design competition led to adoption of Frederick Olmsted's plan for a naturalistic landscape reminiscent of picturesque art, combined with formal elements such as fountains, lakes, and boulevards.[26] The land was marshy and rocky, housing marginal communities at its southern end. Geographer Matthew Gandy notes, 'the erasure of these communities may even have been a significant motivating factor behind the political momentum for the park's creation'.[27] These squatters' shacks were an equivalent of the informal settlements along the railway lines of Manchester in 1844 (Chapter 5). As a sign of what would in the 1980s have been called an underclass, these people threatened the image of the city. There were financial opportunities, too; but the intended perception of Central Park was aesthetic, a non-productive space which alluded in its wilder areas to a growing taste for rambling. Gandy observes tensions within Olmsted's approach: although he shared a desire for a unifying national culture with other educated and elite North Americans, the park 'was never intended as a forum for political debate' but as an extension of the private sphere, 'through the extension of nineteenth-century conceptions of bourgeois domesticity' mapped onto a public arena.[28] Central Park was a place where people might more easily lose sight of others than join them in political endeavours, not unlike a modern art museum later. Tensions remain, as Gandy remarks,

> This streak of green connects two different worlds into a symbolic whole where the innate heterogeneity of urban life is forged into a unified realm. The city's exclusions and delights are thrown together in a tangled mass of human interaction. Here the tensions and contradictions of capitalist urbanization are softened in the shade of oaks, maples, and the remnants of the luxuriant vegetation that once covered Manhattan Island.[29]

Like other sites in New York, Central Park's management has moved towards sanitisation.

But how do people experience public spaces? Anthropologist Setha Low records experiences in Parque Central and Plaza de la Cultura in San José, Costa Rica. The former is a nineteenth-century, tree-lined space with a central bandstand; the latter is modern, with a fountain and a large paved area over an office development. Parque Central 'is full of people. Almost every bench is taken, mostly by men, who stand or sit in groups around a bench or wall ledge; a few are even stretched out full length on a bench.'[30] Part of Plaza de la Cultura is used by tourists and vendors, another part by street performers: 'Children of all social classes, from little boys who sell crafts or shine shoes to children in private school uniforms, come to see and listen to the juggler/clown … adults line up behind them.'[31] Women sit there in the mornings, resting on the way to work or waiting for buses; the stop has moved but they wait in Parque Central anyway, and move to the stop when a bus arrives.[32] A police presence in Plaza de la Cultura suggests 'a physical, social, and metaphorical space for public debate'; Low notes that 'how politicians manipulate the political symbolism of these charged public spaces portrays the plaza's power to elicit civic commentary and social action'.[33]

More often, such sites house interludes of leisure, observed by W.H. Whyte in New York in the 1970s.[34] Whyte used time-lapse photography to evaluate the uses of sites, and found that moveable furniture, variety of spaces, water features, planting and availability of refreshment attracted people. One of the most successful sites was Paley Park, a vest-pocket site (between buildings) near the Museum of Modern Art. Visiting Paley Park in the 1990s, I sensed it was a convivial place of the kind identified with the notion of a liveable city (much debated in the 1980s). Most of its users, whether professionals or older residents, or visitors like me, were middle class. People sat in small groups or alone, talking, reading the paper, creating a semi-private space in public (or watching others, like me). As if to emphasise the de-politicisation of urban public spaces, between Paley Park and the Museum of Modern Art is a small plaza in which people drink coffee at garden tables in front of a section of the Berlin Wall (Figure 6.1). The Wall exhibits the colourful graffiti which meant freedom in the West but was read as a sign of a destructive underclass when it appeared on subway trains – both in the 1980s.

Paley Park suggests the quality of street life celebrated by Jane Jacobs from her experience in Greenwich Village, New York, a picture of a city where streets facilitate social mixing and may create common cause between residents of a neighbourhood (although often in defence against people perceived as outsiders). Jacobs writes of the 'casual public sidewalk life of cities' and claims that, while civic organisation is often assumed by planners 'to grow in direct, common-sense fashion out of announcements

Figure 6.1   A section of the Berlin Wall, Manhattan

of meetings, the presence of meeting rooms, and the existence of problems of obvious public concern', such activity requires a pre-existing, 'informal public life' between public and private realms.[35] Jacobs' view has been influential, although there has been a tendency to map it from streets onto public spaces. For instance, a brochure on redevelopment in the north-west of England states,

> A vibrant public realm is not just a result of quality design, but the way in which a space encourages, enhances and creates opportunities for activity. Think of the best public spaces you know and the chances are they will be places of activity, places to meet, sit, observe, attend local events and engage in social relationships.
>
> The diversity of public life requires spaces that provide for everyone's needs, spaces for intimate and communal activity, places to accommodate necessary, optional (recreational) and social activities. Spaces *must* be flexible and adaptable … [italics added][36]

The rhetoric is well-meaning, fusing Whyte and Jacobs, but it reproduces an assumption that liveliness can be designed into spaces: a disempowering fantasy which Jacobs was careful to reject, writing, '*A city cannot be a work of art.*'[37]

Culture and business

The idea of conviviality permeated the remodelling of public spaces in Birmingham, England, from the 1980s to the 2000s. This has been described elsewhere[38] but I want to draw out three phases, attached to different spaces. The first is Centenary Square, site of the International Convention Centre (ICC), an international chain hotel, the Repertory Theatre, office blocks, a war memorial and (a recent addition) the new public library. It is a civic space with a mix of old and new public monuments but its brick paving is unique, designed by painter and printmaker Tess Jaray working with the city's arts and parks departments. It resembles a vast Persian carpet: a geometric design in colours derived from natural clays by adjusting the firing temperature. Unfortunately, the new library's designers made a large, circular hole in it to expose a view of the book stacks in the basement. Centenary Square is well used because it is a through-route between the railway station, business and shopping streets, the concert hall and the theatre. Site-specific street furniture by Jaray and Tom Lomax lends distinctiveness, but if there is a sense of place, this is produced by people using the square.

In Victoria Square, the next redevelopment scheme, steps embellished by eclectic sculptures and a fountain lead up to the Victorian Town Hall and the City Art Gallery. To one side, there is a rusting iron man by Antony Gormley (commissioned by a bank but supposed to represent the lost iron-working trades of the West Midlands). Victoria Square is a civic space due to its grandiose architectural context and location; like Centenary Square it is well used because it is on the same routes through the city centre. Each December, it is used for a German-style Christmas market.

All this was meant to rescue the image of Britain's second city after de-industrialisation. Public investment was justified by anticipated employment and other economic benefits, but research at Birmingham University showed that the new jobs were mainly low-skilled, low-paid and short-term, while money had been redirected from other, more socially inclined areas of expenditure to pay for the new city centre.[39] Geographer Tim Hall writes of these redevelopments as situated within a tension between two contexts:

> they fit into the international landscapes of post-industrial, postmodern urbanism, landscapes of convention centres, waterside developments, futuristic architecture and upscale urban consumption. However …

they are everyday landscapes through which Birmingham's citizens live their lives and which provide cultural resources from which senses of the city's identity are drawn.[40]

The new squares are public spaces but the preponderance of the ICC suggests that this might be a Central Business District (the model promoted by the Chicago planners of the inter-war years) masked as a cultural district.

Then, third, Brindleyplace, across the canals from the ICC, exhibits an overtly neoliberal form of place-making. Surrounded by quasi-gothic and pseudo-classical motifs in buildings which are steel frames hung with cladding in warm brick, to give a sense of tradition as safety for money, the new plaza is sterile, used, but more or less only by those who have business there or who visit the Ikon Gallery on the square's fourth side. The following statement in a (largely promotional) publication says enough: 'It might have been better if the residential component ... had been of higher density and more closely integrated.... But we had to provide what the market wanted – security, privacy and parking.'[41] As to civic benefit, urbanist Graeme Evans concludes that the evidence of regeneration from major cultural projects is 'limited'; where it exists, 'distributive effects and regeneration objectives ... are generally under-achieved, or they are not sustained ... flagship and major city-centre and waterfront cultural schemes are less about regeneration than the conventional wisdom portrays them.'[42] Sociologist Rosemary Mellor wrote similarly of Manchester's redevelopment that 'there was a business-leisure agenda in which the cosmetic presentation of the city centre was crucial. In this the poorer people of Manchester (whose only centre this is) have no role.'[43]

Other places

City centres do not house populations but are liminal sites visited by diverse publics. Jacobs' idea of villages within a city is unrealistic now that place-based communities are eclipsed, as dwellers increasingly have global links and city-wide social networks.[44] The street, too, has been seen in less convivial, more conflicted ways. Elizabeth Wilson writes, in *Sphinx and the City*, that while 'male writers seem to have seen suburbia as an environment created for women', depicted in women's magazines featuring ideal homes in 'leafy glades' and domestic interiors,[45] and post-war English new towns projected a similar ideal onto the developments into which people were moved to allow clearance of bombed areas and the demolition of working-class streets regarded as chaotic, women on their own in the city were regarded negatively (usually as sex workers). This is found widely in nineteenth-century literature, with its absence of women strollers;[46] but it is also political because, 'women had traditionally always been involved in struggles over housing; they led rent strikes ... and were also involved in ... help in times of sickness or special poverty'.[47] In the 1960s, Wilson continues, women were prominent in community action, 'because more women than men lived in the inner city and mothers and the old were more imprisoned within their localities' and disproportionately afflicted by unemployment.[48] Wilson criticises Jacobs for rejecting planning and leaving cities potentially open to 'unfettered capitalist development'.[49] At the end of the 1980s, she adds, 'what has been forgotten in the optimistic scenarios of Jacobs and Sennett' is how postmodern urbanism relies on the market while the growth of homelessness demonstrates its 'glaring insufficiencies'.[50] Zukin similarly links the urban villages celebrated by Jacobs to gentrification. Urban villages are a mark of new urbanism, indeed, and perhaps the myth of conviviality-by-design is in fact a camouflage for other meanings in public space.

Urban renaissances

The plaza appears in Spain in the sixteenth century, after the voyages of colonisation, adapted from the Spanish colonial city which was itself derived from the conquered societies of the Americas. Low argues that while European cities with a central square, cathedral, administrative offices and houses for the elite reproduced an old-world spatial practice, they were irregular. Cities in pre-Columbian America, in contrast, 'were planned according to a gridiron pattern'.[51] This is found in Europe only in, 'fortress and frontier towns'.[52] Then the Laws of the Indies (1573) formalised a spatial ordering which was quite new to Europe: 'The Spaniards ... admired these exceptional models of urban design and wrote about the grandeur, order and urbanity of these newly discovered cities.'[53] The familiar plaza derives from an intersection of Spanish and indigenous cultures: 'a contested terrain of architectural representation', which is 'an excellent example of how cultural and political meanings of the past are represented in the built environment'.[54] In pre- and post-Colombian cases, the large central square where grid-planned streets opened onto light were not intended for expressions of popular sentiment but for power's display to a passive audience allowed only to gaze at the spectacle.

Meanwhile, 'civic spaces are no longer democratic places where all people are embraced and tolerated' but are given over to consumption.[55] I suggest that the realm of free public mixing is a projection of a present lack onto either adapted pasts or aspirational futures. The street is gendered, coded by new distinctions of affluence; the square might have been a site of power and at rare times of its contestation but is now a consumption site. And the literature of modernity contains many expressions of being alone in a city, as in this passage from Fernando Pessoa's *The Book of Disquiet*:

> It's midday in the deserted office, and I lean out one of the balcony windows overlooking the street down below. My distraction, aware of the movement of people in my eyes, is too steeped in its meditation to see them. I sleep on my elbows propped painfully on the railing and feel a great promise in knowing nothing. With mental detachment I look at the arrested street full of hurrying people, and I make out the details: the crates piled up on a cart, the sacks at the door of the other warehouse, and, in the farthest window of the grocery on the corner, the glint of those bottles of Port wine that I imagine no one can afford to buy. My spirit abandons material dimension. I investigate with my imagination. The people passing on the street are always the same ones who passed by a while ago, always a group of floating figures, patches of motion, uncertain voices, things that pass by and never quite happen.[56]

This is the Baudelairian city belonging to men of several classes but not to women walking alone or to marginal publics. In that sense, I suppose it is not unlike the *agora*.

Following New Labour's victory in the 1997 UK general election, architect Richard Rogers led an Urban Task Force to investigate a perceived decline in cities and towns, leading to a report, *Towards an Urban Renaissance*,[57] and a White Paper, *Our Towns and Cities – The Future: Delivering an Urban Renaissance*.[58] The report was not particularly concerned with public spaces, although parks and play spaces were seen as elements in a liveable city. More central issues were housing design and economic growth, in a vision of citizen participation, good design, good public services, prosperity, safety and sustainability; four 'key steps' were identified in the White Paper:

- Getting the design and quality of the urban fabric right;
- Enabling all towns and cities to create and share prosperity;
- Providing the quality services people need;
- Equipping people to participate in developing their communities.[59]

One outcome of the Urban Task Force report was the establishment of the Commission for Architecture and the Built Environment (CABE), which urged improvements in the design and specification of new housing, and provided advice as well as evaluating performance. It was a progressive organisation, abolished in 2010 in a so-called bonfire of quangos. Another outcome was a call for a 'culture of innovation and enterprise' spanning e-commerce and the creative sector.[60] Aims were over-generalised, and rested on professional expertise for their delivery. It was not clear how disadvantaged groups could join in the fun.

Taking the following as exemplifying top-down optimism:

> We want our towns, cities and suburbs to be places for people: places that are designed, built and maintained on the principle people come first. They should contribute to the quality of life and encourage healthy and sustainable lifestyles. They should be places in which we want to live, work, bring up our children, and spend our leisure time. They should be places which promote economic success and allow people to share in rising prosperity, attracting and retaining successful businesses.[61]

I find some unanswered questions. I cannot argue against the idea that places should be for people (rather than cars, or Martians), but the text mixes platitudes with assumptions as to who constitutes the 'we' involved. This echoes Matthew Arnold's vision of the educated middle class as change-agent, adapted for neoliberalism in an emphasis on what Arnold might have disdained as trade; and reveals a lack of insight as to how marginal or protesting publics gain access to planning processes and decisions. For geographer Loretta Lees, 'social mixing is a one-sided strategy that is seldom advocated in wealthier neighbourhoods',[62] while, with no policy as to what social mixing is expected, 'it is difficult to assess just what kinds of change in neighbourhood character – such as changing ethnicity or class composition – are intended to aid neighbourhood communities in bringing about an urban renaissance'.[63] She concludes:

Socially mixed urban communities created by the in-movement of middle-class people into poor, marginal areas of the inner city are being posited, under the rhetoric of urban renaissance, as the desegregating answer to lives that are lived in parallel or in isolation along class, income, ethnic and tenurial fault lines. It is ironic that a process that results in segregation and polarisation – gentrification – is being promoted via social-mix policies as the positive solution to segregation.[64]

Similarly, urbanist Rowland Atkinson writes that, 'the role of urban design and management in securing public spaces and reducing social exclusion is an explicit part of the government's urban agenda', but that more divisive attitudes prevail.[65] Surveillance has increased, too, with the negative social effects observed by geographer Stephen Graham: 'CCTV control rooms are ridden with racism and sexism ... certain types of young people are targeted with socially constructed suspicion ... scrutinized, followed and harassed.'[66] Geographers Adam Holden and Kurt Iveson quote Rogers that people 'must feel that public space is in their communal ownership and responsibility' to ask if his aim in revitalising public spaces was an attempt to undo 1980s individualism. They add that, although streets are important, 'the physical spaces of a city do not exhaust the potential of spaces through which the meaning of citizenship is constructed and contested'.[67] Reflecting concerns over gentrification, they suggest that cities are remodelled in the interests of 'those people who possess economic value as consumers and residents', while another urban renaissance, 'as a re-regulation of the poor', would mean an 'understanding of cities as arenas of struggle'.[68] This, they argue, is reduced to gestures at 'the kaleidoscopic scale of the local or neighbourhood' to re-align political subjectivities 'in a political space beyond the state'.[69] Holden and Iveson criticise reliance on expertise but see 'a nomadic army' of professionals, 'wandering the land in search of consultancy fees and places to save, parachuting in to localities with plans and designs and then moving on to the next place', who are 'trans-local or inter-local', while 'it is not their localness that gives them legitimacy, it is their expertise' – in contrast to a sense of citizenship made in 'neighbourhood participation'.[70] This includes the consultants who write National Lottery bids (Chapter 4).

Perhaps the threat of giving agency to marginalised publics reproduces the threat attributed to women identified by Wilson: 'Women have fared especially badly in western visions of the metropolis because they have seemed to represent disorder.'[71] Control applies particularly to public squares and streets, but also in covert ways to electronic communications. It may be that, as urbanist Krzysztof Nawratek writes, public space, 'is the space which is fought over' so that whoever appropriates it 'appropriates the city',[72] but the definition of public space may need to include other sites of exchange and networking. Artist Krzysztof Wodiczko similarly claims that 'The democratic process depends on the vitality of public space'[73] but adds that this happens in conditions which enable the marginal and the estranged to find voices. I suggest that this includes the occupation of the metaphorical as well as the material and technological sites of determination. It has been overtaken, post-crash, by urban clearance.

Clearances

On 5 November 2013, *The Guardian* reported that Adrian Glasspool, a teacher and the last resident of the Heygate Estate in south London, expected the bailiffs to call to evict him. He did not owe rent, indeed had bought his flat from the Council, but his continuing occupation of his property was an obstacle to a redevelopment scheme in which the whole estate would be demolished to make way for properties for young professionals.[74] Part of the money raised by Southwark Council was set aside for affordable housing but, one ex-resident said: 'The dispersal of people from the area is pretty shocking. The vast majority of leaseholders have had to move a long way out to afford another property.'[75] Journalist Peter Walker reported:

> Critics say transformation is part of a wider trend in which poor residents are banished from central London neighbourhoods and replaced by wealthy incomers and buy-to-let investors. They point to one planned new towerblock near the site where Lend Lease [Southwark's private-sector partner] successfully argued against including any affordable housing as it would be too costly to build the additional entrances needed to separate social tenants from their richer neighbours.[76]

The Heygate Estate was completed in 1974, providing more than 3,000 council flats and houses in modernist blocks (Figure 6.2). It is easy to dismiss such estates after the demolition of social housing blocks labelled social as well as architectural disasters (notably Ronan Point in east London and the Pruitt-Igoe project, St. Louis). But for those who lived at Heygate, conditions were good: three- and four-bedroom flats with better space and specifications than in most new-build projects today; good public transport; a short distance from work in central London. Timothy Tinker, Heygate's local authority architect, stated:

> I don't think it was in any way a failed estate.... There are failed estates, but this wasn't one of them. The hardware – what we provided in concrete and brick – was relatively OK. The problem was there wasn't the software to run the damn thing.[77]

Film companies used the estate for thrillers; the media homed in on drugs and crime as products of modern architecture.[78] For Glasspool, 'the place was being labelled a problem estate. This is all part of the regeneration discourse ... there's nothing wrong with the buildings, they have to find an excuse to regenerate the place, i.e. knock it down and replace it.'[79]

Heygate is not the only case of forced redevelopment in London. Sally Taylor, a resident of Gibbs Green Estate in west London said, 'We are the wrong sort of people in the right sort of postcode as far as they're concerned. We're sitting on a golden nugget of land. They've never

Figure 6.2   The Heygate Estate, London, 2012

thought for one minute that we're human beings.'[80] The 2012 Olympics were a further excuse for clearance, afflicting housing, allotment land and houseboats on the River Lea. A change in regulation meant that boat-dwellers had to pay ten times as much for permanent moorings as for the continuous cruising licence which low-income individuals and families used to build sustainable lives on the river. Photographer Mike Wells' boat was a mile from the Olympic park: 'it is almost inconceivable that the authorities would allow anything unsightly or tatty during the games. This is social cleansing.'[81] The Olympic link is explicit in a leaked note from British Waterways: 'The urgency ... relates to the objective of reducing unauthorised mooring ... in time for the Olympics.'[82] Iain Sinclair charted the erasure of allotments on the Olympic site in the same period: after a low-ranking official met allotment holders to say that a lot of concrete would be removed and the allotments would return after the games, 'Consultation concluded. Sheds come down, blue fence goes up. Some of the gardeners relocate to a dank swamp and start again, others shrivel like the summer crops they will never see.'[83] Sinclair sums up the chasm between projection and actuality,

> The tacky blue of the perimeter fence does not appear on any of the computer generated versions of the Olympic Park. The prospect from the north is favoured, down towards Canary Wharf, the Thames and the Millennium Dome. The heritage site looks like an airport with one peculiar and defining feature: no barbed wire, no barrier between Expo campus and a network of motorways and rivers. The current experience, in reality, is all fence; the fence is the sum of our knowledge of this privileged mud. Visit here as early as you like and there will be no unsightly tags, no slogans; a viscous slither of blue. Like disinfectant running down the slopes of a urinal trough.[84]

Phil Cohen describes the opening ceremony as resembling (in business terms) a 'mash-up.'[85]

In other places, redevelopment has become a sector in its own right and clears away whatever it regards as in its way. The last hole-in-the-wall oatcake shop in Hanley, Stoke-on-Trent, was closed in 2012 after 80 years of serving the local community; owner Glenn Fowler said, 'It's the last oatcake shop that serves directly onto the pavement. The people who come here are not just customers, they're friends.'[86] The shop was a thriving business, which genuine regeneration should support. More than

5,000 people signed a petition to save it; local MP Tristram Hunt reflected that, 'There's no doubt we've knocked down too much of the city's fabric. The threat is we'll just end up with car parks and Tesco.'[87] In a more wholesale scheme in Liverpool, the local community have been not quite cleared from Victorian terraces near the football ground. A few houses retain signs of habitation such as newly painted doors and windows, and flower baskets. Others are boarded up, row after row after row of them (Figure 6.3). The football club began buying houses to make space (as if it is a neutral category) for a new stadium in the 1990s but never built it. The houses are in limbo, an urban wasteland where a community once lived. Ex-resident Howard Macpherson said:

> Anfield was a good area, all the houses occupied.... The area started to decline in the 1990s with the city's economic problems. But Liverpool football club accelerated the decline, by leaving good houses empty and boarded up. It wasn't a natural decline; it was engineered.[88]

Elsewhere, the Housing Market Renewal Pathfinder scheme launched in 2002 (since closed) displaced residents and boarded up their houses for a scale of demolition resembling 1960s slum clearance. Consultation was minimal and usually a sham. Residents protested but had no agency

Figure 6.3   Boarded-up houses in Anfield, Liverpool

when properties were compulsorily purchased by local authorities. People drifted away and communities were displaced. Journalist Anna Minton wrote, 'across the north of England and the Midlands, many residents ... are bitterly opposed to having their homes demolished, but the programme has been imposed by force'.[89] So much for the liveable city; now it is the profitable city, whatever that means and regardless of who is in the way.

Incidental reclamations

Berger began an essay on the future of art, 'works of art are like the stones of bridges', which people built and crossed together 'because they needed to travel in a particular direction'.[90] In the global city there is no alternative and the prescribed direction is lethal. But the period of mass revolt, of parades carrying red banners and singing collective anthems died at some time in the twentieth century (and ended modernity). New political formations have emerged, such as anti-roads protest in the 1990s,[91] and Occupy in 2011–12. In Chapter 8 I ask what function art might retain but here I want to look at the intersection of urban public space and other readings which might at least offer a glimpse of an alternative public realm – though not a determinative public sphere – in work by Joanna Rajkowska in Warsaw, and Wolfgang Weileder in Washington, DC and Singapore.

Greetings from Jerusalem Avenue is a 15-metre, artificial palm tree at the intersection of two main streets, Aleje Jerozolimskie and Nowy Świat, in the centre of Warsaw, among a mix of recent high-rise and Soviet-era buildings. The project began in 2002 when Rajkowska went to Israel during the second intifada, and the title has a number of nuances: in Polish, to be hit by a palm tree is to think something unthinkable or to act like an idiot. Rajkowska translates, 'it describes a momentary loss of control or logic, or madness, from the point of view of someone who has both feet on the ground'.[92] And while Jerusalem Avenue is the street's name, it alludes to both a city in a state created after the Holocaust (of which memories are complex in Poland) which Rajkowska visited, and to Nowa Jerozolima, an eighteenth-century Jewish village outside Warsaw after which the street (once leading to it) was named. The tree was made from an artificial trunk and leaves fabricated at Escondido on the Mexican-US border. When it was first erected the leaves looked too short, leading to the tree being called parsley. Then the city authorities disowned the project (for which temporary permission had previously been granted). Rajkowska recalls, 'It was not only the ordinary pedestrians who were sceptical. The art world did not greet the project with a warm handshake either – the palm tree was received with utter silence'[93] (Figure 6.4). At the same time:

apart from the after-effects of the Israel conflict and the void left by the Holocaust, there was something in the palm tree that caused people's faces to change.... I had produced an image of desire that sent them off into their private dreams – of trips to warm countries, of a better life, of something that is elsewhere.[94]

People started to bring or add things to the tree: a graphic designer used it in the background to a digital image of Lech Wałęsa; people demonstrated under it, such as the gay club, cultural hub and Left meeting place, Le Madame: 'Demonstrators wearing bathing suits over winter coats [in December] sunglasses, pith helmets and covered with artificial flowers arrived ... with inflatable mattresses, flags and banners.'[95] Five years later, in 2009, there was a Greenpeace protest; later that year a young man undressed under the tree with a large sheet of paper round his waist saying sorry to his girlfriend. In 2012, female pro-Palestinian activists adorned the tree with a keffiyeh in protest at a Polish government visit to Jerusalem when parts of the city were being illegally annexed by Israel. Eventually, in 2012, the project gained support from the city's Museum of Modern Art, but that seems almost incidental as it has sparked public debate and disagreement, and continues to do so, outside the agendas of institutions. Some of the events which *Greetings from Jerusalem Avenue* has drawn to its site are politicised, although none threaten any regime; yet this appears an everyday public realm by other means, unofficial but not inconsequent.

Weileder's *Res Publica* (2012) was the temporary installation of a stainless steel leaflet dispenser outside the Supreme Court in Washington, in the form of a Palladian temple (like the court building, by Cass Gilbert) on a plinth. It contained copies of a manual for a 1:50 scale model of the building; four of these cardboard models were made by art students and sited around the city in places where homeless people congregate. A catalogue states, '*Res Publica* juxtaposed two diametrically different understandings of architecture: one representative of power and prestige and the other a basic shelter for survival.'[96] The leaflet stand toned in with others in the city, which routinely offer tourists maps and advertising. The manuals may have been a surprise to those who took one, but there is more to it: the model is complicated and requires model-making skills to

Figure 6.4   Greetings from Jerusalem Avenue, Joanna Rajkowska, 2002 (continuing), Warsaw (photo: K. Nawratek)

complete; it is a detailed, accurate scale representation but the models once so carefully made are vulnerable (Figure 6.5). If the Palladian form resonates with power, its scale representation is within human grasp and the crumpled, wet models resonate with abjection. They may also remind beholders of the inevitability that power breaks down.

Stilt House (2011) was built from recycled plastic waste at Dhoby Ghaut, Singapore, during an architectural festival. It is one of several temporary house projects by Weileder, most of them built and taken down in

Figure 6.5   Res Publica, Washington, DC, Wolfgang Weileder 2012 (photo by permission of the artist)

public, working with building trainees and students. Weileder says, 'the apprentices themselves ... are a key audience. I discovered that there are far more types of audiences than passers-by. You could say ... there are innumerable hidden stakeholders in any complex project'.[97] The obvious stakeholders might be city authorities and arts funding bodies, or curators and critics, but these projects introduce participants as co-producers (if not as designers) whose ownership of the project adds to an always-unfinished, continually adapted meaning. Weileder opts for prominent sites where people are likely to have expectations: 'the more prominent and understood the site, the more imaginative space there is for my work to question those very things'.[98] But *Stilt House* occupies 'a tiny park, one of the few remnants that remain of the original landscape.... Singapore has been completely transformed into a hi-tech western-style city, and has mostly ignored its own architectural heritage'.[99] The project references that heritage, and recreates a vernacular architecture in a twenty-first-century material produced from recycled plastic. The structure is a viable sustainable building, ephemerally exhibited in a public site which is near the city centre and a metro, a hybrid of a park and residual, overlooked green margin. Weileder was, 'concerned with questioning the nature of public space' and saw the building as squatting a 'highly-visible, extremely public' site, and as 'an experiment to see what would happen', which might 'almost force a reaction' from the audience.[100] This was extended by post-project documentation, for instance on waste management in Singapore, effecting neither representation of the issues nor intervening in the extant processes of decision-making but performing, as it were, its presence in 'a more active engagement between viewer and artwork' than might otherwise occur.[101]

Figure 6.6   Stilt House, Singapore, Wolfgang Weileder, 2013 (photo by permission of the artist)

7

Dissent: Antagonistic Art in a Period of Neoliberal Containment

In the previous chapter I cited John Berger's remark that, 'works of art are like the stones of bridges' which people have crossed together because they 'needed to travel in a particular direction'.[1] I want to unpack that a little now, asking how the direction of travel is decided. In the nineteenth century, the avant-garde sought to lead society towards a better life but if this suggests a priest-like function,[2] and a separation between an avant-garde and the publics for whom they interpret history, this may be at odds with Berger's interest in a process integral to ordinary life. Yet it was the depiction of ordinary life which preoccupied the French Realist painters Gustave Courbet and Jean-François Millet from the 1840s through the 1860s in the depiction of working people with a dignity previously reserved for myth and history painting. They also lived as members of poor rural societies at Barbizon. Although Millet retained a maid there – costs were much lower than in Paris – he and his family walked the 30 miles to Barbizon from Paris in 1849 when they were destitute.[3] After the fall of the Commune in 1871, and Courbet's death impoverished and in exile in 1874 (coincidentally the year of the first Impressionist exhibition), rural life appeared again in the work of Camille Pissarro. Tim Clark argues that Pissarro, as an anarchist, reading tracts by Peter Kropotkin, saw agriculture as a regenerative force. Kropotkin's *The Conquest of Bread* indeed re-imagines rural life 'as a pole of attraction after the revolution'.[4] Like Courbet and Millet, Pissarro paints rural life as a site of dignity but his paintings also contained coded messages for those able to read them, as in anarchist circles. The rural poor, however, remain representations of a future yet to come, which distances their representation from the immediacy of social change after 1871.

In contrast, recent art and literature have introduced participatory practices and oral histories by which non-privileged publics become co-producers of the work, or of stories (rather than formalised narratives) told in their own words. I remember a radio series in the 1970s, *The Long March of Everyman* (when a universal masculine went unchallenged). The programmes were introduced by theme music from Ralph Vaughan Williams' *Masque of Job* (1931), with sequences of slow, rolling cadences (a work partly based on William Blake's illustrations of *The Book of Job* [1826]). The series was quite radical at the time in telling popular histories, although this also reflected the emergence of cultural studies[5] and Raymond Williams' idea of a long revolution through social institutions such as literacy and education.[6] This kind of history-telling denotes a direction of travel which is *produced* (not passively received) by the acts of mass publics, which are conditioned by but which also re-inflect their circumstances.

Autonomy?

In popular history, engagement means sharing the historian's role of narrating past events. A similar model is evident in recent participatory art,[7] which sits uneasily with modernist claims for autonomy. Yet autonomy can be read as the creation of a critical distance both *from* and *in* the conditions in which art is made, which is what Herbert Marcuse meant by an aesthetic dimension.[8] Perhaps aesthetics (going beyond the circumstances of production) is compatible with intervention when it entails the creation of alternative imaginaries which go beyond the mere representation of conditions. Nonetheless, there are issues. Audre Lorde said in 1979:

> Those of us who stand outside the circle of this society's definition of acceptable women, those of us who have been forged in the crucibles of difference … know that *survival is not an academic skill*. It is learning how to stand alone, and how to make common cause with those others identified as outside the structure in order to define and seek a world in which we can all flourish. It is learning how to take our differences and make them strengths. *For the master's tools will never dismantle the master's house.* They may allow us temporarily to beat him at his own game, but they will never enable us to bring about genuine change.[9]

This could be interpreted as a call to junk traditional art forms as being inextricably bound to bourgeois values, yet it is too easy to say the master's tools include media such as oil painting, and too simplistic to say that conceptualism in the 1960s constituted new tools. For instance, the deep humanity of touching hands in Rembrandt's *The Jewish Bride* (1665, Amsterdam, Rijksmuseum) conveys an intimacy that goes beyond the social conditions of the painting's production. For historian John Molyneux, Rembrandt poses, 'deep personal tenderness and intimacy [or] "intimitude" as [Hélène] Cixous calls it' and a, 'solidarity with the oppressed in Dutch society' against Dutch capitalism.[10] Similarly, Marcuse reads French literature in the 1940s as a literature of intimacy which stands against fascism.[11] Marcuse cites Paul Éluard and Louis Aragon, both at times members of the French Communist Party.

Arguments over art's autonomy continue now as they did then;[12] the second avant-garde of early modernism was a revolt of tendencies within art, an oblique disruption of bourgeois society. Marxist art writer Kim Charnley, citing Peter Bürger, argues that avant-gardism is, 'central to the institution of art' today.[13] As artists adopted practices that did not provide objects for sale, dealers traded instead in reputations; artist-run spaces freed artists from the art world's validation but, artist Martha Rosler reflects, this was shaped by the 'alternative cultural spheres, or countercultures'[14] of the 1960s, which dissolved with the New Left. The anti-institutional revolt failed and 'patterns of behaviour and estimations of worth in the art world' resemble those of entertainment.[15] Charnley asks if art can be revolutionary without revolution,[16] which implies a vicious circle: revolutionary art needs revolutions in order to be revolutionary, but is made revolutionary by being within revolutions which are yet to happen. Unless the difficulty is transcribed from temporality to a metaphorical spatiality (allowing co-presence of the new within the old) there is no exit from that. One form of that metaphorical spatiality might be the expanded field.

Jane Rendell, citing Rosalind Krauss,[17] argues that, 'definitions and categorisations of art are occurring across multiple disciplines', which requires 'new terms and modes of thinking that allow us to identify the particularities and differences of the various related practices in ways that go beyond opposition'.[18] Rendell adds that artists operate at sites 'within, at the edge of, between and across' diverse fields, using methods which question disciplinary procedures.[19] An advantage is that the expanded field dispels the idea that artists have a privileged insight, or the kind of free choice once assumed for the idealised subjects of liberal-humanism. Art's production and reception are made – manufactured – in a matrix of factors such as the market (or its refusal), art criticism, and adjacent fields such as architecture, design, landscape, social campaigns and politics; the artist's intention is one of many equally valid indicators of what a work does.[20] This is closer than the model of an avant-garde to the idea of a mass public able to determine the crossing of bridges according to its own needs. This still has limits; citing cultural theorist John Roberts, Charnley argues that 'art cannot claim to be equivalent to political struggle' but is at best a cultural expression of that struggle.[21] Expression, or articulation, still goes beyond representation.

Outside artspace

Artist Gregory Sholette writes that, in the 1980s, socially oriented practices presented 'an interpretive artistic vocabulary' based on social history and cultural identity.[22] He gives the example of the United Victorian Workers Union's participation in the annual Victorian Stroll in Troy, New York, when they carried placards stating, in a Victorian font, Agitate! Educate! Organize! and Our Field The World – Our Cause Humanity. The parade was intended to turn the district into 'a magical stage of song, dance, and family enjoyment' into which this group of artist-activists intervened; 'disarmed business leaders and politicians dressed in Victorian garb looked on in dismay'.[23] The business leaders could not, however, accuse the Union of being visually out of place, which indicates a tactic of working within a given situation to re-inflect its meaning, punning, playing on anticipated readings of reality, subverting without necessarily leading the production of meaning. The author, so to speak, is not dead but the public do complete the work. Sholette also cites Temporary Services, an arts collective in Chicago whose aim is 'to build an art practice that makes the distinction between art and other forms of creativity irrelevant, champions the work of those who are frequently excluded, under-recognized, marginal, non-commercial, experimental, and/or socially and politically provocative' while returning money and cultural capital to 'the work of other artists and publishers'.[24] Temporary Services has set up ephemeral exhibition sites, illicitly added books to a library, fly-posted, distributed leaflets and acted as an unsanctioned public service carrying out surveys of responses to public sculptures. Sholette regards Temporary Services as re-enacting 'an old vanguard desire to dissolve *art into life*', aligned to carnival as an interruption of everyday life as much as to revolutionary movements such as Russian Productivism.[25] I would compare this to Henri Lefebvre's idea of moments of liberation within the routines of capitalism,[26] although carnival was brought into cultural discourse by Mikhail Bakhtin from a concern, not with carnival as such, as a Land of Cockaigne,[27] but for its representation as the grotesque in literature.[28]

Art activism has grown internationally since the 1990s, and Sholette lists 47 arts groups in 19 countries who work this way.[29] Such work can be read as intervention in an expanded field: art as not-society/politics; and as an insertion of alternative histories and critiques in what Walter Benjamin called the relations of production: 'Instead of asking what is the position of a work viv-a-vis the productive relations of its time ... I should like to pose a different one ... what is its position *within* them?[30] Benjamin gives the example of a Soviet writer who participates in the daily life of a collective farm, ordering tractor parts, arranging mass meetings, launching wall-newspapers and introducing travelling film shows. The divide between readers and writers is collapsed, as it is when readers send accounts of collective life for publication.

Bürger cites Dada events as similarly collapsing the divide between production and reception: 'given the avant-gardist intention to do away with art as a sphere that is separate from the praxis of life, it is logical to eliminate the antithesis between producer and recipient'.[31] And Charnley argues that collectivism refuses art's individualism but, citing artist/writer Gerald Raunig,[32] suggests that stresses may arise within art collectives when a group, 'perceives and contests the structuring power' of institutions.[33] There is a further conceptual tension between actualities and their representation, as sociologist Alberto Toscano sees in Soviet cinema, for instance in the work of Dziga Vertov. Toscano raises the idea of, 'an October [Revolution] in cinema' whence '*the art of revolution must never represent the revolution*'.[34] That is, it must *be* the revolution, not its image.

As Charnley notes, the counter-cultural political groups of the 1960s have been succeeded by single-issue campaigns and media activism.[35] Adbusters, for example, operates critically in the realm of advertising, with sophisticated equivalents of its technologies. It was Adbusters, too, who issued the public call for the occupation of Wall Street in 2011. The Yes Men have similarly inserted themselves in dialogues of corporate excess through spoof presentations to neoliberal business conferences in which a dominant logic is stretched to a point at which the dehumanising basis of global capitalism appears (to those who see it) as obviously irrational. Whether this is revolutionary depends on how the idea of living the revolution is interpreted, and whether devices such as parody and irony construct a critical distance or are captured by the culture they critique.

Relational aesthetics

I want to juxtapose the above discussion (a very compressed version of the arguments cited) to an extract from curator-critic Nicolas Bourriaud's introductory text in the catalogue for the Tate Triennial exhibition *Altermodern*, which he curated in 2009. After forays into relational aesthetics,[36] Bourriaud arrived at the metaphor of an archipelago to denote a tendency which has not been pressed into a movement or a new departure from the mainstream, but arises in a Deleuzian nomadism. 'Altermodern' is a term rooted in an 'idea of otherness', suggesting 'a multitude of possibilities, of alternatives to a single route.[37] He sees this as analogous to new kinds of protest: 'In the geo-political world, alter-globalization defines the plurality of local opposition to the economic standardization imposed by globalization,' suggesting an 'image of the archipelago' as a 'constellation of ideas linked by the twenty-first century ... [when] the historical role of modernism ... resides in its ability to jolt us out of tradition; it embodies a cultural exodus, an escape from the confines of nationalism and identity-tagging ...'[38] We'll see. Triennials, biennials and art fairs are key elements in the art market, but there seems also to be a tension between a jolting out of history and a pluralism which could equally be, not a refusal of the trajectory, but its next phase as it is appropriated by the mainstream. Perhaps a more careful construction of the question is required.

Political theorist Seyla Benhabib identifies an equivalent difficulty in intercultural discourses:

Norms of universal respect and egalitarian reciprocity already undergird practices of discursive argumentation: they must be presupposed in some form for practical discourses. This reflects not a vicious circle but a virtuous one: moral and political dialogues begin with the presumption of respect, equality, and reciprocity between the participants. We engage in discourses with an assumed background, and we understand that these norms apply to all participants ... [who] subject these assumed background interpretations to intersubjective validation. Discourses are procedures of *recursive validation* through which abstract norms and principles are concretized and legitimized.... These are dialogic processes through which we not only concretize and contextualize the meaning of such norms; we also determine what kind of a problem is being debated.[39]

The agenda, that is, emerges in the meeting rather than being pre-scripted, and the values contested are *enacted* rather than signposted; and if the means *are* the ends, not a way to the ends, this relocates the problem of change from a temporal trajectory – the golden tomorrow which never dawns – to *another present* which changes what is extant from within rather than constructing a chasm between the extant and its overthrow. For the most part, art criticism still constructs a chasm between art and politics; successive revolts within art may constitute alternatives within the present reality, nonetheless, which brings to mind Herbert Marcuse's justification for aesthetics as what is viable in 'the miserable reality'[40] when political change is unlikely (in the 1970s, or now). I have examined Marcuse's aesthetic theories elsewhere,[41] and here I want to move to the more recent contributions, now, of Jacques Rancière.

Relational aesthetics

In 'Problems and Transformations of Critical Art', Rancière argues that critical art, 'sets out to build awareness of the mechanisms of domination', enabling the spectator to become a 'conscious agent of world transformation'.[42] He identifies three important difficulties: first, understanding does not change things, only the perception of things; second, the exploited do not need explanations of the conditions they experience first-hand; and, third, to dissolve the appearances of things or conditions destroys the necessarily strange encounter with what is to be transformed so that art then risks being 'inscribed in the perpetuity of a world in which the transformation of things into signs is redoubled by the very excess of interpretative signs'.[43] This is a vicious circle, like the one which Marcuse outlined in *The Aesthetic Dimension*: 'Art is committed to that perception of the world which alienates individuals from their functional existence ... to an emancipation of sensibility, imagination, and reason', which in turn requires, 'a degree of autonomy which withdraws art from the ... power of the given'.[44] Toscano reads similarities between Marcuse's and Rancière's positions on the mediation and indirectness of art's praxis.[45] Rancière elaborates, further, on an aesthetics that contains a tension between two kinds of politics: 'the logic of art becoming life at the price of its self-elimination and the logic of art's getting involved in politics on the express condition of not having anything to do with it'.[46] He seems as haunted by the failures of the French Left after 1968 and capital's assimilation of democracy as consumer choice as the Frankfurt School was haunted by the failure of the German Revolution in 1918–19 and subsequent rise of fascism. In 'The End of Politics', Rancière sees politics redefined as the 'management of the social' or 'reciprocal appeasement of the social and the political ... the art of suppressing the political ... [and] a procedure of self-subtraction'.[47] Looking to Brecht, however, he argues that: 'It is by crossing over the borders and changes of status between art and non-art that the radical strangeness of the aesthetic object and the active appropriation of the common world were able to conjoin' as a micro-politics of art appears between art as life and art as 'resistant form'.[48] Rancière writes further of 'a specific sensory experience' that holds the promise of 'the new in art and life.'[49] Paraphrasing Schiller, he says, 'aesthetic experience will bear the edifice of the art of the beautiful *and* of the art of living'.[50] This might not be too far from an art which enacts, as Claire Bishop puts it, a 'desire to create an active subject'[51] able to determine her or his own social and political reality.[52] The rest of this chapter concerns cases of current art practice in which aspects of the above discussion are implicit.

A right to ordinary life: SEFT-1

In 1995, Mexico's railways were privatised. All passenger services were stopped, and 9,000 km of track was closed for passenger and freight services deemed to be unprofitable. Ivan Puig and Andrés Padilla Domene ask, 'Why should public transport have to be profitable?' and cite their indignation at the loss of the passenger services for communities along the lines as the basis for their project *SEFT-1 Abandoned Railways Exploration Probe*.[53] Constructing a working road-rail vehicle based on a small car in a silver, retro-space-age style (SEFT-1), in 2010 to 2012 they travelled in it over the redundant routes. Much of the track had been lifted after closure, so the road-rail vehicle could adapt immediately from rails to empty track-bed. Driving through Mexico and Ecuador, they met local people afflicted by the closures. They made video and photographic records of the journey, collected found objects along the way, posted videos and text on the project website,[54] and staged more than 20 exhibitions of the project, including one in 2014 with a scale model made by local railway modellers at Furtherfield Gallery in Finsbury Park, London (Figure 7.1). This exhibition was organised by The Arts Catalyst, a British arts-science organisation.[55] The link to Britain was historical, too, in that Mexico's railways were first engineered by British companies in the late nineteenth century, linking Mexico City to ports from where ocean-liners sailed to Europe. Alongside abandoned mines, redundant power stations and industrial wastelands – notably sites in the Ruhr, Germany, rehabilitated for community and leisure uses – these engineers' lost work constitutes one of the many ruins of modernity.[56]

Recapturing the past as a model of public service was one dimension of the project, brought into the present in numerous conversations with people along the old lines whose indignation matched that of the artists and remained; another dimension was the imagination of possible futures, implicitly if not realistically the reopening of the lines, explicitly renewing a promise of mobility for people whose lives are restricted by its lack under

Figure 7.1   *SEFT-1* at Furtherfield Gallery, Finsbury Park, London, June, 2014

neoliberalism. Art does not change the world, but without the imagined alternatives it makes visible, or makes tangible in this case as the artists unofficially reopened the lines, change would be permanently remote. The artists write on the design of SEFT-1:

It comes from numberless subconscious references we've consumed from all kinds of media throughout our lives. Besides paraphrasing space exploration, the purpose of building a spaceship-like road-rail vehicle was to reflect on technology as a promise of progress brought with modernity. In that way, the SFET-1 aesthetic is not limited to a specific decade; it works like a timeless allegory of technology; when exploring the railways in ruins it automatically poses the question of what happened with the common good and public benefit technology was supposed to bring.[57]

Puig and Domene encountered ghost towns and places which still supported a community, carrying stories from one abandoned station to the next. With a certain irony, or it might be a refusal of defeat, one such station is called Esperanza (hope). Perhaps this was a vision of a future of desolation and survival, not as the result of a natural disaster but as the systematic denial of rights to a basic livelihood and mobility to the non privileged.

Art critic Jonathan Jones sees the project in context of modern ruins which 'inspire the imagination, incite pleasantly melancholy thoughts, and humanize a landscape', while ruins like those of Mexico's railways, or Detroit with its ruined public buildings and abandoned services, 'are the stuff of 21st-century dreams' telling those who see them that 'we already live in the ruins of modernity'.[58] Looking at photographs from *SEFT-1* he reflects, 'Ruinous desolate stretches of track slowly decay back into the fertile landscape in the pictures they took on their journey that is also an image of some dystopian future when our world is abandoned and reverts to jungle and forest.'[59]

There is a history of such dystopias; in Richard Jeffries' *After London* (1885) the city is submerged under a black swamp. The book has been called Jeffries' revenge on a city which he hated.[60] A view of ruins which is only melancholic leaves out such emotions, however, while the anger of people who are disadvantaged in more practical ways by centralised economic decisions requires a means of visibility. People who are isolated from communities, markets and the horizons of a possible future when a private company closes a public service can speak for themselves – they do not need artists to explain the world; but SEFT-1 demonstrates a capacity to carry their reactions and a view of their predicament to other publics in a global matrix of rising indignation.

A right to ordinary life: IAPDH

The Institute for the Art and Practice of Dissent at Home (IAPDH) was established by Gary Anderson, Lena Simic and their children, Neal, Gabriel and Sid in Liverpool in 2007, in their council house in Everton. Gary and Lena write,

> Frustrated with the way things were, we decided to try an experiment in family activism. We were terrified of bringing up our children to be passive consumers of corporate commodities and looming on the horizon was the Liverpool 08 European Capital of Culture. There we saw explicit links between art making and capitalism and it made us feel sick. It made us worry about our children. It made us worry about ourselves. The celebrations of commodification were appalling to us and ... no-one really seemed to be complaining. So, we wanted to create a space for doing things a little bit differently, with our eyes on the prize of a workable model for cultural dissent based in a family.... We promised that, whatever we do we'll do it with financial transparency ... [and that] it would be fun.[61]

The Institute is funded by 10 per cent of members' net earnings. It has published pamphlets and arranged events including a performance of August Strindberg's play *Miss Julie* adapted as *Miss Julie in Utopia*, picnics, readings of Marx, short-term residencies by artists and writers, and performance projects in Zagreb, London, Bristol, Manchester and Newcastle as well as Liverpool.

Miss Julie was written in 1888, the year in which an authorised translation of *The Communist Manifesto* appeared in England, and Eugène Pottier wrote the 'Internationale'. Pissarro painted *Apple Picking at Eragny* (Dallas, Museum of Art) in 1888, and Paul Gauguin painted *Vision after the Sermon* (Edinburgh, National Gallery) in Brittany, in retreat from the materialism of Paris (and his failure as a stockbroker). There is nothing special about 1888, and most of the radical art and literature which appeared then is ambivalent in its politics. An equivalent list of events could be made for most years but apparent coincidences still indicate a direction of travel. That is, after the defeat of the Commune, with the rise of militarism in Germany, when the British Empire still seemed robust, stirrings of unrest grew under the surface in societies whose elites represented them as stable and secure. The agency of these stirrings was seen (or determined) later, as any incipient change is seen only in retrospect when enabling factors for its instantiation have prevailed over disabling factors. It may be that in 2007 – which saw the end of the agrarian age when a majority of the world's human population lived in cities, also a writers' strike in North America, the Year of the Dolphin, the criminalisation of slavery in Mauritania, a World Economic Forum report putting the US (as usual until 2010) at the top of its global competition chart, and the financial services crisis, as well as the foundation of IAPDH – similar stirrings gathered strength under a surface of news of economic melt-down and the redirection of vast sums of public money to failing banks. *Miss Julie in Utopia* was performed on Saturday, 21 June 2008. Anderson and Simic write of their subversion of the model of public–private partnerships, of New Labour's 'emptying out of accountable public services into ... an unregulated private ownership [which is] by definition unaccountable', by allocating a bedroom in their house (domestic space, the private realm) for meetings and artist's residencies (as a form of public realm). They used their house and garden as well for *Miss Julie in Utopia*.

Strindberg's original play is problematic:

> Strindberg was a left-winger, who had a demonstration of Dock Workers campaign for a state pension for him on his 63rd birthday ... [but he was] also an insufferable misogynist, a woman-hater subscribing to ideas about the weak dying out making way for the stronger.[62]

Gauguin had problematic but more prolific relationships with women, and invited Strindberg to write a preface for the catalogue of a sale of his works prior to his departure for the South Seas. Strindberg nonetheless exposed the dysfunctionality of bourgeois family life in his plays while Gauguin revealed, or re-presented for a European audience, a promise of joy in Tahitian society as a radical other to European bourgeois society. Both men led flawed lives and produced works of ambivalent meaning but both contributed, too, to the aesthetics of a new social imaginary in which the revolutionary subject is present and active. In IAPDH's adaptation of the play, Julie articulates her self-doubt: 'I dream the people are coming. I stand waiting to greet them, dressed as one of them.... I hear the murmur of their song.... Then it occurs to me I haven't learnt the words.'[63] The bind reappears: to join the revolution needs a revolutionary consciousness which is gained only within the processes of revolution. If, as said above, an exit from an insoluble conceptual dilemma is to set aside the trajectory in which freedom is tomorrow, ushering in an insurgent co-present, perhaps a form of this, on a domestic scale, is IAPDH's setting aside of a room in their house as a site for critical cultural work into which to invite likeminded others. This is a little tenuous, but home-made aesthetics might be able to oppose capitalism; and a home-made adaptation of literature may offer a glimpse of emancipation extricated from its historically or conventionally compromised form, for a public of family and friends: revolutionary moments at home. This directly refutes the conventional model in which access to the arts is widened for a supposedly general public, or an excluded public in New Labour's rhetoric of social inclusion. That strategy failed in Liverpool's year as European Capital of Culture in 2008 (L08) when, from research on the programmes' reception in outlying parts of the city, up to 80 per cent of people surveyed felt it would have no impact on their neighbourhoods.[64]

In an IAPDH booklet, Bruce Bennett and Imogen Tyler explain the need for disobedience:

> Alongside the rising levels of economic and social inequality, Britain has witnessed the erosion of workers' rights, civil liberties and human rights, legal protections are seen to interfere with and distort competitive markets. The systematic tearing up of the new social contract that was instituted after the Second World War can be tracked through the period that extends from the 1970s through the rollback of the welfare state, the decomposition of trade unions, the securitization of borders, and a redefining of British citizenship. At the same time, formal and informal modes of democratic protest ... have been seriously undermined. Britain is becoming more unequal and less democratic.[65]

They continue, in a commentary on IAPDH, that the capacity to object is eroded when sites in public spaces which are privatised become scarce. Perhaps, I would add, a prevailing culture of consumption reduces the urge to seek alternatives, in the familiar workings of alienation identified by Marx, and in the media's manufacture now of false needs.

Beside groups such as the Laboratory for Insurrectionary Imagination and its offshoot, the Clandestine Insurgent Rebel Clown Army, IAPDH merges playfulness with global critique, and merges critique with home-made tactics of refusal. Bennett and Tyler end, 'Rejoicing in the absurdity of an avant-garde art practice that is based in the spare bedroom of a council house, as well as in the normality of this situation, [their] work offers a model of domestic radical art practice.'[66] Since that was written, Gary, Lena, Neal, Gabriel, Sid and baby James (Figure 7.2) have moved to a larger house bought with a mortgage. They maintain a group practice which is critically performative and refuses to conform to art world expectations.

Figure 7.2   The Institute for the Art and Practice of Dissent at Home, joining the march for Gaza, August 2014 (photo by permission of IAPDH)

Alternative imaginaries: scepticism, art and money

Matthew Cornford and David Cross, working as Cornford & Cross, began working together in 1987 as students in London. They have made installations for specific outdoor and gallery sites, and exhibited project proposals which were rejected by selection panels (in some cases when the proposal drew out contradictions in the brief). Their work has a metaphorical and playful quality underpinned by a commitment to an open society, particularly in relation to cities. They write that rather than taking an oppositional stance, they 'encourage a reflective scepticism towards individual actions and their collective results. Our practice is not separate from the economic and political spheres.'[67] For the most part, their projects begin with a co-written text worked and re-worked through discussion. This is an important part of the work, not notes in a margin. If a proposal is accepted, the text becomes part of it; if it is not, the text and any visual material may be exhibited or published later. Most of the projects which are realised are of short duration, so more people see them in documentation than directly, which lends photography a key role in the work's development, production and reception. Cornford & Cross state:

> We maintain that as well as producing aesthetic experiences, a key function of contemporary art … is to test concepts, assumptions and boundaries.… Our interventions are often disruptive of everyday life, so realizing them calls for close interaction with the organization and people who occupy places and influence events.… Every art project we have carried out has encountered obstacles, which were only overcome with the flexibility shown by people prepared to take risks, go beyond conventional interpretations of their roles and become active participants.[68]

The latter observation is echoed by John Roberts, writing that they inhabit a post-Thatcherite world of, 'deracinated public cultures, hysterical faith in markets, and bland and ahistorical multiculturalisms' where, instead of offering plain defiance they, 'hang around, so to speak, melding their interests and views of their interlocutors'.[69] Roberts asks what form of sensual practice – reminiscent of the phrase 'practical human-sensuous activity' in Marx's fifth Thesis on Feuerbach[70] – follows self-ironisation, finding an answer in 'art's negation in a world of art's social positivisation'.[71] So, to endorse a practice 'as a process of dialogue with certain intractable material interests ... as the basis for the transformation of part of the world in the name of art, is to insist that art must risk its own failure if its sensuousness is not to emerge as ... empty affirmation'.[72] Roberts cites the work *New Holland* (1997), a mass-produced turkey shed which Cornford & Cross installed in the grounds of the Sainsbury Centre for Visual Arts at the University of East Anglia (Figure 7.3).

Figure 7.3   Cornford & Cross, *New Holland*, 1997 (photo by permission of the artists)

New Holland juxtaposes two minimal architectures: Norman Foster's partly underground, glass-fronted centre, and the metal shed placed between the centre's façade and a sculpture by Henry Moore. This also re-inflects two Englands: one of a Romantic pastoralism, another of the region's agribusiness. Cornford & Cross say, 'The structure was entirely appropriate yet uncomfortably out of place in its physical setting and institutional context.'[73] The shed had no door; recorded house and garage music sounded loudly from its inaccessible inside like an underground rave, suggesting an antagonistic sensuous activity, or a 'space of controlled rebellion'.[74]

In *The Abolition of Work* (2007), the artists' fee and production costs for an installation at The Exchange – a new art gallery converted from the redundant telephone exchange in Penzance, Cornwall, part of the new wave of arts venues (Chapter 4) – was converted into 1p coins which were then placed on the gallery floor until the entire exhibition space was filled (Figure 7.4). The resulting copper floor has a resonance with Cornwall's copper industry, which began in the Bronze Age; and its craft production (not only of the familiar studio pottery but also of copper-work); and with minimalist sculptures such as Carl Andre's *Equivalent VIII* (1972), an installation of 120 fire bricks, or Walter de Maria's *The Broken Kilometre*

Figure 7.4   Cornford & Cross, installing *The Abolition of Work*, 2007, The Exchange Gallery, Penzance (photo by permission of the artists)

(1979), an installation of 500 brass rods. Cornford writes of 'the willingness of gallery volunteers to literally get down on their hands and needs and help us lay the coins on the floor', so that what had been anticipated as tedious labour 'turned into an enjoyable and social occasion'.[75] The artists are grateful to Claire Benson, Rachel Campbell, Rebecca Griffiths, Ann Haycock, Louise Hedges, Yasmin Ineson, Victoria Lingard, Jess Morgan, Jane Pitts, Judi Rea, Jo Tabone and Karen Thomas for their help, and assistance in completing the work.

The work's title has multiple resonances: for the artists the source was an essay of the same title by the anarchist artist Bob Black, in which he argues that work is the source of nearly all misery in the world, advocating a society based instead on play. This reflects an emphasis on play in 1960s counter-culture, and ideas advanced by Kropotkin. Indeed, the abolition of toil is central to utopian socialism and anarchism, articulated in a mediated form in the idea of a society in which each person works according to ability and takes from the common product according to need. Today this might imply a life of voluntary simplicity; but, for Kropotkin, the advent of factory production and new agricultural methods was a solution to the economic problem of scarcity and the social divide it produced. But mass production was turned into commodity fetishism, built-in obsolescence and the dehumanising toil of the production line. In this context, Cornford & Cross point out that the 1p coin has been debased: minted for the transition to decimal currency in 1971, it was initially in bronze but, by 1992, the metal was worth more than the coin's exchange value; bronze was replaced by copper-plated steel. The copper, as it was called, became a sham. The 700,000 plus copper-plated coins were placed on the floor of The Exchange as they came, heads or tails up, and returned to circulation via the gallery's bank account after the show. The artists write, 'Although the multitude of coins does not represent anything, it may resemble many things', so that the work becomes like 'a vast puzzle' in which 'all the pieces are the same', inviting reflection on labour, and on 'the paradoxes of the relationship between art, money and the value of time'.[76]

People beg for coins, but money in this form may soon be encapsulated in a past as remote as revolution while, political scientist Adolpho Gilly says, 'the violence of money' advances technologically as it seeks 'the commodification of every domain and interstice of society' and the eradication of 'whoever resists this plundering or fails to enter into the universal valorization of capital'.[77]

Alternative Imaginaries: fracking in the gallery

Fracking Futures (2013) was an installation by the artists' group HeHe –
Helen Evans and Heiko Hansen, based in Paris – at FACT (Foundation for
Art and Creative Technology) in Liverpool, co-commissioned by The Arts
Catalyst. Hydraulic fracturing (fracking) is a way to extract gas or oil from
rock by pumping fluid into its fissures at high pressure. In North America,
it has poisoned water sources, destroyed farms, caused methane leaks,
explosions and earthquakes, and wrecked some of the sites it afflicts. The
industry says that techniques have been refined and that fracking is now
safe but, in 2013, a test site at Balcombe in rural Sussex attracted a protest
camp. Fracking is contentious both in terms of safety and in context of
the need to reduce reliance on unsustainable fossil fuels. In Britain, as I
write in 2014, it is seen by government as vital to future energy security.
Evans writes, 'Inspired by the debate,' HeHe made the gallery space, 'a
temporary, experimental drilling site for hydraulic fracking ... [making]
a fracked landscape'.[78] Tiles were ripped up from the gallery floor, and
a micro-scale drilling rig mounted in the space, causing tremors and
an 'unquantifiable subterranean noise' as water seemingly polluted by
fracking chemicals bubbled in a pit, a flame signalled a periodic release of
gas, and gallery visitors were, 'introduced to the sounds and sensations of
hydraulic fracturing, allowing them to become more deeply connected to
the contentious issues that surround the process'[79] (Figure 7.5).

Figure 7.5   HeHe, *Fracking Futures*, FACT, Liverpool, 2013 (photo by permission
of the artists)

The installation was part of FACT's tenth anniversary exhibition, *Turning FACT Inside Out*, which also included work by Uncoded Collective; Katarzyna Krakowiak; Manifest AR; Nina Edge; and Steve Lambert, who installed a 6-metre neon sign in nearby Rope Walks saying, Capitalism Works For Me. People were invited to agree or disagree (capitalism lost). FACT Director Mike Stubbs sees these events as handing over the site to artists, mainly in collaborative practices, able to 'reverse the narrative of objects, deconstruct the museum as part of its continuing development', by bringing art, people and technology together 'to rethink FACT's place in Liverpool and the international cultural field'.[80] Visitors to *Fracking Futures* may have thought that gas was being extracted, or that test explorations were being undertaken, as if FACT was trying to be self-sufficient in energy. Evans writes that the installation illustrated the potential dangers, 'but also considers the fact that fracking attempts to produce an alternative source of energy and has the potential for commerce and growth. Whether this last point is genuine or tongue-in-cheek is for the visitor to decide.'[81]

I recall graffiti in Belfast asserting 'No Fracking Eire'. The transition to an F-word indicates a negative public reaction similar to the response to genetically modified crops, or Frankenstein foods as a tabloid journalist called them (after which supermarkets competed to remove them from their shelves). A two-year study of fracking conducted in Los Angeles, funded by the oil industry, has decided there is no physical danger.[82] Perhaps a more important issue is the link between a fossil-fuelled future and climate change: fracking is less overtly scarring of the land than open-cast mining, and evades the unionisation which was integral to coal, but the reserves are finite; the idea that fracking will prevent future energy crises is a fantasy which merely distracts from the urgency of a non-fossil-fuel future. It is an urgent issue for north-west England because a large number of licences have been sold for test drilling there, many around the declining seaside resort of Blackpool. Industry and government may think that unemployment and reliance on tourism will reduce opposition there, but an anti-fracking camp was set up near Blackpool in August, 2014, organised by local people with protesters from Sussex. Tina Rothery, a protester in Blackpool, said: 'As mothers and grandmothers we don't care about anything they want to talk about except the safety of our young.... we wear headscarves and aprons. We're not eco-terrorists.'[83]

Art will not stop fracking: only people can do that and it will be difficult. *Fracking Futures* lends the issue a dramatic, confrontational visibility. Despite its neutral presentation in both the artists' statement and the reality rather than representation of a drilling rig in the gallery, *Fracking Futures* is a provocation; and HeHe is included in a website listing the top ten anti-fracking artists.[84] In an earlier project, *Nuage Vert* (2008, continuing), HeHe created a practical demonstration of reduced energy consumption, inviting people in the area served by the Salmisaari combined heat and power plant in Helsinki to switch off their appliances for a specific hour. The impact was monitored and visualised as a shrinking green laser projection of a cloud onto the real emission cloud.[85] These two projects, I think, construct an axis of creative tension between provocation and invitation, or between an allusion to a destructive industry and a form of what might be called (from Marx), practical human-sensuous activity. Ripping up the gallery floor, of course, also alludes to histories of anti-art as anti-bourgeois revolt.

Revolutionary art after revolutions

In 2003, Andy Hewitt and Mel Jordan, working as Hewitt + Jordan, installed a billboard in Sheffield stating:

> THE FUNCTION OF PUBLIC ART IS TO INCREASE
> THE VALUE OF PRIVATE PROPERTY

It was the first in a series of billboard works, presented on site and photographed to be re-sited in galleries and published in documentation and on their website. It began as *I won an artist in a raffle*, in which Hewitt + Jordan offered their labour in making a work as the first prize in a raffle at Public Art Forum's 2003 conference. The second prize was a nice box of paints. As it happened, the winner let them do what they liked, possibly unsettled by the contradiction between Hewitt + Jordan's approach and the efforts of the public art establishment to become insiders in the regeneration industry, dealing in place-making, employment, social inclusion and whatever their market (both public- and private-sector) required.

Further billboards stated:

> THE AESTHETIC FUNCTION OF PUBLIC ART IS TO CODIFY
> SOCIAL DISTINCTIONS AS NATURAL ONES

and

THE SOCIAL FUNCTION OF PUBLIC ART
IS TO SUBJECT US TO CIVIC BEHAVIOUR

The three texts were re-presented together as a poster in public sites in Leeds in 2005. Hewitt and Jordan stated their aim as, 'to examine the tensions and contradictions that exist within public art practice [and] to explain how public art ... functions in support of the dominant ideology'.[86] I was initially drawn to Hewitt + Jordan's work by their refusal of the prevailing rhetoric around public art (which has become highly institu-tionalised and sanitised), and the combination of an incisive, politicised critique. I was also drawn by the aesthetic quality of the work as I perceived it: an economy of means; the exact relations of image, colour, text and site; and the artists' inclusion of themselves – human presences inviting engagement yet distanced by the photographic image and often partly obscured by a banner or card bearing a text – in carefully posed photographic images.

Hewitt + Jordan now work with Dave Beech as Freee Art Collective. At an exhibition at the International Projects Space in Bourneville, Birmingham in 2007, they exhibited two works stating:

PROTEST IS BEAUTIFUL

made from yellow silk flowers like an elaborate funeral wreath, held by the artists facing the spectator. In one version they stood in a park, in the other against the blue of a photographic backdrop. The open-air version was then mounted above the entrance to an art gallery in a converted shop in East London. Like much of Freee's work, the images involved an elaborate production process of scripting, siting, performance and photography to produce the public image. At first, I read the artificial flowers as implying a degree of irony; the artists refuted this,[87] which I accept. Perhaps, instead, a sense of lament emerges like a wreath for the joyful protest I remember from the 1960s, which will not return. Freee also exhibited the following wall-scale text:

The concept of public space, beloved of lonely myopic
law-abiding right-on gushing morons, can only
imagine the public as a mass of bodies.

The concept of the public realm, preferred by shifty-piss-guzzling
half-witted busy-body nerve-wracked self-serving technocrats,
can only imagine the public as a mass to be administered.
The concept of the public sphere, in the radical tradition of
Critical Theory, imagines the public producing itself
through politicized acts of cultural exchange.[88]

In a book produced from the project *Futurology* in 2004 at the New Art
Gallery, Walsall – in which artists were commissioned to work with local
people and schools to imagine what the Black Country might be like in
2024 – Jordan and Hewitt write, 'Within the new cultural settlement, in
which art is dominated by two massive emerging economic structures,
namely culture-led regeneration and biennale style art fairs, art production
has become a highly visible constituent of the enlarged culture industry of
a global economy.'[89] Freee inserts the collaborative production of art in
such situations, taking arts funding as appropriate, prepared to bite, or at
least shake vigorously, the hand that feeds them by using given settings to
critically challenge the assumptions on which they rely.

In *Futurology*, they categorise art's publics in three ways: reformers,
conservatives and the avant-garde; reformers include 'culture-led
regeneration lobbyists and government agencies' – whom I would put in
context of liberal reformism (Chapter 5) – of whom they say, 'the art that is
provided represents the values of middle-class culture for a working-class
audience'; for conservatives, 'autonomy is a key issue here … autonomy as
isolation …', derived from a Kantian disinterest translated into modernist
value-free art; and on the avant-garde they say, 'artists contribute to the
critique of contemporary society and help shape our visions of a better
future, even though the radical departures of the avant-garde are often
absorbed back into commodity systems and capital'.[90] I might want to
debate the difference between value-free art, autonomy and critical
distance but, leaving that aside, much of what they say echoes arguments
I rehearse in this book on the alignment of urban redevelopment to liberal
reform and neoliberalism, and its context in what Freee pointedly call the
culture industry, a term previously used by Theodor W. Adorno to denote
a mechanism of mass deception.[91]

In 2008, Freee showed a series of billboard posters at the Collective
Gallery, Edinburgh in the project *How To Be Hospitable*. One, depicting
Hewitt, Jordan and Beech holding mugs inscribed, I'M A LOCAL

OUTSIDER, I'M A MIGRANT WORKER and I'M A FOREIGN CITIZEN, plays on ambiguities in the reception of foreign workers. Freee state:

> Responding to the recent wave of Polish immigrant workers in the UK … [we] do not make works that address these issues in a thematic way – Polish experience is not the content of the work – rather [we] hope to trigger debate about the underlying issues of global capitalism that Polish immigration is part of.[92]

See Figure 7.6. The composition cuts off the top half of the male faces in a framing inherited from photography, which lends anonymity; Jordan, however, in the centre, is seen full face and grins inanely. I read this as ambivalent: the grin is submissive, as if for an employer (or gritting teeth at the low wages and vile conditions suffered by many migrant workers); it also remains a smile, a basic mode of human invitation to friendship. Rembrandt counter-posed humanity to capitalism (as Molyneux says, above); across different media and three and a half centuries, I read a glimpse of a similar counter-gesture here, if held in check, distanced and confined by the medium of photography and the device of framing. Perhaps, still, the smile does at least convey a latent, only just glimpsed memory of real hospitality. But Freee's refusal to follow the conventional path of making affirmative images of Polish culture, which would objectify

Figure 7.6   Freee Art Collective, *How to be Hospitable*, Edinburgh, 2008 (photo by permission of the artists)

subjects as subject-matter, is itself a tactic of re-humanisation, set in a world of increasingly brutal labour de-regulation.[93]

Finally, I want to return to revolutionary art after the period of revolutions. Standing in the largest slate quarry in England, at Bayston Hill, Shropshire, Freee hold an orange-red banner saying, in blue letters:

PROTEST DRIVES HISTORY

As the wind blows ferociously (access to the site was limited to a short period on grounds of safety), they stand defiantly. It is bleak, a space of dark, unforgiving geology; metaphorically Freee stand against an almost but not quite overpowering force of history, dark as the rock, as if proclaiming a truth (if it is one) which few would now accept as the political form of mass revolt is encapsulated in history (Figure 7.7).

The photographic image was displayed as a billboard-scale poster in the bar of the Institute of Contemporary Art, London, and on billboards outside. In the privileged space of an art bar in the metropolis, it may have seemed a gesture or a nod to dialectics; or the splash of bright colour as the banner is reflected on the water's dark surface might yet hint of a

Figure 7.7   Freee Art Collective, *Protest Drives History*, 2008, Bayston Hill (photo by permission of the artists)

latent utopian memory, no less contained but also no less real than that of the migrant worker.

Protest Drives History has several possible contexts: the conditions of its production; other work by Freee; and political aesthetics. The former include the dismantling of the post-war welfare state and the seeming futility of mass protests against the Iraq war and student fees, and other single-issue campaigns. In these conditions, when protest is actively restricted, it could appear that, far from driving history, protest is hopeless. But the work is no more ironic than *Protest is Beautiful*. Jordan says of *Protest Drives History*:

> The presentation of the slogan begins as a performance in a deserted private outside space with no passers-by, no audience and no public.... The typically deemed public space of the street is not necessarily so ... making things public operates beyond a spatial placing of an object in the public realm. The way the work is designed tests the notion of primary and secondary audiences, and asks what constitutes private and public.[94]

Billboards are part of the vocabulary of advertising; the red banner is part of the vocabulary of mass insurgency. To carry an orange-red banner in 2008 requires explanation. Part of it is ordinary: the orange-red waterproof material was bought in a Sheffield market for £1 per metre; blue was chosen for the lettering as the complementary to orange. The text, too, is part of a continuing dialectic in Freee's work. The work's third context is the politics of modernism.

Although I doubt that protest *drives* history, this can happen informally in ordinary life and may become extraordinary for a moment in demonstrations and mass protests, not so much as a move to change policy as a consciousness of being present with others in a shift of public feeling (like crossing the bridge as Berger puts it, above) which changes the world. In most cases, the shift is almost imperceptible at the time but moments linger and are transformative long after.

In 2014, Freee reused the banner in Stockholm (where Strindberg's 63rd birthday was celebrated by the workers' parade, cited above),[95] standing with four other participants on the waterfront. The posed photographic image is upside down in this version. The stone paving of the quay is above, the sky is below in a world turned upside down, which is what historian Christopher Hill called the English Revolution of the

1640s.[96] This is a deliberate reference[97] to a revolution which arrived at radical democracy, if for a while. Refusing to give in, the text is the right way up (Figure 7.8).

Figure 7.8   Freee Art Collective, *Protest Drives History*, 2014, Stockholm (photo by permission of the artists)

8

Limits to Culture:
Art after Occupy

In May 2014, on Falgi Tee at the edge of the Old Town in Tallinn, a musician played an old Estonian tune on an accordion. I watched, sitting on the low wall of a public garden above the street. Most people walked by; a few put a coin in the musician's hat and then a tourist began to film him, walking round and round to record from all angles (Figure 8.1). After several minutes, the tourist produced some sheet music from his bag and showed it to the musician, who read it and began to play again. I thought it might be another tune that the tourist wanted to hear, but the musician played the same tune; the tourist pointed to the music, gesturing and singing along. After several minutes, they stopped; as far as I could see the musician asked to keep the music; the tourist agreed, and put a coin or two in the hat. When the tourist had gone, the musician went on playing for a while to the indifference of tourist groups walking from their coaches to the Old Town. Then he packed the accordion into its case, picked up the coins, put on his hat and left. Later, by chance, I met the tourist elsewhere in the city and politely asked him about the encounter. He explained that he was a member of a visiting choir researching traditional Estonian music. The musician played a song the visitor knew but had not heard in vernacular style, and did not have the sheet music (which the visitor did). Both parties gained from the exchange but the musician did not really need the music since he knew the tune by heart. To be given the music in a written form was nice, perhaps, but not essential. All this is incidental except that it illustrates an unplanned encounter between vernacular culture and a version of it formalised and lent the authority of print, which could not have been contrived. Both parties had culture, but of different kinds which they were prepared to exchange. There was no plan, and probably no further outcome. I went on my way, too, for an engagement at the university.

Figure 8.1   Tallinn street musician

Delegated culture

In 1996, Swedish artist Annika Eriksson worked with the Copenhagen Postmen's Orchestra, playing a song by a British pop group; a year later, coincidentally, British artist Jeremy Deller employed the Williams Fairey Brass Band to interpret acid house music in *Acid Brass* (1997). Claire Bishop suggests that, beyond an aesthetic frisson in the merging of two kinds of popular music, the appeal rests on the use of 'real bands' and the acts of working-class collaborators.[1]

Bishop interprets these projects as humorous cases of what she calls delegated performance, a means to signify difference through, 'a metonymic shorthand for politicized identity' where the act of delegation allows 'irony, wit, and distance.'[2] One type of delegated performance is the outsourcing of performance to non-professionals who are asked to act an aspect of their identities, often in the gallery or exhibition.[3] A less witty

form of this, exemplified for Bishop by Spanish artists Santiago Sierra, is
the use of a large number of people to, 'undertake banal or humiliating
tasks for the minimum wage', as in his *250cm Line Tattooed on 6 Paid
People* (1999).[4] The figures stand with their bare backs to the camera,
anonymous and objectified, a tattooed line formally (in a visual sense)
holding them in line. Bishop admits that controversy surrounded the
work, which intentionally reproduces the inequities of the global South
where it was staged, but claims that it does so to draw attention to unjust
economic conditions; and notes that Sierra includes details such as the
use of a recruitment agency in descriptions of the work, to insert it into
economic debate.[5]

A second type of delegated performance involves the hiring of
professional actors or singers, or students, at market rates, to do what they
have been trained in but in a gallery context. For instance, Tino Sehgal's
This Objective of That Objective entails a staged quasi-philosophical debate
among a cast of philosophy students, re-staged in different galleries. When
a spectator enters, she or he can participate but the script is not changed;
if she or he is silent, the actors wilt onto the floor until someone else walks
in.[6] Bishop reads this art of instruction to the performers as evoking the
'invisible theatre' (also called Forum theatre) of Augusto Boal. Bishop
admits, however, that the artists whom she cites do not, 'subscribe to his
political agenda',[7] which I think misses the point that Boal's theatre for
the oppressed, in which the audience *can* change the script, is *primarily*
political. Boal refuses Aristotelian poetics as a repressive form producing
a catharsis which affirms injustice: 'if … we want to stimulate the
spectator … to engage in revolutionary action … we will have to seek
another poetics!'[8] As Audre Lorde said (Chapter 7), the master's tools
will never dismantle the master's house, and the difficulty that delegated
performance raises for me is that it subsumes potentially new ways of
operating in an art-world form of complicity.

Bishop defines a third type of delegated performance in filmed
encounters which resemble reality television but have roots in
documentary and Neorealist cinema (Roberto Rossellini's employment
of non-professional actors, 'to stretch the prevailing boundaries of what
was then considered realism', for example).[9] Bishop concludes that the
three strands are linked by performance and the artist's role in scripting
or directing the action. The question, however, is again whether delegated
performance mimics exploitation in a way that might be banal but, as high
culture in art fairs, loses its critical function.

Bishop cites the exhibition *La Monnaie Vivante* (*Living Currency*) by French curator Pierre Bal-Blanc, staged in Paris (2006), Louvain (2007), London (2008), Warsaw and Berlin (both 2010), in which several delegated performance works were exhibited. In Tate Modern, Tania Bruguera's *Tatlin's Whisper #5* involved two mounted policemen demonstrating techniques of crowd control, circling six dancers holding poses and salivating onto the floor in a work by Annie Vigier and Franck Apertet.[10] Bishop cites an eponymous, 'near impenetrable' book by Pierre Klossowski as source of the exhibition's title, and suggests that the genre is in part a critique of industrialisation, and the triumph of reproduction over pleasure in industrialised society, leading artists to redefine transgression 'by making a dual appeal to the reification of the body ... [and] the embodiment of the object'.[11] Through the function of the audience, 'the artist outsources authenticity and relies on his [sic] performers to supply this more vividly'.[12] I am not convinced that art can offer authenticity (which is pre-linguistic, unmediated, while art is always a mediation), nor that these works would have the same or any evident meaning outside art space and art's institutional validation. Bishop seeks a nuanced understanding of this kind of art, to be fair, and raises issues beyond a plain Marxist idea of reification. Yet when she writes that this art offers, 'an alternative form of knowledge about capitalism's commodi-fication of the individual' in a space where social norms are suspended, and which may be morally troubling,[13] I wonder, again, to what extent it is subsumed in the relentless quest for a competitive edge at art fairs (which may be too cynical).

My difficulty with much delegated-performance art (of which I admit I have almost no direct experience), is that it seems to be captured by, rather than critically revealing, the inequities it reproduces aesthetically. The shock value of banality becomes mere artifice in its mediation as high culture. In response, I advance two passages from Adorno's *Aesthetic Theory*: one on art going beyond banality; the other on the quest for the new, which I read as analogous to the quest for an authenticity in high culture via appropriation (the working class as new natives):

The surplus of reality amounts to its collapse; by striking the subject dead, reality itself becomes deathly; this transaction is the artfulness of all antiart, and in Beckett it is pushed to the point of the manifest annihilation of reality. The more total society becomes, the more completely it contracts to a unanimous system, and all the more do the

artworks in which this experience is sedimented become the other of
this society.... At ground zero, where Beckett's plays unfold like forces
in infinitesimal physics, a second world of images springs forth, both
sad and rich, the concentrate of historical experiences that otherwise,
in their immediacy, fail to articulate the essential: the evisceration
of subject and reality. This shabby, damaged world of images is the
negative imprint of the administered world.[14]

And:

The relation to the new is modelled on a child at the piano searching
for a chord never previously heard. This chord, however, was always
there; the possible combinations are limited and actually everything
that can be played on it is implicitly given in the keyboard. The new
is the longing for the new, not the new itself. That is what everything
new suffers from. What takes itself to be utopia remains the negation of
what exists and is obedient to it.... art must be and wants to be utopia
... yet at the same time art may not be utopia in order not to betray it by
providing semblance and consolation.[15]

Perhaps delegated performance is semblance. I have a similar difficulty
in response to much of what is called participatory or socially engaged
art. Bishop writes of the contrast, or the opposition, between, 'a discourse
of spectacle' (which I take as the kind of work seen at art fairs and in
flagship venues) and, 'a renewed affirmation of collectivity' against liberal
and neoliberal individualism.[16] She continues:

Participatory projects in the social field therefore seem to operate with
a twofold gesture of opposition and amelioration. They work against
dominant market imperatives by diffusing single authorship into
collaborative activities that, in the words of [Grant] Kester, transcend
'the snares of negation and self-interest.' Instead of supplying the
market with commodities, participatory art is perceived to channel art's
symbolic capital towards constructive social change.... this art arguably
forms what avant-garde we have today: artists devising social situations
as a dematerialized, anti-market, politically engaged project to carry on
the avant-garde call to make art a more vital part of life.[17]

This is art's social turn, parallel to the cultural turn in urban policy which this book critiques; and it might be the avant-garde today, notably for me in the work of collectives rather than of individuals. I agree with Bishop when she says that the conscription of culture to the agenda of social inclusion is, 'less about repairing the social bond' than an attempt to turn everyone into, 'self-administering, fully-functioning consumers who do not rely on the welfare state and who can cope with a deregulated, privatised world'.[18] This aggravates my anxiety about art's capture by the market, however angry it seems, and Bishop does argue that the blurring of creativity as art and entrepreneurialism is problematic: 'through the discourse of creativity, the elitist activity of art is democratized, although today this leads to business rather than to Beuys'.[19] I also share Bishop's caution about such art that it aims to go beyond art but not, 'to the point of comparison with comparable projects in the social domain'.[20] This is why I am not persuaded by delegated performance (without going into the aesthetics of specific cases). I suggest, also, that socially engaged and participatory art retains the artist's privileged voice as project director or, in the worst cases, coloniser of the fabled community, just as culturally led urban regeneration affirms the privileged role of property-owning elites. Art, furthermore, which draws attention to exploitation says nothing new to those who are exploited (as said in Chapter 7), while the displacement of the political to a realm of high culture may reduce its ethical force in the context of capital's attempted containment of all aspects of life – drawing on Peter Sloterdijk's argument (Chapter 3).[21] As Boal says, 'For those who make the laws, all is well. But what about those who do not make them? ... they rebel, not wishing to accept the criteria of inequality provided by present reality.'[22] And, as cultural theorist Davide Panagia says, 'Democracies are noisy creatures.... There are no adequate testimonies to this noise.'[23] There are actions which need no representation to those present and which seek no validation by cultural or social institutions. These may be everyday experiences or moments of clarity, or they may be collective manifestations in which another reality *appears*.

Occupy the means of ...

In the winter of 2011, Occupy emerged amid the austerity regimes imposed after the financial services crisis. It refused the criterion by which 1 per cent of the world's people had amassed most of its wealth at the expense of the other 99 per cent. Occupy re-occupied public spaces because they are usually unfenced and because it is easier to negotiate with public authorities than with private-sector owners and private security firms. Occupy was not a formalised movement; like previous anti-austerity protests, it contained divergent publics. Radical anthropologist David Graeber observes that Marxists described anti-austerity protests in Athens as 'real democracy' while anarchists called them 'direct democracy', and that the General Assembly – of which all present are members, as used by the Indignados in Madrid and anti-austerity protesters in Athens – adopted 'direct democracy'.[24] This is coded; real democracy alludes to the really-existing socialism of the ex-East bloc; direct democracy alludes to the experimental processes of determination evolved by the Diggers in the English Revolution of the 1640s, as by the New Diggers in New York and elsewhere in the 1960s, to refuse representation. This is not about authenticity – a form of aesthetic judgement – but simply about being there.

For Graeber, direct action is protest in which the form of the action *itself* is a model of a free society.[25] The means enact new values, and *are* the end, not a sign towards the end. Occupy was, I speculate, also an extension of the call to take over the means of production. This leap of reason derives from Lenin's reading of Hegel; as Esther Leslie says, it is a, 'grasping at historical transfiguration'.[26] Occupy Wall Street occupied a public space and organised free social and health services; as activist Marina Sitrin wrote, 'education is organized, food is cooked and distributed ... legal advice is dispensed ... people's physical and mental health is attended to ... [by] a team of volunteer nurses and psychologists'.[27] Occupy occupied the *site of the state*, which is abandoned under neoliberalism, as well as spaces.

Noam Chomsky argued at Occupy Boston in 2011 that de-industrialisation enabled a rise of worker-owned industries, and, although many efforts failed, this 'spawned other efforts. Now there's a network of worker/community-owned enterprises spreading over the region.'[28] The significance is more than networking; it is the living-out of a new society within the dominant society, demonstrating its possibility. Similarly, the university and factory occupations which took place in France in May 1968 indicated a capacity to enact the revolution.

Culture appeared in May '68 in the protest posters and songs, in spontaneous occupations at the universities in Nanterre and the Sorbonne, and Hornsey School of Art, London.[29] Marcuse wrote, 'the piano with the jazz player stood well between the barricades; the red flag well fitted the statue of the author of *Les Misérables*.'[30] In other words, May '68 produced its own culture. In a related sense, Julia Kristeva argues that the legacy of '68 is a revolution in social attitudes: 'Group sex, hashish, etc., were experienced as a revolt against bourgeois morality and family values ... an unprecedented reordering of family life.'[31]

The composition of the revolutionary movement was disputed: Marcuse saw it as students and a young intelligentsia; Lefebvre pointed out that millions of French workers had joined the general strike.[32] What is not in dispute is that factory occupations in 1968 adopted the tactic of occupation from anti-fascist activism in 1936 as, Kristin Ross explains, 'a mark of the strength and the seriousness of the strike ... a clear departure from tired, artificial forms like meetings and petitions ...' and from demands for higher pay.[33] Perhaps, then, to take over the means of production is to create a Commonwealth. Occupy was accused of lacking a political programme, which ignores that to be present among others in common purpose *is* a revolution and *is* a Commonwealth. Occupy was not an avant-garde, either. Student activist Daniel Cohn-Bendit asserted in conversation with Jean-Paul Sartre that:

> What has happened ... [is] a refutation of the famous theory of the revolutionary vanguard as the force leading a popular movement. At Nanterre and Paris there was simply an objective situation ... [in which the active minority] was more conscious theoretically and better prepared ... able to light the fuse and make the breach. But that is all.[34]

Social critic Henry Giroux writes, in 2012, that real democracy is 'measured by the smoothness in which private troubles can be translated into larger social issues and vice versa', a precondition for which is an educational realm in which time is not instrumentalised but 'made available for individuals to speak, deliberate, learn, engage in critical dialogues, and develop the habits of self- and social reflexivity'.[35] For sociologist John Holloway, 'The opening of cracks is the opening of a world that presents itself as closed. It is the opening of categories that on the surface negate the power of human doing ... to discover at their core the doing that they deny and incarcerate.'[36] This is the leap: 'the doing that we pitch against labour is the struggle to open each moment, to assert our own determination against all pre-determination, against all objective laws of development'.[37] There is no delegation, and cannot be: delegated direct action is nonsensical.

Art after Occupy?

It is not for me to say what artists should do. But there must at least be a question as to what artists can do to open a dialectical space which is conducive to a leap of reason. Cohn-Bendit speaks of an objective situation (above), but after May '68, radical politics migrated to single-issue campaigns and direct action (previously used by the peace movement, and by Gandhi in India). In contrast to direct action, art is indirect, trading in representations even as it breaks the bind of representation in techniques such as montage which use disjunction. In critical cultural theory, the distancing produced in art critically re-presents the gap between the lived reality and freedom (and is easier to state theoretically than in art, as passages above suggest). But how to cross it? I have dismissed delegated performance, and have little more interest in socially engaged art which is too often compromised by ineptitude. I have even less interest in the staging of quasi-social encounters in art spaces of the kind exemplified by, say, Rirkrit Tiravanija's *untitled 1993 (fladlesuppe)*, where a table, two benches, industrial metal shelving and basic cooking equipment were provided to build a sense of community among the artists preparing for the group show *Backstage* in Hamburg. This operated only in the lead-in period, not during the show, producing, Bishop says, a 'greater exclusivity'[38] for an audience able to see only the remnants of the escapade. If art trading in faked encounters cannot enact alternative scenarios, the question does not go away as to what those scenarios are.

Returning to Krzysztof Nawratek's *City as a Political Idea* (Chapter 6), the city as *polis* was a democratic political community but of a relatively small scale, which is weakened to a point of no return in neoliberalism. The city, 'fragments, spatially and socially, losing its urban properties' so that its re-establishment as a real community 'seems to be impossible'.[39] Hence Nawratek looks to a porosity based in sharing and non-commodified exchange, while lack and imperfection are recognised as aspects of the human-urban condition, so that 'space in the city becomes a medium which enables flows to fill holes … its porous structure is constantly being filled and emptied', as flows interfere with its existing structure and, where the structure is weak, remodel it.[40] The re-modelling could be xenophobic, of course, or show some other nasty human attribute. Democracy is messy and conflictual. Yet, political theorist Alessandro Ferrara argues, like Nawratek, that democracy cannot any more be a gathering of the populace together in a public space, moving to representation whereby citizens are only nominal authors of laws, and that it needs to go beyond this through a 'political imagination' which can envisage, 'what new form this founding notion of authorship' assumes in 'post-national ... contexts no longer characterized by the conjunction of one nation, one state apparatus, one economy, one culture and one constitution'.[41] Ferrara means a political not an artistic imagination, but both require leaps of reason beyond pervading self-coercion. I want to pursue this speculatively in two ways: through the material culture of activism presented in a recent exhibition, and the precedent read by curator Gavin Grindon in performative Dada; and through a construct of art as not-politics, from the model of an expanded field advanced in the 1970s by art historian Rosalind Krauss (Chapter 6), and further reflections on the ideas of critical aesthetics developed by Jacques Rancière. Underlying this is a tentative question as to whether art can occupy the vacated site of politics. Occupy enacted social autonomy with no need for art (having its own culture and no need for interpretations of its experiences), and this question is more challenging than the insight that, in a society in which the division of art from everyday life has been collapsed, the category of Art is redundant.

Carnival and activism's material culture

Grindon writes of a Dadaist parade in Berlin in February 1919, a month after the failure of the Spartacist revolt and the murder by far-Right armed gangs of its leaders Rosa Luxemburg and Karl Liebknecht. The parade was accompanied by a brass band wearing frock coats and silk hats: 'Along the streets of grubby tenements, riddled by the machine-gun fire of the Spartacist struggle ... our Dada-carnival was greeted with delight', while a pamphlet, *Every Man His Own Football*, sold out along the way.[42] Grindon reads the parade as a parody, and viable because it was as if below the radar, using tunes played for members of the far-Right Freikorps while following the exact route of Liebknecht's funeral.

Dada parades were integral to the political upheaval of 1918–19: but, 'by engaging with the art forms and relations of production particular to social movements, they lost the historical visibility of official cultural spaces of production' and have disappeared from art's and other histories.[43] Activism still produces things like the Dada pamphlet and the placards, however, and many of them were shown in an exhibition curated by Grindon and Catherine Flood at the Victoria & Albert Museum, London, in 2014.

Disobedient Objects included home-made placards used at demonstrations, badges, posters, leaflets, spoof newspapers and spoof road signs, manuals for making tools for direct action, defaced coins, overprinted banknotes, and artefacts from a history of a culture of radicalism, such as fine china cups bearing Suffragette emblems from 1910. To give three examples randomly picked from the catalogue: a dollar bill is overprinted with a red line in the middle, demarking the share of wealth owned by the richest 400 and the 150 million poorest people; dolls made by women in Chiapas, using pre-Columbian techniques, depict leaders of the Zapatista Army of National Liberation; and a spoof cover for a populist cook book by Delia Smith (who features in bestseller lists) is called *Basic Blockading*.[44] Like the Dada street parades, the acts of insurgent groups tend to fall out of recorded history; one reason for this exhibition was to demonstrate that protest has developed distinct, historically specific material cultures which are not mere representations of those cultures. Grindon and Flood write:

> Exhibitions are moments of collective meaning-making. Bringing these objects and histories together, and presenting them to an audience that never encounters them outside mass media, makes the museum a site for difficult questions and tests its claim to be a public space.... Rather than assuming a straightforward opposition between radical integrity and institutional separation, we attempted a more grounded approach to the re- and de-composition of these always-unfinished objects in relation to the making of movements.[45]

Despite the separation of museums from the streets outside, they can be sites of interruption in an internal institutional revolt. A similar kind of interruption can equally occur outside the museum: for instance, *A User's Guide to Demanding the Impossible* was drafted by Grindon and John Jordan of the Laboratory of Insurrectionary Imagination in a lull between student demonstrations which had included a teach-in at Tate during the presentation of the 2010 Turner Prize. I end this section by quoting two passages:

> Art is useless, so they tell us, as soon as it truly affects the world it loses its status as art.... The strange thing is that those who tell us this are often the same people who put art to the crudest instrumental use – the art market. Maybe what they mean is that art is useless when it's not ultimately used to make a profit. Perhaps it's the same logic as that

which argues that education has no use outside slotting us into the mutilated world of work and consumption.[46]

And:

To dismantle and reinvent institutions or systems we have to start at the roots, with the culture that supports them. Culture is the material substratum of politics, the muddy foundations upon which it is built, but these foundations can't be changed in the same way that you can undo a law – they are transformed by infiltrating them at the molecular level, through the fault lines, pores and gaps, burrowing away like an old mole opening up millions of potential north-west passages. Luckily for you, that's where you are already.[47]

Expanding the expanded field

An obstacle to rethinking art is the art world's capacity to absorb departures from its norms, while the institutional revolt has at best to coexist with validation by the structures it refuses. Outside the gallery, participation can be a cosmetic solution to infrastructure failures. I do not wish to denigrate the efforts of artists working for social justice[48] but this art can become as much encapsulated in the art world as any other kind. To go further may require a departure from art altogether; or it may be viable to expand the fields of both art and politics. For example, the London-based group Platform sees itself in terms of art, activism, education and research, and has been called a human rights group;[49] founder-member James Marriott sees himself as 'working in the city'[50] on the global oil industry's disregard for human rights and environmental care.[51] Platform uses guided walks in London's financial district followed by discussion among a small, diverse group of participants; they also distribute spoof newspapers to unidentified publics, such as *London Late*, issued during the 2012 Olympics and headlined: 'The Big Money Games Have Begun'.[52] Inside stories include awards for brand policing, Olympic sweatshop chic and an item on Liberate Tate's attempt to donate a wind turbine blade to Tate Modern.[53]

Art activism begins to collapse the divide between art and everyday life, if paradoxically, as the critical distancing inherent in the autonomy claimed for modernism collides with street-level interactions and contested power relations. Without an alternative imaginary, however, there is little prospect of articulating alternative scenarios, which is perhaps where a creative-critical practice contributes to change. Neither artists nor writers (nor cultural theorists) have a monopoly on alternative imaginaries, which are produced elsewhere, as in protest from anti-roads to anti-fracking camps (Chapter 7). But I wonder to what extent both activist cultures and traditional (high) culture offer glimpses of another world which is already articulated in what Walter Benjamin saw as the phantasmagoric world of the arcades.[54]

Ernst Bloch, who spent days in conversation with Benjamin in Paris in the 1920s, writes of a utopian memory latent in everyone's consciousness which is aroused by images which, in dark times, go beyond the conditions of their production. I have to compress the argument, but I think that Bloch projected a redemptive light which shines as if back from the end of history (which, for Bloch, is a trajectory the objectively given end of which is freedom). He ends *The Principle of Hope*: 'in real democracy, there arises in the world something which shines into the childhood of all and in which no one has yet been: homeland'.[55] For Herbert Marcuse the task is to reveal the irrationality inherent in the dominant reality, to which beauty is the radical other. The plays of Brecht and Greek tragedy are interruptions: 'a work of art can be called revolutionary if … it represents … the prevailing unfreedom and the rebelling forces, thus breaking through the mystified (and petrified) social reality, opening the horizon of change (liberation)'.[56] And Rancière offers a related argument that, 'the identification between art, autonomy, and modernity collapsed in the last decade of the twentieth century', as new forms of social life and commodity culture prevented the maintenance of the boundaries between art and commodity, or between high and low culture.[57] The politics of aesthetic autonomy divides into 'two poles of aesthetics … two communities of sense'.[58] Aesthetics is historically aligned to the equality proclaimed in the French Revolution, ending the hierarchy of subject-matters in art, and erasing the frontier between art and non-art; and Kantian disinterest offers freedom from the criterion of ordinary visual perception. The latter disconnects the equality inherent in the former, to restage, Rancière says, the issue of communities of sense as a new opposition between communities of connection and disconnection.[59] On one side is alienated life; on the other is a 'homogeneous appearance of aestheticized life and commodity culture' resisted by 'the community framed by the autonomy of aesthetic experience, by its heterogeneity to all other forms of experience'.[60] Hence, the 'political act of art is to save the heterogeneous sensible ... [its] power of emancipation'.[61]

In the nineteenth century – Rancière cites Zola – the sense of radical otherness was produced by 'border crossings' between cultural categories.[62] Hence:

> Making fictions does not mean telling stories. It means undoing and rearticulating the connections between signs and images, images and times, or signs and space that frame the existing sense of reality. Fiction invents new communities of sense ... new trajectories between what can be seen, what can be said, and what can be done.... It is no coincidence that some of the most interesting artworks today engage with matters of territories and borders. What could be the ultimate paradox of the politics of aesthetics is that perhaps by inventing new forms of aesthetic distance or indifference, art today can help frame, against the consensus, new political communities of sense. Art cannot merely occupy the space left by the weakening of political conflict. It has to reshape it, at the risk of testing the limits of its own politics.[63]

Like Adorno and Marcuse, Rancière advances and modifies concepts, constructing a creative tension in which the question remains open. A basic form of this critical tactic is the relation of art and the social: art's aesthetic dimension disables its social agency; its social agency, as propaganda, disables its aesthetic quality. For Marcuse, art draws away from the reality of the My Lai massacre in the Vietnam war because it cannot, inherently, represent suffering 'without subjecting it to aesthetic form, to the mitigating catharsis, to enjoyment. Art is inexorably infested with this guilt.'[64] There is no exit from the difficulty.

Art might still test its limits by reshaping the political: *dissensus* as refusal of an affirmative *consensus*; but, again, artists have no monopoly; the literature of citizen or civic participation is more developed than that of art, and I cite the following:

> Viewing participation as a contingent, contested process highlights the micropolitics of encounters in participatory arenas.... [Studies] situate this micropolitics in sites with very different histories of state–citizen interaction, configurations of political institutions, and political cultures. From post-conflict Angola to New Labour's Britain, from rural Bangladesh to urban Brazil ... [they] range across contexts

with distinctively different histories and cultures. While persistent inequalities and forms of embedded exclusion exist in all, their dimensions and dynamics differ, as do notions of citizenship, and the degree and kinds of social mobilisation and state-supported efforts to redress systemic discrimination, whether on the basis of gender, race, caste or class.[65]

Outside

Outside institutions and academies, protest and indignation at the destruction of the common wealth continue, localised and small scale, featured in the global media if celebrities appear but mainly circulated via social media. Indignation is seen in fly-posting (Figure 8.2) and what I might call street-writing to differentiate it from street-art (Figure 8.3). This lacks the coherence of a revolutionary manifesto, but there will be no more revolutions in which crowds carry red banners and sing the 'Internationale'. In Statue Park outside Budapest, in a garden for Soviet-era monuments surrounded by electricity pylons, the statues silently replay sentiments once heartfelt but which declined into slogans. Protest happens in the indignation of the vacuum.

I end at Stokes Croft, a district near the centre of Bristol in south-west England. The People's Republic of Stokes Croft was set up as a community

Figure 8.2   Fly-posting, George W. Bush, terrorist, Lisbon

Figure 8.3   Street-writing, Jail the Bankers, Coimbra

interest company in 2007 to coordinate artists and volunteers in mural production and the decoration of shop-fronts and façades, in street-art styles. In 2010, it produced a spoof sign announcing Stokes Croft as winner of the Britain in Bloom competition in 2012, 2013 and 2015; and that it was twinned with the arts districts of St Ives, Montmartre and Wan Chai in Hong Kong.[66] In press reports, Stokes Croft was described as an arts district, but had avoided gentrification.

Then the cultural turn turned nasty. The area gained media notice when a supermarket opened after sustained objections from local people and small traders, and was trashed in a late-night civil disturbance. In the planning process, Stokes Croft's 'alternative culture' was said to be the antithesis of supermarket values: 'it has built its identity on being nonconformist, being all about independence, all about creativity'.[67] Then it became known that Tesco was the new owner of the site; objectors sent letters to the council, and organised demonstrations. A squat occupied a building on the main road, and a mural (which remains, in 2014) asked people to boycott Tesco (Figure 8.4). On 21 April 2011, a small demonstration was met by police who also attempted to clear the squat, leading to a presence of 160 officers and a violent confrontation. Tesco's windows were marked Closing Down Sale in red, and broken. Banksy lost

Figure 8.4   Opposition to Tesco, Stokes Croft, Bristol

no time in capitalising on the event's media profile and issued a print of a Tesco Molotov cocktail. Tesco reopened three weeks later.

Geographers Michael Buser, Carlo Bonura, Maria Fannin and Kate Boyer read Stokes Croft as visually 'carnivalesque', quoting a local MP's description of the demonstration: 'a typical Stokes Croft atmosphere. There was someone playing a saxophone on a bus shelter ... people walking around with lampshades on their heads.'[68] This sounds like Marcuse's description of Paris in May '68 (above) but it isn't. The aim in Stokes Croft was not to change the regime or the world but to stop Tesco. This can be compared to the acts of militant farmers in the south of France who resisted fast food outlets in 1999[69] as a localised resistance to globalisation, or, if the cultural turn still has currency, the failure to stop Tesco may be a prelude to the turning of an arts district that turned nasty into the next property market discovery.

Geographer Erik Swyngedouw argues that, 'emblematic projects' such as the Guggenheim in Bilbao or Abu Dhabi's Masdar eco-city indicate that cities adapt their built environments in a post-political consensus which eliminates any 'space of disagreement'.[70] A visual cacophony in Barcelona, mixing political and cultural references, expresses fracture not dissensus (Figure 8.5).

I remember the accordion player in Tallinn: vernacular culture needs no artistic intervention. An art of dissensus would be different: provoking, pointing, irritating, colliding with capital's regime of relentless consumerism; yet there was a moment of joy in the accordionist's tune, to which I cling.

Figure 8.5   Fly-posting, Plaça dels Angels, Barcelona

Notes

Introduction

1. Illich, I., *De-schooling Society*, New York, Harper Row, 1970.
2. Freire, P., *Pedagogy of the Oppressed*, Harmondsworth, Penguin, 1972.
3. Illich, *Limits to Medicine – Medical Nemesis: The Expropriation of Health*, London, Marion Boyars, 1976, p. 130.
4. Ibid., p. 206.
5. Marcuse, H., 'Liberation from the Affluent Society', in Cooper, D. (ed.), *The Dialectics of Liberation*, Harmondsworth, Penguin, 1968, pp. 175–92.
6. Illich, *Limits to Medicine*, pp. 135–36.
7. Sloterdijk, P., *In the World Interior of Capital*, Cambridge, Polity, 2013, p. 176 (first published as *Im Weltinneraum des Kapital*, Frankfurt, Suhrkamp, 2005).

Chapter 1

1. Dunham-Jones, E., 'Irrational Exuberance: Rem Koolhaas and the 1990s', in Deamer, P. (ed.), *Architecture and Capitalism, 1845 to the Present*, London, Routledge, 2014, p. 161.
2. Hatherley, O., *Guide to the New Ruins of Great Britain*, London, Verso, 2010, pp. 150–51.
3. Ibid., p. 155.
4. Ibid., p. 156.
5. Crary. J., 24/7, London, Verso, 2013, p. 11.
6. Žižek, S., *Living in the End Times*, London, Verso, 2011.
7. Marcuse, H., 'Society as a Work of Art', in Kellner, D. (ed.), *Art and Liberation*, London, Routledge, 2007, pp. 123–29; see also Toscano, A., 'Destructive Creation, or the Communism of the Senses', in Watson, G., van Noord, G. and Everall, G. (eds), *Make Everything New: A Project on Communism*, London, Bookworks, 2006, pp. 119–28.
8. Edgar, A. and Sedgwick, P., 'Adorno, Oakeshott and the Voice of Poetry', in Adam, B. and Allan, S. (eds), *Theorizing Culture: An Interdisciplinary Critique after Postmodernism*, London, UCL Press, 1995, p. 106.
9. Lefebvre, H., 'The Theory of Moments', in *Critique of Everyday Life: II, Foundations for a Sociology of the Everyday* (2nd edn), trans. Moore, J., London, Verso, 2008, pp. 340–58 (first published as *Critique de la vie quotidienne II: Fondements d'une sociologie de la quotidienneté*, Paris, L'Arche, 1961).

10. Clark, T.J., *Farewell to an Idea: Episodes from a History of Modernism*, New Haven, CT, Yale University Press, 1999, p. 8.

11. Albrow, M., *The Global Age*, Stanford, CA, Stanford University Press, 1996, pp. 121–22.

12. Bauman, Z., *Globalization: The Human Consequences*, Cambridge, Polity, 1998, pp. 65–66.

13. Sloterdijk, P., *In the World Interior of Capital*, trans. Hoban, W., Cambridge, Polity, 2013, p. 177 (first published as *Im Weltinneraum des Kapitals*, Frankfurt, Suhrkamp, 2005).

14. Ridgeway, J., *It's All for Sale: The Control of Global Resources*, Durham, NC, Duke University Press, 2004, p. 167.

15. Klein, N., *The Shock Doctrine*, London, Penguin, 2007, p. 299.

16. Hatherley, *Guide to the New Ruins*, p. 238.

17. Widgery, D., *Some Lives! A G.P.'s East End*, London, Sinclair-Stevenson, 1991, p. 41, cited in Ambrose, P., *Urban Process and Power*, London, Routledge, 1994, p. 182.

18. Sassen, S., *Cities in a World Economy*, Thousand Oaks, CA, Pine Forge, 2006.

19. Widgery, *Some Lives!*, p. 164, cited in Ambrose, *Urban Process and Power*, p. 184.

20. Bauman, *Globalization*, p. 23.

21. Hall, P., *Cities of Tomorrow* (updated edn), Oxford, Blackwell, 1996, p. 422.

22. Bauman, *Globalization*, p. 51.

23. Sheller, M., 'Demobilizing and Remobilizing the Caribbean Paradise', in Sheller, M. and Urry, J. (eds), *Tourism Mobilities: Places to Play, Places in Play*, London, Routledge, 1994, pp. 13–21.

24. Bloch, E., *The Principle of Hope*, Cambridge, MA, MIT, 1959, p. 813 (first published as *Das Prinzip Hoffnung*, Frankfurt, Suhrkamp, 1959).

25. Bird, J., 'Dystopia on the Thames', in Bird, J., Curtis, B., Putnam, T., Robertson, G. and Tickner, L. (eds), *Mapping the Futures: Local Cultures, Global Change*, London, Routledge, 1993, p. 124.

26. Ibid., p. 126.

27. See also Dunn, P. and Leeson, L., 'The Art of Change in Docklands', in Bird et al., *Mapping the Futures*, pp. 136–49.

28. Bird, 'Dystopia on the Thames', p. 126.

29. Miles, S., *Spaces for Consumption*, London, Sage, 2010, p. 27.

30. Augé, M., *Non-Places: Introduction to an Anthropology of Super-modernity*, London, Verso, 1995.

31. Miles, S., *Spaces for Consumption*, p. 28.

32. Chakrabortty, A., 'The Shard is the Perfect Metaphor for modern London', *The Guardian*, G2, p. 5, 26 October 2012.

33. Ibid.

34. Ibid.

35. Buck-Morss, S., 'Radical Cosmopolitanism', *Third Text*, 23, 5, p. 548, 2009.

36. See: www.arca.co.uk/projects/tate-liverpool (accessed 11 May 2014).

37. Gilmore, A., 'Popular Music, Urban Regeneration and Cultural Quarters: The Case of the Rope Walks, Liverpool', in Bell, D. and Jayne, M. (eds), *City of Quarters: Urban Villages in the Contemporary City*, Aldershot, Ashgate, 2004, p. 110.

38. Evans, G., 'Cultural Industry Quarters: From Pre-Industrial to Post-Industrial Production', in Bell and Jayne, *City of Quarters*, p. 72.

39. Zukin, S., *Loft-living: Culture and Capital in Urban Change*, New Brunswick, NJ, Rutgers University Press, 1989.

40. Zukin, S., *Naked City: The Death and Life of Authentic Urban Places*, Oxford, Oxford University Press, 2010, pp. 238–39.

41. Sadler, S., 'Spectacular Failure: The Architecture of Late Capitalism at the Millennium Dome', in Deamer, *Architecture and Capitalism*, p. 198.

42. See: www.tate.org.uk/about/who-we-are/history (accessed 11 May 2014).

43. Leslie, E., 'Tate Modern: A Year of Sweet Success', *Radical Philosophy*, 109, p. 2, 2000.

44. Ibid., p. 3.

45. Miles, M., *Eco-Aesthetics: Art, Literature and Architecture in a Period of Climate Change*, London, Bloomsbury, 2014, pp. 158–64.

46. Degen, M.M. and Garcia, M., 'The Transformation of the Barcelona Model: An Analysis of Culture, Urban Regeneration and Governance', *International Journal of Urban and Regional Research*, 36, 5, p. 1022, 2012, citing Evans, G., 'Measure for Measure: Evaluating the Evidence of Culture's Contribution to Regeneration', *Urban Studies*, 42, 5/6, p. 968, 2005.

47. Degen and Garcia, 'The Transformation of the Barcelona Model', p. 1024.

48. Cerdá, I., 'Teoria de la viabilidad urbana y reforma de la de Madrid', para. 1149 [1861], in Soria y Puig, A. (ed.), *Cerdá: The Five Bases of the General Theory of Urbanization*, Madrid, Electa, 1999, p. 369.

49. Dodd, D., 'Barcelona, the Making of a Cultural City', in Dodd, D. and van Hemel, A. (eds), *Planning Cultural Tourism in Europe: A Presentation of Theories and Cases*, Amsterdam, Boeckman Stichting, 1999, pp. 57–58.

50. See: www.lonelyplanet.com/spain/barcelona (accessed 11 May 2014).

51. *Barcelona Nous Projectes, Octubre 1999*, Barcelona, Ajuntament de Barcelona, 1999, p. 16.

52. Degen and Garcia, 'The Transformation of the Barcelona Model', p. 1033.

53. Miles, S., *Spaces for Consumption*, p. 9, citing Pryce, W., *Big Shed*, London, Thames & Hudson, 2007, p. 218.

54. Pryce, *Big Shed*, p. 221.

55. Miles, S., *Spaces for Consumption*, p. 93.

56. National Statistics Institute (INE), and Basque Statistics Office (EUSTAT), cited in Sainz, M.A., '(Re)building an Image for a City: Is a Landmark Enough? Bilbao and Guggenheim Museum, 10 Years Together', *Journal of Applied Social Psychology*, 42, 1, p. 106, 2012.

57. González, J.M., 'Bilbao: Culture, Citizenship and Quality of Life', in Bianchini. F. and Parkinson, M. (eds), *Cultural Policy and Urban Regeneration: The West European Experience*, Manchester, Manchester University Press, 1993, p. 85.

58. Sainz, '(Re)building an Image for a City', p. 116.

59. Sudjic, D., *The Edifice Complex*, London, Allen Lane, 2005, p. 278.

60. Fraser, M. and Kerr, J., 'Beyond the Empire of the Signs', in Borden I. and Rendell, J. (eds), *Intersections: Architectural Histories and Critical Theories*, London, Routledge, 2000, p. 139.

61. Ibid., p. 141, citing Fernandez-Galiano, L., 'Bilbao Song', in *ANY 21: How the Critic Sees*, New York, Anyone Corporation, 1997, p. 18.

62. Cited in 'Finns Say No to Guggenheim Plan', *The Guardian*, 3 May 2012, p. 20 (Reuters report).

63. See: www.designguggenheimhelsinki.org (accessed 4 September 2014).

64. Tremlett, G., 'Spain Can't Afford the Other Guggenheim', *The Guardian*, 4 October 2011, p. 17.

Chapter 2

1. Atwood, M., *Cat's Eye*, London, Bloomsbury, 1989.

2. Ibid., p. 8.

3. Ibid., p. 14.

4. Ibid., p. 42.

5. Ibid., p. 43.

6. Ibid., p. 85.

7. Ibid.

8. There are varied interpretations from the Hebrew; proverbially, 'The writing is on the wall' means that someone's days are numbered; see also Rembrandt's painting *The Feast of Belshazzar* (1635, London, National Gallery).

9. Atwood, *Cat's Eye*, p. 225.

10. Ibid., p. 226.

11. Ley, D., 'Artists, Aestheticization and the Field of Gentrification', *Urban Studies*, 40, 12, 2003, p. 2534.

12. Cited in ibid., p. 2534.

13. Ibid., p. 2535.

14. Klemek, C., *The Transatlantic Collapse of Urban Renewal: Postwar urbanism from New York to Berlin*, Chicago, University of Chicago Press, 2012, p. 171.

15. Becker, H., *Art Worlds*, Berkeley, CA, University of California Press, 1982, p. 306.

16. Sennett, R., *The Corrosion of Character: The Personal Consequences of Work in the New Capitalism*, New York, Norton, 1998, p. 147.

17. Benjamin, W., 'Theses on the Philosophy of History, VIII', in *Illuminations*, London, Fontana, 1973, p. 259.

18. Gottdiener, M., *The Social Production of Urban Space*, Austin, TX, University of Texas Press, 1985, p. 28.

19. Park, R.E., Burgess, E.W. and McKenzie, R.D. (eds), *The City*, Chicago, University of Chicago Press, 1925.

20. Ibid., p. 9, cited in Hall, P., *Cities of Tomorrow* (updated edn), Oxford, Blackwell, 1996, p. 367.

21. Ibid., p. 367.

22. Park et al., *The City*, p. 22, cited in ibid., p. 367.

23. Hall, *Cities of Tomorrow*, p. 372.

24. Ibid., p. 371.

25. Florida, R., *The Rise of the Creative Class*, New York, Basic Books, 2002, p. 4.

26. Ibid.

27. Ibid., pp. 4–5

28. Wilson, E., *Bohemians: The Glorious Outcasts*, London, I.B. Tauris, 2003, p. 231.

29. Ibid.

30. McGuigan, J., *Cool Capitalism*, London, Pluto, 2009, p. 49.

31. Ibid.

32. Florida, *The Rise of the Creative Class*, p. 113.

33. Ibid.

34. Standing, G., *The Precariat: The New Dangerous Class*, London, Bloomsbury, 2011, p. 15.

35. Ibid., p. 33.

36. Florida, *The Rise of the Creative Class*, p. 115.

37. Ibid.

38. Bauman, Z., *Globalization: The Human Consequences*, Cambridge, Polity, 1998, p. 85.

39. McRobbie, A., 'Clubs to Companies: Notes on the Decline of Political Culture in Speeded Up Creative Worlds', *Cultural Studies*, 16, 4, p. 522, 2002.

40. Ibid.

41. Ibid.

42. Ibid., p. 523.

43. Hetherington, K., *Capitalism's Eye: Cultural Spaces of the Commodity*, London, Routledge, 2002, p. 177.

44. Ibid.

45. Ibid., p. 179.

46. Zukin, S., *Naked City: The Death and Life of Authentic Urban Places*, Oxford, Oxford University Press, 2010, p. 231.

47. Scott, A.J., *The Cultural Economy of Cities*, London, Sage, 2000, p. 209.

48. Florida, *The Rise of the Creative Class*, p. 74.

49. Robins, K., 'Prisoners of the City: Whatever Could a Postmodern City Be?', in Carter, C., Donald, J. and Squires, J. (eds), *Space and Place: Theories, Identity and Location*, London, Lawrence & Wishart, 1993, pp. 321–23, cited by McGuigan, J., *Culture and the Public Sphere*, London, Routledge, 1996, cited in Miles, S., *Spaces for Consumption*, London, Sage, 2010, p. 44.

50. Zukin, S., *The Cultures of Cities*, Oxford, Blackwell, 1995, pp. 7–8.

51. Ibid., p. 1.

52. Ibid., p. 23.

53. Harris, A., 'Financial Artscapes: Damien Hirst and the City of London', *Cities*, 33, p. 33, 2013.

54. Miller, T., 'From Creative to Cultural Industries', *Cultural Studies*, 23, 1, p. 93, 2008.

55. Zukin, *The Cultures of Cities*, p. 22.

56. Ibid., p. 118.

57. McCracken, G., *Culture and Consumption*, Bloomington, IN, Indiana University Press, 2005, p. 143.

58. Florida, *The Rise of the Creative Class*, p. 166.

59. Miles, S., *Spaces for Consumption*, p. 58.

60. Ibid.

61. Toulmin, S., *Cosmopolis: The Hidden Agenda of Modernity*, Chicago, University of Chicago Press, 1990, p. 104.

62. Duncan, C., *Civilizing Rituals: Inside Public Art Museums*, London, Routledge, 1995, pp. 102–32.

63. Grunenberg, C., 'The Politics of Representation: The Museum of Modern Art, New York', in Pointon, M. (ed.), *Art Apart: Art Institutions and Ideology across England and North America*, Manchester, Manchester University Press, 1993, p. 197.

64. O'Connor, J., 'Popular Culture, Cultural Intermediaries and Urban Regeneration', in Hall, T. and Hubbard, P. (eds), *The Entrepreneurial City*, Chichester, Wiley, 1998, p. 231.

65. Wynne, D. and O'Connor, J. (eds), *From the Margins to the Centre: Cultural Production and Consumption in the Post-Industrial City*, Aldershot, Ashgate, 1996.

66. Glass, R., 'Introduction: Aspects of Change', in Centre for Urban Studies (ed.), *London: Aspects of Change*, London, MacGibbon & Kee, 1964.

67. Lees, L., 'A Reappraisal of Gentrification: Towards a Geography of Gentrification', in Lees, L., Slater, T. and Wyly, E. (eds), *The Gentrification Reader*, London, Routledge, 2010, p. 387.

68. Smith, N., *The New Urban Frontier: Gentrification and the Revanchist City*, London, Routledge, 1996 and *Uneven Development: Nature, Capital and the Production of Space*, Oxford, Blackwell, 1984.

69. McCall, B., 'Top Brokers Spot the Hot New Neighbourhoods', *New Yorker*, 6 December 2004, p. 128; reproduced in Lees et al., *Gentrification*, pp. 40–41.

70. Ibid., p. 41.
71. Ibid., pp. 50–68; Smith, N., 'Toward a Theory of Gentrification: A Back-to-the-city Movement by Capital, not People', *Journal of the American Planning Association*, 45, 4, pp. 538–48.
72. Short, J.R., 'Yuppies, Yuffies and the New Urban Order', *Transactions of the Institute of British Geographers*, 14, 2, pp. 173–88, 1989.
73. Bell, D., *The Coming of Post-Industrial Society: A Venture in Social Forecasting*, New York, Basic Books, 1973, cited in Lees et al., *Gentrification*, p. 91. For Ley see note 11.
74. Lees et al., *Gentrification*, p. 92, citing Ley, D., *The New Middle Class and the Remaking of the Central City*, Oxford, Oxford University Press, 1996, p. 15.
75. Lees et al., *Gentrification*, pp. 99–100, citing Rose, D., 'A Feminist Perspective of Employment Restructuring and Gentrification: The Case of Montreal', in Wolch, J. and Dear, M. (eds), *The Power of Geography: How Territory Shapes Social Life*, Boston, MA, Unwin Hyman, 1989, pp. 118–38.
76. Florida, *The Rise of the Creative Class*, p. 256, cited in Lees et al., *Gentrification*, p. 108.
77. Lees et al., *Gentrification*, p. 107.
78. Peck, J., 'Struggling with the Creative Class', *International Journal of Urban and Regional Research*, 29, 4, pp. 744–45, cited in Lees et al., *Gentrification*, p. 107.
79. Degen, M.M., *Sensing Cities: Regenerating Public Life in Barcelona and Manchester*, London, Routledge, 2008, p. 110.
80. Ibid., citing 'D, El Raval councillor'.
81. Ibid., citing 'D, El Raval councillor'.
82. Ibid., p. 110.
83. Ibid., p. 111, citing 'planner L'.
84. Ibid., p. 112, citing 'spokesperson E'.
85. Ibid., p. 112, citing 'planner L'.
86. Ibid., p. 112.
87. Harris, A. and Moreno, L., *Creative City Limits: Urban Cultural Economy in a New Era of Austerity*, London, Urban Laboratory, University College London, 2011, pp. 3–4.
88. Rushton, R., 'Fashion Feature', *i-D*, February 2001, n.p., cited in McRobbie, A., 'Clubs to Companies: Notes on the Decline of Political Culture in Speeded Up Creative Worlds', *Cultural Studies*, 16, 4, p. 525, 2002.
89. Lees et al., *Gentrification*, pp. 99–100 (see note 75).
90. Jay, M., *Adorno*, Cambridge, MA, Harvard University Press, 1984, pp. 38–40.
91. Leslie, E., 'Tate Modern: A Year of Sweet Success', *Radical Philosophy*, 109, p. 3, 2001.
92. Campkin, B., *Remaking London: Decline and Regeneration in Urban Culture*, London, I.B. Tauris, 2013, p. 135.
93. Ibid., p. 133.

94. Ibid., p. 134.
95. Ibid., p. 138.
96. Ibid., p. 142.

Chapter 3

1. Judt, T., *Postwar: A History of Europe Since 1945*, London, Pimlico, 2007, p. 163.
2. Jones, S., 'A War-weary Nation in an Age of Austerity – Must Be Time for a New Festival of Britain', *The Guardian*, 22 April 2011, p. 3.
3. Kelly, J., in Southbank Centre press release, 7 September 2011, p. 2.
4. Ibid.
5. Jones, 'A War-weary Nation', p. 3.
6. See: http://tomlynham.wordpress.com/2012/11/01/southbank-2011 (accessed 7 July 2014).
7. Ibid.
8. Seth-Smith, N., www.opendemocracy.net/ourkingdom/niki-seth-smith/festival-of-britain-2011 (accessed 7 July 2014).
9. Sandercock, L., 'Cosmopolitan Urbanism: A Love Song to Our Mongrel Cities', in Binnie, J., Holloway, S., Millington, S. and Young, C. (eds), *Cosmopolitan Urbanism*, London, Routledge, 2006, p. 47.
10. Ibid., p. 48.
11. Kynaston, D., *Austerity Britain 1945–51*, London, Bloomsbury, 2007, p. 509.
12. Jacobson, D., quoted in Kynaston, *Austerity Britain*, p. 509 (no source given).
13. Langford, G., quoted in Kynaston, *Austerity Britain*, p. 592 (no source given).
14. Quoted in Kynaston, *Austerity Britain*, p. 253 from Mass Observation (no source given).
15. Judt, *Postwar*, p. 162.
16. Ibid., p. 77.
17. Turner, B., *Beacon for Change: How the Festival of Britain Shaped the Modern Age*, London, Aurum, 2011, p. 8.
18. Ibid., p. 11, citing Greenhalgh, P., *Ephemeral Vistas*, Manchester, Manchester University Press, 1998 (no page reference given).
19. Turner, *Beacon for Change*, p. 4.
20. Barry, G. (unpublished papers), in Turner, *Beacon for Change*, p. 151.
21. Ibid., p. 152.
22. Turner, *Beacon for Change*, p. 117.
23. Ibid., p. 125.
24. Orwell, G., 'The Lion and the Unicorn: Socialism and the English Genius', in Davison, P. (ed.), *A Patriot After All, 1940–1944*, London, Secker & Warburg, 2002, p. 409.
25. Turner, *Beacon for Change*, p. 129.

26. Mass Observation, *Puzzled People: A Study in Popular Attitudes to Religion, Ethics, Progress and Politics*, London, Victor Gollancz, 1947, p. 128.

27. Ibid., p. 129.

28. Ibid., p. 131.

29. Quoted in Taylor, B., *Art for the Nation: Exhibitions and the London Public 1747–2001*, New Brunswick, NJ, Rutgers University Press, 1999, p. 173; see also p. 276, n. 20: Taylor notes that Bevin's address was reported in the *Daily Telegraph*, 11 April 1946 (no page stated), but he was unable to locate the text.

30. Taylor, *Art for the Nation*, p. 171 fig. 77.

31. Charter of Incorporation, 9 August 1946, quoted in Taylor, *Art for the Nation*, p. 175.

32. Read, H., *To Hell with Culture*, London, Kegan Paul, Trench & Trubner, 1941, p. 25.

33. Ibid.

34. Ibid., p. 22.

35. Ibid., p. 46.

36. Ibid., p. 52.

37. Ibid., p. 57.

38. Read, H., *Education through Art*, London, Routledge, 1943.

39. Ibid., p. 141, cited in Taylor, *Art for the Nation*, p. 173.

40. Keynes, J.M., 'The Arts Council: Its Policy and Hopes', *The Listener*, 12 July 1945, pp. 31–32, cited in Taylor, *Art for the Nation*, p. 175.

41. Williams, R., 'The Arts Council', *Political Quarterly*, Spring 1979, p. 166, cited in Taylor, *Art for the Nation*, p. 176.

42. Willett, J., *Art in a City*, London, Methuen, 1967, pp. 203–04.

43. Ibid., p. 204.

44. Pearson, N., *The State and the Visual Arts*, Milton Keynes, Open University Press, 1982, p. 63.

45. McGuigan, J., 'The Social Construction of a Cultural Disaster: New Labour's Millennium Experience', *Cultural Studies*, 17, 5, p. 670, citing Toynbee, P., 'I Paid Up, Queued Up, and Now I'm Thoroughly Fed Up', *The Guardian*, 5 January 2000, p. 20; 'The £758 Million Disaster Zone', *Daily Mail*, 6 January 2000, pp. 6–7.

46. Hatherley, O., *A Guide to the New Ruins of Great Britain*, London, Verso, 2010, p. 295.

47. McGuigan, 'The Social Construction of a Cultural Disaster', p. 672, citing Blair, T., 'Why the Dome Is Good for Britain', speech, Royal Festival Hall, 24 February, 1998, p. 3.

48. Quoted in Nicholson, A., *Regeneration – The Story of the Millennium Dome*, London, HarperCollins, 1999, p. 2, cited in McGuigan, 'The Social Construction of a Cultural Disaster', p. 673.

49. Matthews, N.M., *Paul Gauguin: An Erotic Life*, New Haven, CT, Yale University Press, 2001, p. 262.

50. Sadler, S., 'Spectacular Failure: The Architecture of Late Capitalism at the Millennium Dome', in Deamer, P. (ed.), *Architecture and Capitalism, 1845 to the Present*, London, Routledge, 2014, p. 191.

51. Ibid.

52. Ibid., p. 194.

53. Ibid., pp. 195–96.

54. Sloterdijk, P., *In the Interior World of Capital*, trans. Hoban, W., Cambridge, Polity, 2013 (first published as *Im weltinnenraum des Kapitals*, Frankfurt, Suhrkamp, 2005).

55. Chernyshevsky, N., *What is To Be Done?* [1863], London, Virago, 1982.

56. Sloterdijk, *In the Interior World of Capital*, p. 170.

57. Ibid., pp. 170–71.

58. Ibid., p. 173; see Benjamin, W., *The Arcades Project*, trans. Eiland, H. and McLaughlin, K., Cambridge, MA, Harvard University Press, 1999.

59. Sloterdijk, *In the Interior World of Capital*, p. 176.

60. Marcuse, H., *One-Dimensional Man*, Boston, Beacon Press, 1964.

61. Lodziak, C., *The Myth of Consumerism*, London, Pluto, 2002.

62. Ibid., p. 68, citing Gorz, A., *Reclaiming Work: Beyond the Wage-based Society*, Cambridge, Polity, 1999.

63. Lodziak, *The Myth of Consumerism*, p. 74.

64. Gormley, A., quoted in Higgins, C., 'Oyez! Oyez! The Plinth Has Come: Gormley Begins his Picture of Britain', *The Guardian*, 7 July 2009, p. 1.

65. Miles, M., '*One & Other*: A Picture of the Nation in a Period of Cosmopolitanism?' *Journal of Architecture*, 16, 3, pp. 347–64, 2011.

66. Bauman, Z., *Liquid Modernity*, Cambridge, Polity, 2000, p. 62.

67. Standing, G., *The Precariat: The New Dangerous Class*, London, Bloomsbury, 2011, p. 34.

68. McGuigan, J., *Cool Capitalism*, London, Pluto, 2009, p. 1.

69. Ibid., p. 2.

70. Ibid., p. 6.

71. Ibid., p. 7.

72. Zukin, S., *The Cultures of Cities*. Oxford, Blackwell, 1995, p. 9.

73. McGuigan, *Cool Capitalism*, p. 92.

74. Sadler, 'Spectacular Failure', p. 195.

75. Landry, C., *The Creative City: A Toolkit for Urban Innovators*, London, Earthscan, 2000.

76. Ibid., p. 14.

77. Ibid., pp. 14–15.

78. Ibid., p. 15.

79. Ibid., p. 17.

80. Chatterton, P., 'Will the Real Creative City Please Stand Up?, *City*, 4, 3, 2001, p. 392.
81. Landry, *The Creative City*, p. 38.
82. Ibid., p. 59.
83. Ibid., p. 124.
84. Levitas, R., 'The Concept of Social Exclusion and the New Durkheimian Hegemony', *Critical Social Policy*, 16, pp. 5–20, 1996.
85. Atkinson, R., 'Combating Social Exclusion in Europe: The New Urban Policy Challenge', *Urban Studies*, 37, 5/6, p. 1041, 2000.
86. Ibid., p. 1042.
87. Landry, *The Creative City*, p. 39.
88. Belsey, C., *Shakespeare and the Loss of Eden*, Basingstoke, Palgrave, 2001, p. 7.

Chapter 4

1. Barrett, J., *Museums and the Public Sphere*, Chichester, Wiley-Blackwell, 2012, p. 109.
2. Ibid., p. 111.
3. Wright, P., 'The Quality of Visitors' Experiences in Art Museums', in Vergo, P. (ed.), *The New Museology*, London, Reaktion, 1898, p. 119.
4. Vergo, P., 'The Reticent Object', in Vergo, *The New Museology*, p. 47.
5. Ibid., p. 58.
6. Fuller, N.J., 'The Museum as a Vehicle for Community Empowerment: The Ak-Chin Indian Community Ecomuseum Project', in Karp, I., Kreamer, C.M. and Lavine, S.D. (eds), *Museums and Communities: The Politics of Public Culture*, Washington, DC, Smithsonian, 1992, p. 328.
7. Fuller, 'The Museum as a Vehicle for Community Empowerment', pp. 328–29.
8. McGuigan, J., *Culture and the Public Sphere*, London, Routledge, 1996, p. 66.
9. Ibid., p. 67.
10. Bishop, C., *Radical Museology: or What's Contemporary in Museums of Contemporary Art?*, London, Koening Books, 2013, p. 5, citing Krauss, R., 'The Cultural Logic of Late Capitalism', *October*, 54, 1990, p. 14.
11. Bishop, *Radical Museology*, p. 11.
12. Amin, A. and Thrift, N., *Cities: Reimagining the Urban*, Cambridge, Polity, 2002, p. 24.
13. Nordgren, S., 'Preface', in *B. Year One: Baltic, The Centre for Contemporary Art, Gateshead July 2002–2003*, Gateshead, Baltic, 2003, p. 6.
14. Hatherley, *Guide to the New Ruins*, London, Verso, 2010, pp. 163–64.
15. Ibid.
16. McIntyre, K., 'The Ubiquitous B.', in *Year One: Baltic*, p. 16.
17. Caruso St John architects, cited in Fowle, K., 'A Different Perspective', in Smith, D. (ed.), *The New Art Gallery Walsall*, London, Batsford, 2002, p. 73.

18. Grunenberg, C., 'The Politics of Presentation: The Museum of Modern Art, New York', in Pointon, M. (ed.), *Art Apart: Art Institutions and Ideology across England and North America*, Manchester, Manchester University Press, 1994, pp. 192–211.
19. See: www.thenewartgallerywalsall.org.uk (accessed 11 July 2014).
20. Ibid.
21. Ibid.
22. Ryan, R., *Cool Construction: David Chipperfield, Waro Kishi, Eduardo Suoto de Moura, Tod Williams and Billie Tsein*, London, Thames & Hudson, 2001, p. 28.
23. Ibid., inside cover.
24. Gray, F., *Designing the Seaside: Architecture, Society and Nature*, London, Reaktion, 2006, pp. 266–71.
25. Pomery, V., *Turner Contemporary: Our History*, Margate, Turner Contemporary and Jigsaw Publishing, 2013, p. 11.
26. Cited in ibid., p. 23.
27. McGuigan, J., *Rethinking Cultural Policy*, Maidenhead, Open University Press, 2004, p. 94.
28. Myerscough, J., *The Economic Importance of the Arts in Britain*, London, Policy Studies Institute, 1988.
29. McGuigan, *Rethinking Cultural Policy*, p. 94.
30. Matarasso, F., *Use or Ornament? The Social Impact of Participation in the Arts*, Stroud, Comedia, 1997.
31. Merli, P., 'Evaluating the Social Impact of Participation in Arts Activities', *International Journal of Cultural Policy*, 8, 1, p. 108, 2002, cited in McGuigan, *Rethinking Cultural Policy*, p. 95.
32. McGuigan, *Rethinking Cultural Policy*, p. 95.
33. Belfiore, E. and Bennett, O., *The Social Impact of the Arts: An Intellectual History*, Basingstoke, Palgrave, 2008.
34. Jowell, T., 'Why Should Government Support the Arts?', *Engage*, 17, p. 6, 2005.
35. Ibid.
36. See: www.thepublicwestbromwich.co.uk (accessed 10 July 2014).
37. Clayton, P., 'Development Woes of West Bromwich', letters page, *The Guardian*, 15 August 2013.
38. Ibid.
39. Ibid.
40. See: http://mancunian1001.wordpress.com/2013.03 (accessed 10 July, 2014).
41. The Earth Centre, 'The Future Works' (publicity brochure), 1999, not paginated.
42. Ibid.
43. Bishop, *Radical Museology*, p. 33.
44. Ibid., p. 34.
45. Ibid., pp. 37–45.

46. Ibid., p. 62.
47. Ronson, J., 'This Was Once a Floating Nightclub. Now It Needs the Tide to Turn', *The Guardian*, 3 March 2012, p. 6.
48. Ibid.
49. Hatherley, O., *A New Kind of Bleak: Journeys through Urban Britain*, London, Verso, 2012, p. 45.
50. Ibid., p. 38.
51. Ibid., p. 48.
52. Amin and Thrift, *Cities*, p. 27.
53. Ibid.

Chapter 5

1. Porter, B., *Plots and Paranoia: A History of Political Espionage in Britain 1790–1988*, London, Unwin Hyman, 1989, p. 85.
2. Ashton, O., Fyson, R. and Roberts, S. (eds), *The Chartist Legacy*, Woodbridge, Merlin Press, 1999.
3. Porter, B., *The Origins of the Vigilant State: The London Metropolitan Police Special Branch before the First World War*, London, Weidenfeld & Nicolson, 1987, p. 11.
4. Porter, *The Origins of the Vigilant State*, p. 12.
5. Porter, *Plots and Paranoia*, p. 86.
6. Arnold, M., *Culture and Anarchy* (popular edition), London, Smith Elder, 1889, p. 21.
7. Ibid.
8. Ibid., p. 22.
9. Ibid., p. 36.
10. Ibid., pp. 36–37.
11. Ibid., p. 37.
12. Ibid., p. 158.
13. Ibid., p. 159.
14. Duncan, C., *Civilizing Rituals: Inside Public Art Museums*, London, Routledge, 1995, p. 7.
15. Coombes, A., *Re-inventing Africa – Museums, Material Culture and Popular Imagination*, New Haven, CT, Yale University Press, 1994.
16. Duncan, *Civilizing Rituals*, p. 8.
17. Hobsbawm, E., 'The Making of the English Working Class', in *Uncommon People: Resistance, Rebellion and Jazz*, London, Abacus, 1999, pp. 79–81.
18. Hobsbawm, *Uncommon People*, p. 85.
19. *The Times*, 23 July 1897, cited in Taylor, B., *Art for the Nation: Exhibitions and the London Public 1747–2001*, New Brunswick, NJ, Rutgers University Press, 1999, p. 119.
20. *Norwood Press*, 21 August, 1897, cited in Taylor, *Art for the Nation*, p. 124.

21. *Daily Graphic*, 17 August, 1897, cited in Taylor, *Art for the Nation*, p. 124.
22. *Pall Mall Gazette*, 14 October, 1889, cited in Taylor, *Art for the Nation*, p. 125.
23. Taylor, B., *Art for the Nation*, p. 87 illustrated, from *The Graphic*, 8 February 1879.
24. Taylor, *Art for the Nation*, p. 123.
25. Ibid., p. 124.
26. Hobsbawm, *Uncommon People*, p. 89.
27. Porter, *The Origins of the Vigilant State*, p. 3.
28. Ibid.
29. Taylor, B., *Art for the Nation*, p. 100.
30. Ibid.
31. Ibid., p. 105.
32. Ibid., p. 112.
33. *Daily News*, 3 November 1892, cited in Taylor, *Art for the Nation*, p. 114.
34. Cited in Taylor, *Art for the Nation*, p. 116.
35. Great Britain Royal Commission on the Housing of the Working Classes, I, p. 4, London, 1885, cited in Hall, P., *Cities of Tomorrow*, Oxford, Blackwell (updated edn), 1996, p. 19.
36. Mearns, A., *The Bitter Cry of Outcast London: An Inquiry into the Condition of the Abject Poor*, London, James Clarke, 1883, p. 4, cited in Hall, *Cities of Tomorrow*, p. 17.
37. Engels, F., *The Condition of the Working Class in England in 1844* [1845], London, Allen & Unwin, 1892, pp. 45–54, extract in Donald, J., *Imagining the Modern City*, London, Athlone, 1999, p. 35.
38. Donald, *Imagining the Modern City*, p. 35.
39. Mearns, *The Bitter Cry*, p. 7, cited in Hall, *Cities of Tomorrow*, p. 17.
40. Hall, *Cities of Tomorrow*, p. 17.
41. Ibid., p. 24.
42. Webb, B., *My Apprenticeship*, London, Longman Green, 1926, p. 155, cited in Hall, *Cities of Tomorrow*, p. 24.
43. Hall, *Cities of Tomorrow*, p. 26.
44. Booth, C., 'The Inhabitants of Tower Hamlets: Their Condition and Occupations', *Journal of the Royal Statistical Society*, 50, p. 335, cited in Hall, *Cities of Tomorrow*, p. 28.
45. Booth, 'The Inhabitants of Tower Hamlets', p. 332, cited in Hall, *Cities of Tomorrow*, p. 30.
46. Taylor, *Art for the Nation*, p. 117.
47. *Daily News*, 2 December 1893, cited in Taylor, *Art for the Nation*, p. 266, n. 71.
48. Taylor, *Art for the Nation*, p. 124.
49. Greig, H., *The Beau Monde*, Oxford, Oxford University Press, 2013, p. 196.
50. Ibid., p. 116.
51. Rendell, J., *The Pursuit of Pleasure: Gender, Space and Architecture in Regency London*, London, Athlone, 2002, pp. 63–64.

52. Sennett, *Flesh and Stone*, London, Faber & Faber, 1995, p. 321.

53. Greig, *The Beau Monde*, p. 14.

54. Ibid., p. 15.

55. Ibid., p. 18.

56. Rendell, *The Pursuit of Pleasure*, pp. 100–01.

57. Ibid., p. 101.

58. Ibid., p. 31.

59. Ibid., p. 101.

60. Ibid., p. 103.

61. Ibid., p. 69, citing Castle, T., *Masquerade and Civilization: Carnivalesque in Eighteenth-century English Culture and Fiction*, Stanford, CA, Stanford University Press, 1986; Ogborn, M., *Spaces of Modernity: London's Geographies 1680–1780*, New York, Guildford Press, 2009.

62. Greig, *The Beau Monde*, p. 72.

63. Ibid., p. 74.

64. Ibid.

65. Ibid., p. 77.

66. Ibid., p. 98.

67. Ibid.

68. Taylor, *Art for the Nation*, p. 31.

69. Carey, J., *A Descriptive Catalogue of a Collection of Paintings by British Artists in the Possession of Sir John Flemming Leicester*, London, 1819, cited in Taylor, *Art for the Nation*, p. 31.

70. Taylor, *Art for the Nation*, p. 33.

71. Ibid., p. 43.

72. Ibid.

73. Arnold, M. [1880], cited in Williams, R., *The Long Revolution*, Harmondsworth, Penguin, 1965, p. 190 (no source given).

74. Jardine, L., 'SFMOMA', *Modern Painters*, Spring, 1997, p. 84.

75. Ibid., p. 85.

76. Ibid., p. 87.

Chapter 6

1. Berger, J., *Lilac and Flag*, London, Granta, 1991, p. 154.

2. Madanipour, A., *Public and Private Spaces of the City*, London, Routledge, 2003, p. 193.

3. Ibid., pp. 193–94.

4. Ibid., p. 194.

5. Urry, J., *Consuming Places*, London, Routledge, 1995, p. 176.

6. Lefebvre, H., *The Production of Space*, trans. Nicolson-Lord, D., Oxford, Blackwell, 1991, pp. 38–39.

7. Sennett, R., *Flesh and Stone*, London, Faber & Faber, 1995, p. 52.

8. Arendt, H., *The Human Condition*, Chicago, University of Chicago Press, 1958, p. 26.

9. Sennett, *Flesh and Stone*, p. 155.

10. Ibid.

11. Ibid., p. 158.

12. Ibid.

13. Ibid., p. 159.

14. Ibid., p. 215.

15. Deutsche, R., 'Uneven Development: Public Art in New York City', in Ghirado, D. (ed.), *Out of Site: A Social Criticism of Architecture*, Seattle, WA, Bay Press, 1991, p. 159.

16. Zukin, S., *The Cultures of Cities*, Oxford, Blackwell, 1995, p. 27.

17. Ibid., p. 35.

18. Figes, O., *A People's Tragedy: The Russian Revolution 1891–1924*, London, Pimlico, 1996, p. 472.

19. Tolstoy, V., Bibikova, I. and Cooke, C., *Street Art of the Revolution: Festivals and Celebrations in Russia 1918–33*, London, Thames & Hudson, 1990, pp. 137–39.

20. Sennett, R., *The Fall of Public Man* [1974], New York, Norton, 1992, p. 81, citing Eyton, E., *The Penny Universities*, London, Secker & Warburg, 1956, ch. 9.

21. Habermas, J., *The Structural Transformation of the Public Sphere: An Inquiry into a Category of Bourgeois Society*, Cambridge, MA, MIT Press, 1991, p. 33.

22. Rendell, J., *The Pursuit of Pleasure: Gender, Space and Architecture in Regency London*, London, Athlone, 2002, pp. 63–64.

23. Sennett, *The Fall of Public Man*, p. 81.

24. Soria y Puig, A. (ed.), *Cerdá: The Five Bases of the General Theory of Urbanization*, Madrid, Electa, 1999.

25. Gandy, M., *Concrete and Clay: Reworking Nature in New York City*, Cambridge, MA, MIT, 2002, p. 83.

26. Ibid., p. 87.

27. Ibid., p. 88.

28. Ibid., p. 99.

29. Ibid., p. 79.

30. Low, S., *On the Plaza: The Politics of Public Space and Culture*, Austin, TX, University of Texas Press, 2000, p. 3.

31. Ibid., p. 20.

32. Ibid., p. 15.

33. Ibid., p. 32.

34. Whyte, W.H., *The Social Life of Small Urban Spaces*, Washington, DC, Conservation Foundation, 1980.

35. Jacobs, J., *The Death and Life of Great American Cities*, New York, Vintage, 1961, p. 57.

36. Renew Northwest, *Places Matter! Creating Inspirational Spaces: A Guide for Quality Public Realm in the Northwest*, Liverpool, Renew Northwest, n.d., p. 7.

37. Jacobs, *The Death and Life of Great American Cities*, p. 372.

38. Kennedy, L. (ed.), *Remaking Birmingham: The Visual Culture of Urban Regeneration*, London, Routledge, 2004; Miles, M., *Art, Space and the City*, London, Routledge, 1997, pp. 115–17.

39. Loftman, P. and Nevin, B., 'Pro-growth Local Economic Development Strategies: Civic Promotion and Local Needs in Britain's Second City, 1981–1996', in Hall, T. and Hubbard, P. (eds), *The Entrepreneurial City: Geographies of Politics, Regime and Representation*, Chichester, Wiley, 1998, pp. 129–48.

40. Hall, T., 'Public Art, Civic Identity and the New Birmingham', in Kennedy, *Remaking Birmingham*, p. 65.

41. Madelin, R., 'Lessons from Brindleyplace', in Latham, I. and Swenarton, M. (eds), *Brindleyplace: A Model for Urban Regeneration*, London, Rightangle Publishing, 1999, p. 47.

42. Evans, G., 'Measure for Measure: Evaluating the Evidence of Culture's Contribution to Regeneration', *Urban Studies*, 42, 5/6, 2005, p. 975.

43. Mellor, R., 'Hypocritical City: Cycles of Urban Exclusion', in Peck, J. and Ward, K. (eds), *City of Revolution: Restructuring Manchester*, Manchester, Manchester University Press, 2002, p. 216.

44. Albrow, M., 'Travelling Beyond Local Cultures: Socioscopes in a Global City', in Eade, J. (ed.), *Living the Global City: Globalization as local process*, London, Routledge, 1997, pp. 37–55.

45. Wilson, E., *The Sphinx in the City: Urban Life, the Control of Disorder, and Women*, Berkeley, CA, University of California Press, 1991, pp. 106–07.

46. Ibid., pp. 47–64.

47. Ibid., p. 118.

48. Ibid.

49. Ibid., p. 115.

50. Ibid., p. 152.

51. Low, *On the Plaza*, p. 86.

52. Ibid.

53. Ibid., p. 103.

54. Ibid., p. 125.

55. Ibid., p. 34.

56. Pessoa, F., *The Book of Disquiet*, trans. Zenith, R., London, Penguin, 2001, p. 127.

57. Department of Environment, Transport and the Regions (DETR), *Towards an Urban Renaissance*, London, DETR, 1999.

58. DETR, *Our Towns and Cities – The Future: Delivering an Urban Renaissance*, London, DETR, 2000.

59. Ibid., 1.11.

60. Ibid., 1.21.
61. Ibid., 4.3.
62. Lees, L., 'Gentrification and Social Mixing: Towards an Inclusive Urban Renaissance?', *Urban Studies*, 45, 12, 2008, p. 2460.
63. Ibid., p. 2462.
64. Ibid., p. 2463.
65. Atkinson, R., 'Domestication by *Cappuccino* or a Revenge on Urban Space? Control and Empowerment in the Management of Urban Space', *Urban Studies*, 40, 9, 2003, p. 1829.
66. Graham, S., 'Spaces of Surveillant Simulation: New Technologies, Digital Representations, and Material Geographies', *Environment and Planning D*, 16, 1998, p. 491, cited in Atkinson, 'Domestication by *Cappuccino*', p. 1833.
67. Holden, A. and Iveson, K., 'Designs on the Urban: New Labour's Urban Renaissance and the Spaces of Citizenship', *City*, 7, 1, p. 57.
68. Ibid., p. 60.
69. Ibid., p. 62.
70. Ibid., p. 66.
71. Wilson, *The Sphinx in the City*, p. 157.
72. Nawratek, K., *City as a Political Idea*, Plymouth, University of Plymouth Press, 2011, p. 142.
73. Wodiczko, K., 'Art, Trauma and Parrhesia', *Art and the Public Sphere*, 1, 3, 2011, p. 293.
74. Walker, P., 'Bailiffs Will Sound Death Knell for Vast London Estate', *The Guardian*, 5 November 2013, p. 18.
75. Flynn, J., quoted in Walker, 'Bailiffs Will Sound Death Knell for Vast London Estate', p. 18.
76. Walker, 'Bailiffs Will Sound Death Knell for Vast London Estate', p. 18.
77. Tinker, T., quoted in Moss, S., 'Homes Under the Hammer', *The Guardian*, 4 March 2011, section 2, p. 9.
78. See: http://heygate.heroku.com/after-the-heygate (accessed 25 April 2012).
79. Glasspool, A., quoted in Moss, 'Homes Under the Hammer', p. 7.
80. Taylor, S., quoted in Hill, D., 'The Battle of Earl's Court', *The Guardian*, 9 March 2011, Society section, p. 3.
81. Wells, M. quoted in Griffiths, I., 'In the Shadow of the Olympics, Houseboaters Fear They Are Being Socially Cleansed', *The Guardian*, 10 March 2011, p. 3.
82. Quoted in Griffiths, 'In the Shadow of the Olympics', p. 3.
83. Sinclair, I., *Ghost Milk – Calling Time on the Grand Project*, London, Penguin, 2011, p. 72.
84. Ibid., pp. 72–73.
85. Cohen, P., *On the Wrong Side of the Track? East London and the Post Olympics*, London, Lawrence & Wishart, 2013, p. 292.

86. Fowler, G., quoted in Doward, J. and Simpson, D., 'Potteries Mourn Passing Era as Developers Claim Last Oatcake Shop', *The Guardian*, 4 March 2012, p. 13.
87. Hunt, T., quoted in Doward and Simpson, 'Potteries Mourn Passing Era', p. 13.
88. Macpherson, H., quoted in Conn, D., 'Anfield: The Victims, the Anger and the Shame', *The Guardian*, 7 May, 2013, Sport, p. 1.
89. Minton, A., *Ground Control: Fear and Happiness in the Twenty-first-century City*, London, Penguin, 2009, pp. 86–87.
90. Berger, J., *Permanent Red*, London, Methuen, 1969, p. 205.
91. McKay, G., *Senseless Acts of Beauty: Cultures of Resistance since the Sixties*, London, Verso, 1996.
92. Rajkowska, J., *Where the Beast is Buried*, Winchester, Zero Books, 2013, p. 12.
93. Ibid., p. 11.
94. Ibid., p. 13.
95. Ibid., p. 19.
96. Weileder, W., project notes, in Robinson, A. (ed.), *Continuum*, Bielefeld, Kerber Art, 2013, p. 143; see also Wells, R., 'Housing Justice', in Hollinshead, R. (ed.), *Magnificent Distance*, New York, Grit and Pearl, 2012, pp. 77–89.
97. Weileder, W., interview, in Robinson, *Continuum*, p. 79.
98. Ibid., p. 80.
99. Ibid.
100. Ibid., p. 79
101. Guy, S., Henshaw, V. and Heidrich, O., 'Climate Change, Adaptation and Eco-Art in Singapore', *Journal of Environmental Planning and Management*, 10, 2013, p. 12.

Chapter 7

1. Berger, J., *Permanent Red*, London, Methuen, 1969, p. 205.
2. Nochlin, L., 'The Invention of the Avant-Garde: France 1830–80', in Hess, T.B. and Ashbery, J. (eds), *Avant-Garde Art*, New York, Macmillan, 1967, pp. 1–24.
3. Clark, T.J., *The Absolute Bourgeois: Artists and Politics in France 1848–1851*, London, Thames & Hudson, 1973, pp. 75–77.
4. Clark, T.J., *Farewell to an Idea: Episodes from a History of Modernism*, New Haven, CT, Yale University Press, 1999, p. 119.
5. Lee, R.E., *Life and Times of Cultural Studies: The Politics and Transformation of Structures of Knowledge*, Durham, NC, Duke University Press, 2003.
6. Williams, R., *The Long Revolution*, Harmondsworth, Penguin, 1965.
7. Kester, G.H., *The One and the Many: Contemporary Collaborative Art in a Global Context*, Durham, NC, Duke University Press, 2011.
8. Marcuse, H., *The Aesthetic Dimension*, Boston, Beacon Press, 1978.

9. Lorde, A., 'The Master's Tools Will Never Dismantle the Master's House', Second Sex conference, New York, 29 September 1979, in Rendell, J., Penner, B. and Borden, I. (eds), *Gender Space Architecture: An Interdisciplinary Introduction*, London, Routledge, 2000, p. 54 (italics original).

10. Molyneux, J., *Rembrandt and Revolution*, London, Redwords, 2001, pp. 82–83, citing Cixous, H., 'Bathsheba or the Interior Bible', in *Stigmata: Escaping Texts*, London, 1998, pp. 15–16.

11. Marcuse, H., 'Some Remarks on Aragon: Art and and Politics in the Totalitarian Era', in *Technology, War and Fascism (Collected Papers*, vol. 1, edited by D. Kellner), New York, Routledge, 1998, pp. 199–214; Miles, M., *Herbert Marcuse: An Aesthetics of Liberation*, London, Pluto, 2011, pp. 65–84.

12. Bishop, C., 'The Social Turn: Collaboration and Its Discontents', *Artforum*, 44, 6, 2006, pp. 178–83; see also Kester, G., 'Another Turn', *Artforum*, 44, 9, 2006, p. 22; Bishop, 'Claire Bishop Responds', *Artforum*, 44, 9, 2006, p. 24.

13. Charnley, K., 'The Art Collective as Impurity', *Art & the Public Sphere*, 1, 3, 2011, p. 245, citing Bürger, P., 'Avant-Garde and Neo-Avant-Garde: An Attempt to Answer Certain Criticisms of *Theory of the Avant-Garde*', *New Literary History*, 41, 4, 2010, pp. 695–715.

14. Rosler, M., 'Place, Position, Power, Politics', in Becker, C. (ed.), *The Subversive Imagination: Artists, Society and Social Responsibility*, New York, Routledge, 1994, p. 56.

15. Ibid., p. 57.

16. Charnley, 'The Art Collective as Impurity', p. 245.

17. Krauss, R., 'Sculpture in the Expanded Field', in Foster, H. (ed.), *Postmodern Culture*, London, Pluto, 1985, pp. 31–42.

18. Rendell, J., *Art and Architecture: A Place Between*, London, I.B. Tauris, 2006, p. 43.

19. Ibid.

20. Baxandall, M., *Patterns of Intention: On the Historical Explanation of Pictures*, New Haven, CT, Yale University Press, 1987.

21. Ibid.

22. Sholette, G., *Dark Matter: Art and Politics in the Age of Enterprise Culture*, London, Pluto, 2011, p. 62.

23. Ibid., p. 90 (illustrated, p. 89).

24. Temporary Services, cited in ibid., p. 100; see www.temporaryservices.org (accessed Jan. 2015).

25. Sholette, *Dark Matter*, p. 106.

26. Shields, R., *Lefebvre, Love and Struggle*, London, Routledge, 1996, pp. 58–64.

27. Bloch, E., *The Principle of Hope*, Cambridge, MA, MIT Press, 1995, p. 813 (first published as *Das Prinzip Hoffnung*, Frankfurt, Suhrkamp, 1959).

28. Bernard-Donals, M., 'Knowing the Subaltern: Bakhtin, Carnival, and the Other Voices of the Human Sciences', in Bell, M.M. and Gardiner, M. (eds), *Bakhtin and the Human Sciences*, London, Sage, 1998, pp. 112–27.

29. Sholette, *Dark Matter*, p. 107.

30. Benjamin, W., 'The Author as Producer', in *Understanding Brecht*, London, Verso, 1983, p. 87 (from an address to a meeting of Communist writers, Paris, 1934).

31. Bürger, P., *Theory of the Avant-Garde*, Minneapolis, MN, Minnesota University Press, 1984, p. 53.

32. 'Instituent Practices: Fleeing, Instituting, Transforming', in Ray, G. and Raunig, G. (eds), *Art and Contemporary Practice: Reinventing Institutional Critique*, London, Mayfly, pp. 3–12.

33. Charnley, 'The Art Collective as Impurity', p. 248.

34. Toscano, A., 'Destructive Creation, or The Communism of the Senses', in Watson, G., van Noord, G. and Everall, G. (eds), *Make Everything New: A Project on Communism*, London, Bookworks and Dublin, Project Arts Centre, 2006, p. 127 (italics original).

35. Charnley, 'The Art Collective as Impurity', p. 259.

36. Bourriaud, N., *Relational Aesthetics*, Dijon, Les presses du réel, 2002 (first published as *Esthétique relationelle*, 1998).

37. Bourriaud, N., 'Altermodern', *Altermodernism* (exhibition catalogue), London, Tate, 2009, p. 12.

38. Ibid.

39. Benhabib, S., *The Claims of Culture: Equality and Diversity in the Global Era*, Princeton, NJ, Princeton University Press, 2002, p. 12.

40. Marcuse, *The Aesthetic Dimension*, p. 1.

41. Miles, M., *Herbert Marcuse*.

42. Rancière, J., 'Problems and Transformations of Political Art', in *Aesthetics and its Discontents*, Cambridge, Polity, 2004, p. 45.

43. Ibid., pp. 45–46.

44. Marcuse, *The Aesthetic Dimension*, p. 9.

45. Toscano, 'Destructive Creation', p. 124.

46. Rancière, 'Problems and Transformations of Political Art', pp. 45–46.

47. Rancière, J., 'The End of Politics', in *On the Shores of Politics*, London, Verso, 1995, pp. 11–12.

48. Rancière, 'Problems and Transformations of Political Art', pp. 50–51.

49. Rancière, J. 'The Ethical Turn of Aesthetics and Politics', in *Dissensus: On Politics and Aesthetics*, London, Continuum, 2010, p. 115.

50. Ibid., p. 116.

51. Bishop, C., 'Introduction: Viewers as Producers', in *Participation*, London, Whitechapel Art Gallery and Cambridge, MA, MIT Press, 2006, p. 13.

52. Bishop, *Participation*, p. 12.

53. E-mail to the author, 12 August 2014.

54. See: www.seft1.net (accessed Jan. 2015).

55. See: www.artscatalyst.org (accessed Jan. 2015).

56. Hell, J. and Schonle, A. (eds), *Ruins of Modernity*, Durham, NC, Duke University Press, 2010.

57. E-mail to the author, 12 August 2014.

58. Jones, J., 'The Ruin-hunters Who Drove a Car down Mexico's Forgotten Railways', *The Guardian*, 11 June 2014, www.theguardian.com/artanddesign/jopnathanjonesblog/2014/jun/11/ruins-hunters (accessed 24 June 2014).

59. Ibid.

60. Woodward, C., *In Ruins*, London, Vintage, 2002, p. 74.

61. IAPDH, *Five: The Institute for the Art and Practice of Dissent at Home 2008–2012*, Liverpool, IAPDH, 2014 p. 4.

62. Ibid., p. 43.

63. Ibid., p. 41.

64. Impacts 08, 'Neighbourhood Impacts: A Longitudinal Study into the Impact of the Liverpool European Capital of Culture on Local Residents', Liverpool, Impacts 08, 2010, pp. 21, 22.

65. IAPDH, *Five*, p. 10.

66. Ibid., p. 13.

67. See: www.cornfordandcross.com/introduction (accessed 13 August 2014).

68. Ibid.

69. Roberts, J., 'Fade Out', in Cornford and Cross, *Cornford & Cross*, London, Black Dog, p. 13.

70. See Fischer, E., *Marx in His Own Words*, Harmondsworth, Penguin, 1973, pp. 152–58.

71. Roberts, 'Fade Out', p. 14.

72. Ibid.

73. Cornford & Cross, *Cornford & Cross*, p. 48; see also Miles, M., *Urban Avant-Gardes: Art, Architecture and Change*, London, Routledge, 2004, pp. 167–68.

74. Ibid.

75. E-mail to the author, 7 July 2014.

76. Ibid.

77. Gilly, A., 'Globalization, Violence and Revolutions: Nine Theses', in Foran, J. (ed.), *The Future of Revolutions: Rethinking Radical Change in the Age of Globalization*, London, Zed Books, 2003, p. 117.

78. Evans, H., 'Fracking Futures: A Taste of What's to Come', *New Internationalist*, 6 November 2013, http://newint.org/blog/2013/06/11/fracking-futures-fact-exhibition (accessed 13 August 2014).

79. Ibid.

80. Paraphrased from e-mail to the author, 13 August 2014.

81. Evans, 'Fracking Futures'.

82. Ravillious, K., 'Art Installation Brings You Face to Face with Fracking', *New Scientist*, 18 July 2013, www.newscientist.com/article/dn23889-art-installation-brings-you-face-to-face-with-fracking (accessed 13 August 2014).

83. Rothery, T.L., quoted in Vaughan, A., 'Anti-fracking Protesters Set Up Camp outside Blackpool', *The Guardian*, 12 August 2014, p. 13; see also www.frack-off.org.uk

84. See: www.dazeddigital.com/artsandculture/article/16925/top-ten-anti-fracking-artists (accessed 13 August 2014).

85. Miles, M., *Eco-Aesthetics: Art, Literature and Architecture in a Period of Climate Change*, London, Bloomsbury, 2014, pp. 153–56.

86. See: www.freee.org.uk/works/the-threee-functions (accessed 14 August 2014).

87. Conversation, March 2010.

88. Freee Art Collective (photocopied leaflet in the author's possession), 2007.

89. Hewitt, A. and Jordan, M. (eds), *Futurology: Issues, Contexts and Conditions for Contemporary Art Practice Today*, Walsall, New Art Gallery, 2008, p. 13.

90. Ibid., pp. 15–16.

91. Adorno, T.W., *The Culture Industry: Selected Essays on Mass Culture*, London, Routledge, 1991.

92. See: www.freee.org.uk/works/how-to-be-hospitable (accessed 7 July 2014).

93. Hewitt, A., 'Freee Art Collective and Third Way Cultural Policy' (from unpublished PhD thesis, University of the Arts, London), 2012.

94. E-mail to the author, 5 December 2013.

95. Williams, R., *The Politics of Modernism*, London, Verso, 1996, p. 49.

96. Hill, C., *The World Turned Upside Down: Radical Ideas during the English Revolution*, Harmondsworth, Penguin, 1976.

97. Conversation, 21 June 2014.

Chapter 8

1. Bishop, C., *Artificial Hells: Participatory Art and the Politics of Spectatorship*, London, Verso, p. 221.

2. Ibid., p. 222.

3. Ibid., p. 220.

4. Ibid., p. 222.

5. Ibid., p. 223.

6. Ibid., p. 224.

7. Ibid., p. 225.

8. Boal, A., *Theatre of the Oppressed*, London, Pluto, 2000 (new edition, first published 1979), p. 47.

9. Bishop, *Artificial Hells*, p. 229.

10. Ibid., p. 233.

11. Ibid., p. 234.

12. Ibid., p. 237.

13. Ibid., p. 238.

14. Adorno, T.W., *Aesthetic Theory*, trans. Hullot-Kentor, R., London, Athlone, 1997, p. 31.
15. Ibid., p. 32.
16. Bishop, *Artificial Hells*, p. 12.
17. Ibid., pp. 12–13, citing Kester, G., *Conversation Pieces: Community and Communication in Modern Art*, Berkeley, University of California Press, 2004, p. 29.
18. Bishop, *Artificial Hells*, p. 14.
19. Ibid., p. 16.
20. Ibid., p. 19.
21. Sloterdijk, P., *In the World Interior of Capital*, trans. Hoban, W., Cambridge, Polity, 2013, p. 177 (first published as *Im Weltinneraum des Kapitals*, Frankfurt, Suhrkamp, 2005).
22. Boal, *Theatre of the Oppressed*, p. 24.
23. Panagia, D., *The Political Life of Sensation*, Durham, NC, Duke University Press, 2009, p. 52.
24. Graeber, D., *The Democracy Project: A History, A Crisis, A Movement*, London, Penguin, 2014, p. 21.
25. Ibid., p. 233.
26. Leslie, E., *Walter Benjamin: Overpowering Conformism*, London, Pluto, 2000, pp. 203–04, citing James, C.L.R., *Notes on Dialectics: Hegel, Marx, Lenin*, London, Allison & Busby, 1948, pp. 99–101.
27. Sitrin, M., 'One No, Many Yeses', Taylor, in A., Gessen, K. and editors from n+1, *Occupy! Scenes from Occupied America*, London, Verso, 2011, p. 9.
28. Chomsky, N., *Occupy*, London, Penguin, 2012, p. 61.
29. Tickner, L., *Hornsey 1968: The Art School Revolution*, London, Frances Lincoln, 2008.
30. Marcuse, H., *An Essay on Liberation*, Harmondsworth, Penguin, 1969, p. 30.
31. Kristeva, J., *Revolt, She Said*, Los Angeles, Semiotext(e), 2002, p. 18.
32. Merrifield, A., *Henri Lefebvre: A Critical Introduction*, London, Routledge, 2006, p. 26.
33. Ross, K., *May '68 and its Afterlives*, Chicago, University of Chicago Press, 2002, p. 70.
34. Cohn-Bendit, D. (interview with Sartre, J.-P.), in Bourges, H. (ed.), *The French Student Revolt: The Leaders Speak*, New York, Hill & Wang, 1968, p. 77.
35. Giroux, H.A., *Twilight of the Social: Resurgent Publics in the Age of Disposability*, London, Pluto, 2012, p. 115.
36. Holloway, J., *Crack Capitalism*, London, Pluto, 2010, p. 9.
37. Ibid., p. 254.
38. Bishop, *Artificial Hells*, p. 209.
39. Nawratek, K., *City as a Political Idea*, Plymouth, University of Plymouth Press, 2011, p. 114.
40. Nawratek, *City as a Political Idea*, p. 115.

41. Ferrara, A., 'Politics at Its Best: Reasons that Move the Imagination', in Bottici, C. and Challand, B. (eds), *The Politics of Imagination*, Abingdon, Birkbeck Law Press, 2011, p. 53.

42. Mehring, W., *Berlin Dada: Ein Chronik mit photos und dokumenten*, Zurich, der Arche, 1959, quoted in Grindon, G., 'Autonomy, Activism, and Social Participation in the Radical Avant-Garde', *Oxford Art Journal*, 34, 1, 2011, p. 91.

43. Grindon, 'Autonomy, Activism, and Social Participation', p. 92.

44. Flood, C. and Grindon, G. (eds), *Disobedient Objects* (exhibition catalogue), London, Victoria & Albert Museum, 2014.

45. Flood and Grindon, *Disobedient Objects*, p. 23.

46. Grindon, G. and Jordan, J., *A User's Guide to Demanding the Impossible*, London, Minor Compositions, 2010, p. 2.

47. Grindon and Jordan, *A User's Guide to Demanding the Impossible*, p. 12

48. Kester, G.H., *The One and the Many: Contemporary Collaborative Art in a Global Context*, Durham, NC, Duke University Press, 2011; Lippard, L., *The Lure of the Local: Senses of Place in a Multicentred Society*, New York, The New Press, 1997.

49. Macalister, T., 'Invest in Iraq and You Repeat Past Mistakes, Investors tell BP Board', *The Guardian*, 18 April 2008.

50. Conversation, 9 May 2008.

51. Marriott, J. and Minio-Paluello, M., *The Oil Road: Journeys from the Caspian Sea to the City of London*, London, Verso, 2012.

52. This and related material can be downloaded from www.platformlondon.org/publications (accessed 17 July 2014).

53. Miles, M., *Eco-Aesthetics: Art, Literature and Architecture in a Period of Climate Change*, London, Bloomsbury, 2014, pp. 158–64.

54. Leslie, *Walter Benjamin*, pp. 100–22.

55. Bloch, E., *The Principle of Hope*, Cambridge, MA, MIT Press, 1986, p. 1376 (first published as *Der Prinzip Hoffnung*, Frankfurt, Suhrkamp, 1959); see also Boldyrev, I., *Ernst Bloch and His Contemporaries*, London, Bloomsbury, 2014, p. 153.

56. Marcuse, H., *The Aesthetic Dimension*, Boston, Beacon Press, 1978, p. xi.

57. Rancière, J., 'Contemporary Art and the Politics of Aesthetics', in Hinderlitter, B., Kaizen, W., Maimon, V., Mansoor, J. and McCormick, S. (eds), *Communities of Sense: Rethinking Aesthetics and Politics*, Durham, NC, Duke University Press, 2009, p. 33.

58. Ibid., p. 36.

59. Ibid.

60. Ibid.

61. Ibid.

62. Ibid., p. 43.

63. Ibid., p. 50.

64. Marcuse, *The Aesthetic Dimension*, p. 55.

65. Cornwall, A. and Coelho, V.S.P., 'Spaces for Change? The Politics of Participation in New Democratic Arenas', in Cornwall, A. and Coelho, V.S.P. (eds), *Spaces for Change? The Politics of Citizen Participation in New Democratic Arenas*, London, Zed Books, 2007, p. 11.

66. Buser, M., Bonura, C., Fannin, M. and Boyer, K., 'Cultural Activism and the Politics of Place-making', *City*, 17, 5, 2013, p. 615.

67. Chalkley, C. and Anon., Tesco Express Public Hearing, Bristol City Council, 8 December 2010, cited in Buser et al., 'Cultural Activism', p. 617.

68. McCarthy, K., cited in Buser et al., 'Cultural Activism', p. 620, from the *Bristol Evening Post*, 21 April 2011 (no pagination given).

69. Bové, J. and Dufour, F., *The World is Not for Sale: Farmers Against Junk Food*, London, Verso, 2001.

70. Swyngedouw, E., *Designing the Post-Political City and the Insurgent Polis*, London, Bedford Press, 2011, pp. 17, 22.

Index